COMMUNICATION

LAW AND POLICY

| Volume 9 | Autumn 2004 | Number 4 |

SPECIAL ISSUE:
New York Times Co. v. Sullivan Forty Years Later:
Retrospective, Perspective, Prospective

COMMUNICATION LAW AND POLICY

Volume 9   Autumn 2004   Number 4

Editor
W. Wat Hopkins, Ph.D.
Virginia Tech

Founding Editor
Robert Trager, Ph.D., J.D.

Editor Emeritus
Thomas A. Schwartz, Ph.D.

COMMUNICATION LAW AND POLICY

| Volume 9 | Autumn 2004 | Number 4 |

EDITOR'S NOTE

Shortly after Justice William J. Brennan, Jr., delivered the opinion for the Court in *New York Times Co. v. Sullivan*,[1] he received a handwritten note from Justice Hugo Black commenting on the impact of the decision. It read, in part:

> [Y]ou have done a great service to the freedoms of the First Amendment. For your opinion I believe will inevitably lead to a later holding that people have complete immunity from having to pay damages for criticism of government or its officials in the performance of their public duties. Most inventions even of legal principles come out of urgent needs. The need to protect speech in this area is so great that it will be recognized and acted upon sooner or later. The rationalization for it is not important—the result is. What counts in your opinion I think will be the point from which this result will be achieved.[2]

Justice Black was wrong, of course. The Court never adopted the rule that public officials were constitutionally barred from advancing libel suits based on criticisms of their official actions, the stance he took in his concurring opinion in *Times v. Sullivan*.[3] But on the broader plane, he was correct. The need to protect speech on matters of governing importance, more than any other element of government, is the defining factor of a free society. It is what sets apart the governing structure of the United States from any other. And nowhere in the law is that prospect more clearly explained than in Justice Brennan's majority opinion in *Times v. Sullivan*.

While Oliver Wendell Holmes may have been the first justice to make reference to a *duty* by citizens to participate in debate about the government,[4] it was Justice Brennan who first declared that the

---

[1]376 U.S. 254 (1964).

[2]Brennan Papers, Box 107, Manuscript Division, Library of Congress.

[3]376 U.S. at 293 (Black, J., concurring).

[4]*See* Whitney v. California, 274 U.S. 357, 375 (1927) (Holmes, J., dissenting) ("public discussion is a political duty").

duty was at the central meaning of the First Amendment.[5] The purpose of the Amendment, he wrote, drawing upon one of his earlier majority opinions, was to ensure an unfettered exchange of ideas about matters of public importance.[6] In order for government to thrive, the governed must thrive, and for that to happen there must be the assurance of a wide-open, robust debate about matters of public concern.[7]

Three of Justice Brennan's colleagues on the Court—Justices Black,[8] William O. Douglas[9] and Arthur Goldberg[10]—believed one way to accomplish that goal was to insulate critics of public officials from libel suits altogether. A majority of the Court, however, took the more pragmatic approach suggested by Justice Brennan, and held that public officials could only win libel actions by proving that allegedly defamatory material was published with actual malice – that is, with knowledge of falsity or with reckless disregard for its truth.[11]

The rule was not new,[12] and was very nearly an anti-climax to Justice Brennan's eloquent statement of the purpose of the First Amendment. Indeed, there were efforts to dissuade Justice Brennan from advancing it as a constitutional rule. In a brief note to Justice Brennan during the negotiations on the opinion in *Times v. Sullivan*, for example, in an apparent effort to have the justice back off the actual malice rule, Justice Douglas wrote: "As I recall, some of the prosecutions under the Alien & Sedition laws were for 'malicious' statements—perhaps it was in all of them."[13] In addition, Justices Black[14] and Goldberg[15] both criticized the actual malice rule in their concurring opinions. And the controversy among the justices on whether the Court should apply the actual malice rule to the facts of the case very nearly scuttled Justice Brennan's efforts.[16]

---

[5]376 U.S. at 273.

[6]*Id.* at 269 (quoting Roth v. United States, 354 U.S. 476, 484 (1957)).

[7]*Id.* at 270–71.

[8]*Id.* at 297 (Black, J., concurring).

[9]*Id.* (Black, J., concurring) (joined by Justice Douglas); *id.* at 304 (Goldberg, J., concurring in judgment) (joined by Justice Douglas).

[10]*Id.* at 304 (Goldberg, J., concurring in the result).

[11]*Id.* at 279–80.

[12]*See, e.g.,* W. WAT HOPKINS, ACTUAL MALICE 49–68 (1989).

[13]Brennan Papers, *supra* note 2.

[14]376 U.S. at 293 (Black, J., concurring).

[15]*Id.* at 298, 300 (Goldberg, J., concurring in the result).

[16]*See* W. Wat Hopkins, *Justice Brennan, Justice Harlan and* New York Times Co. v. Sullivan: *A Case Study in Supreme Court Decision Making,* 1 COMM. LAW & POL'Y 469 (1996).

Over the years, however, actual malice has remained one of the most durable rules in free speech jurisprudence, though it has never been accepted with affection.[17] While the Court has expanded the rule to encompass protection for critics of public figures,[18] defendants against whom punitive damages are sought in libel actions,[19] persons sued for false light invasion of privacy[20] and defendants in intentional infliction of emotional distress actions,[21] for example, justices have continued to question its effectiveness. In 1986, for example, Chief Justice Warren Burger advocated eliminating the actual malice rule altogether.[22] He was joined in his opinion by Justice William H. Rehnquist, who, possibly as a testament to the durability of the rule, would later recant his disapproval of actual malice in his majority opinion in *Hustler Magazine v. Falwell*.[23]

Both actual malice in particular and *Times v. Sullivan* in general, therefore, remain as testaments to the nation's commitment to protecting wide-open and robust debate about matters of public concern. It is because of the opinion's contribution to this commitment that *Communication Law and Policy* is commemorating the fortieth anniversary of the decision. It is my hope, and that of the Editorial Board, that the essays and articles herein provide an example of the breadth and scope of *Times v. Sullivan* and the ways in which the case continues to impact the jurisprudence of free expression.

The special issue is introduced by two essays designed to provide an overview of the opinion. Constitutional historian Kermit Hall provides some insights into the origins of the dispute the Court was called upon to settle. He describes the culture in which the case was cultivated and various disputes from which it grew. Then Robert O'Neil of the Thomas Jefferson Center for the Protection of Free Expression and a law clerk for Justice Brennan during the term immediately preceding *Times v. Sullivan*, reflects upon the novelty and significance of the case, placing it in modern law.

The four articles that follow the essays are testimony to the breadth of the opinion. With one exception, they deal with aspects of the case not often considered. Greg Lisby, for example, makes the ar-

---

[17]*Compare* DONALD GILMOR, POWER, PUBLICITY AND THE ABUSE OF LIBEL LAW (1992), *with* HOPKINS, supra note 12, at 186–87.

[18]*See* Curtis Publishing Co. v. Butts, 388 U.S. 130 (1967).

[19]*See* Gertz v. Robert Welch, Inc., 418 U.S. 323 (1974).

[20]*See* Time, Inc. v. Hill, 385 U.S. 374 (1967).

[21]*See* Hustler Magazine v. Falwell, 485 U.S. 46 (1988).

[22]*See* Coughlin v. Westinghouse Broad., 476 U.S. 1187 (1986) (Burger, C.J., dissenting from denial of *certiorari*) (joined by Justice Rehnquist).

[23]485 U.S. at 56.

gument that the Court did not go far enough in defining the parameters of actual malice, allowing the law of criminal libel to thrive when it should have been strangled. Susan Dente Ross and Kenton Bird, in one article, and Robert Kerr, in another, examine commercial speech as related to *Times v. Sullivan*. Professors Ross and Bird explore how Justice Brennan's judicial activism advanced advocacy advertising, and Professor Kerr decries the possibility that what he calls "the noble purpose" of the case will be subverted to protect false advertising. Finally, doctoral student and attorney Carlo Pedrioli examines Justice Brennan's judicial philosophy and how that philosophy impacted his opinion for the Court in the case.

The essays and articles all demonstrate the lasting significance of what may be the most important free expression case the Court has delivered. Other cases are important. *Schneck v. United States*[24] is important, among other reasons, because it was the Court's first substantive decision involving freedom of expression. *Gitlow v. New York*[25] is important because it imposed upon the states the same requirement to protect expression. And *Near v. Minnesota*[26] is important because it was the Court's first pronouncement that prior restraint is not allowed under the Constitution.

But the significance of *Times v. Sullivan* is that, for the first time, it defined—clearly and succinctly—who we are as a free society. It is our hope that this special issue contributes to the campaign that we not forget.

— W. Wat Hopkins

---

[24]249 U.S. 47 (1919).
[25]268 U.S. 652 (1925).
[26]283 U.S. 697 (1931).

"LIES, LIES, LIES": THE ORIGINS OF *NEW YORK TIMES CO. V. SULLIVAN*

KERMIT L. HALL*

New York Times v. Sullivan *stands as a monument to the proposition that robust and open political discourse is the best guarantee of democratic self-governance. Some scholars have connected the case to the civil rights movement, of which it was surely a part. Others have noted the negative impact* Sullivan *had on the civility of public discourse. This essay approaches the case from the perspective of white moderates in Montgomery who believed that the law of libel should protect the so-called "best men" by upholding habits and manners of civility. The* Sullivan *case is notable, then, for the sectionally bound social assumptions of the white moderates that animated the litigation in the first place and whose exuberance in doing so ultimately undermined the values they sought to protect.*

Justice William J. Brennan's opinion for a unanimous Supreme Court of the United States in *New York Times v. Sullivan*[1] was this nation's greatest constitutional pronouncement on the law of political libel. It was, as well, Justice Brennan's most important contribution to constitutional law up to that time, and, of the Court's work during the 1963 term, only the Reapportionment Cases matched it's significance.[2] *Sullivan* was also a remarkable incident in modern

---

*President and professor of history, Utah State University.

[1] 376 U. S. 254 (1964).

[2] On Justice Brennan's impact on libel law during the Warren Court, see BERNARD SCHWARTZ, SUPER CHIEF: EARL WARREN AND HIS SUPREME COURT—A JUDICIAL BIOGRAPHY 531–541, 566–568, 612–617, 650–652 (1983). For the Reapportionment Cases, *see* Davis v. Mann, 377 U. S. 656 (1964); Lucas v. Forty-Fourth General Assembly of Colorado, 377 U. S. 713 (1964); Maryland Committee for Fair Representation v. Taws, 377 U. S. 656 (1964); Reynolds v. Sims, 377 U. S. 533 (1964); Roman v. Sincock, 377 U. S. 695 (1964); WMCA v. Lomenzo, 377 U. S. 633 (1964). The Court also handed down major rulings in Bell v. Maryland, 378 U. S. 226 (1964); Escobedo v. Illinois, 378 U. S. 478 (1964); and Malloy v. Hogan, 378 U. S. 1 (1964).

American cultural history, and an appreciation for its origins reveals
how contending social demands shaped and were, in turn, shaped by
expectations about the meaning of the First Amendment.[3] Historians and legal scholars have regularly insisted that *Sullivan* compels our attention because of its connection to the civil rights
movement of the 1960s. *Sullivan*, in this view, was a necessary step
in the legal confirmation of the movement, one that shielded its leadership   from   exposure   to   the   constraining   effects   of
state-administered, common law rules of political libel. The white
public officials of the South that brought *Sullivan* and other libel actions, according to this literature, were provincial racists, who hypo-
critically complemented the force and violence they used against the
movement with a cynical invocation of the law's sweet reason. From
this perspective, Justice Brennan wisely collapsed traditional lines of
constitutional understanding in the face of massive, pent-up demands for racial equality.[4]

---

[3]The continuing analysis of the relationship between the press and public figures
has generated a huge bibliography, and most of that published since 1964 takes account of *Sullivan*. The best historical introduction to the subject of political libel law
is NORMAN L. ROSENBERG, PROTECTING THE BEST MEN: AN INTERPRETIVE HISTORY
OF THE LAW OF LIBEL (1986), and on *Sullivan* in particular *see* W. WAT HOPKINS,
ACTUAL MALICE: TWENTY-FIVE YEARS AFTER TIMES V. SULLIVAN (1989). The law review literature is very full. For a general discussion of the tort and constitutional
ramifications of *Sullivan*, *see* RANDALL P. BEZANSON, GILBERT CRANBERG & JOHN
SOLOSKI, LIBEL AND THE PRESS: MYTH AND REALITY (1987); LOIS G. FORER, A
CHILLING EFFECT (1987); RODNEY SMOLLA, SUING THE PRESS: LIBEL, THE MEDIA, AND
POWER (1986); Arthur L. Berney, *Libel and the First Amendment*, 51 VA. L. REV. 1
(1965); William J. Brennan, *The Supreme Court and the Meikeljohn Interpretation
of the First Amendment*, 79 HARV. L. REV. 1 (1965); Harry Kalven, *The New York
Times Case: A Note on "The Central Meaning of the First Amendment,"* 1964 SUP.
CT. REV. 191; Anthony Lewis, *New York Times v. Sullivan Reconsidered: Time to
Return to "The Central Meaning of the First Amendment,"* 8 COLUM. J. ART & L. 1
(1983); Alexander Meiklejohn, *Public Speech and the First Amendment*, 55 GEO. L.
J. 234 (1966); Melvill Nimmer, *The Right to Speak from Times to Time*, 56 CALIF. L.
REV. 935 (1968); Bruce L. Ottley, John Bruce Lewis & Younghee Jin Ottley, *New
York Times v. Sullivan: A Retrospective Examination*, 33 DEPAUL L. REV. 741
(1984); Willard H. Pedrick, *Freedom of the Press*, 49 CORNELL L. REV. 581 (1964);
Samuel R. Pierce, *The Anatomy of An Historic Decision: New York Times Co. v.
Sullivan*, 43 N. C. L. REV. 315 (1965); Frederick Schauer, *"Public Figures,"* 25 WM.
& MARY L. REV. 905 (1984); Anthony Lewis, *Annals of Law: The Sullivan Case*, NEW
YORKER, Nov. 5, 1984, at 53.

[4]On *Sullivan* and the civil rights movement, *see, e.g.*, TAYLOR BRANCH, PARTING
THE WATERS: AMERICA IN THE KING YEARS 1954–63, 289 (1989); DAVID GARROW,
BEARING THE CROSS: MARTIN LUTHER KING, JR., AND THE SOUTHERN CHRISTIAN
LEADERSHIP CONFERENCE 131, 135, 155, 310 (1986); HARRY KALVEN, THE NEGRO
AND THE FIRST AMENDMENT (1965); ANTHONY LEWIS, MAKE NO LAW: THE SULLIVAN
CASE AND THE FIRST AMENDMENT (1991); Ottley, Lewis & Ottley, *supra* note 3.
There is, however, another body of literature that raises questions about the impact
of the *Sullivan* decision as it relates to the nature of public discourse and the relative

Scholars writing from this perspective of legal liberalism have taught us much.[5] Yet, they have done so by giving a remarkably truncated reading to the events that generated the case in the first place and by ignoring the commitment of southern public officials to habits and manners of civility in public discourse.[6] Southern courts, far more than their northern counterparts, had historically protected these values through common law rules of political libel. Justice Brennan erased this tradition and, with it, the historical assumptions that had sustained the moderate southern position. The liberal interpretation of *Sullivan* and the events surrounding it incorrectly dismisses the possibility that—quite apart from the substantive issues of racial equality—the moderate, southern, white vision of civil discourse had intrinsic worth. By tracking the origins of the case, we are better able to illuminate how those assumptions prevailed and how, in the end, the proponents of southern moderation created the circumstances that prompted the legal destruction of the values they had so fervently hoped to preserve.

MONTGOMERY, ALABAMA: A PLACE IN TIME

Montgomery, Alabama, in 1960 was just beginning to experience the effects of the revolution wrought by the air conditioner on the South's economy, politics and social order. Sun Belt cities like Montgomery beckoned businesses from the chill winds, high wages and organized labor of the North, but new money and new people—outsiders—posed a Hobbesian choice to the city's established, white political leadership: It could either accept economic

---

freedom of the press. *See, e.g,* ROBERT POST, CONSTITUTIONAL DOMAINS: DEMOCRACY, COMMUNITY, MANAGEMENT (1995); Robert Post, *Review Essay: Defaming Public Officials: On Doctrine and Legal History,* AM. B. FOUND RES. J. 539 (1987); Robert Post, *The Social Foundations of Defamation Law: Reputation and the Constitution,* 74 CAL. L. REV. 691 (1986);

[5] *See* LAURA KALMAN, THE STRANGE CAREER OF LEGAL LIBERALISM (1986).

[6] My point is not that muzzling the leadership of the civil rights movement through libel law was either a *good* or a *wise* strategy on the part of southern segregationists. Nor do I intend this essay as a paen either to southern racism or to the section's alleged gentility. Such an argument would stand the region's history so completely on its head as to beggar reality. Nonetheless, I do believe that viewing *Sullivan* from the perspective of the southern, white elite can help to cast in sharper relief the implications of Justice Brennan's opinion, not just for the civil rights movement (as important as that was) but for our understanding of the competing vision of public discourse that informed the moderate segregationist position in the first place. In short, by dismissing the moderate segregationists, we miss an opportunity to better understand their time, the civil rights movement, and the meaning of public discourse as it was handed down to us in *Sullivan*. See *supra* note 4.

growth and, in so doing, threaten the traditional social and political order, or it could seek to sustain that order at the risk of further economic erosion. Montgomery had been the first capital of the Confederacy, the place where Jefferson Davis took the oath as its president, an important commercial center in the cotton culture of the Black Belt, and, in the twentieth century, the decayed but proud relation of industrialized and unionized Birmingham to the north. The white social ethos of Alabama's state capital exuded deference to one's betters and a paternalistic scheme of race relations that purchased social harmony through segregation. By 1960, however, the pressures for change threatened these social and political arrangements, battered as they were by a new, populist form of municipal politics, in which fear of racial change and outside influences became the controlling issues, and by an increasingly aggressive civil rights movement that demanded a place for blacks in determining the course of the city's fate.[7]

During most of the first half of the twentieth century, William A. Gunter, Jr., dominated Montgomery politics. He served as mayor from 1910 to 1915 and from 1919 to his death in 1940. Gunter was a charismatic figure, an Episcopalian, a patrician, and the descendant of a family of wealthy antebellum planters. To secure his political hold over the upper classes in the friends-and-neighbors politics of the city, Gunter had bested the Hill family, whose most famous member was U.S. Senator Lister Hill. Gunter secured his victory when voters installed a city commission form of government—one that divided duties among three commissioners, the most important of which was the commissioner of public safety. With the Hills eliminated, the only significant threat to Gunter's political rule came from lower-class whites, many of whom were associated with the Ku Klux Klan, followers of the Anti-Saloon League—who condemned Gunter's disapproval of prohibition—and fundamentalist Baptists and Methodists, who chaffed at Gunter's easygoing and tolerant life-style. Gunter retained influence through a shrewd distribution of city patronage, a willingness during the Great Depression to provide city jobs to hundreds of persons (even at the cost of running up a debt that frightened fiscal conservatives), and the unwavering support of the *Montgomery Advertiser*, the city's influential morning

---

[7]Much of the discussion on Montgomery and its politics is derived from J. Mills Thornton, The Montgomery Bus Boycott and the Pattern of Montgomery Municipal Politics (Mar. 14, 1988) (paper delivered to the Department of History, University of Florida); and J. Mills Thornton, The Montgomery Freedom Rider Riots (Apr. 28, 1984) (paper delivered at the Annual Meeting of the Alabama Historical Association).

newspaper, and its editor, Grover C. Hall, Sr. At each turn, the *Advertiser* sustained Gunter, especially in his attack on the Klan.

After Gunter's death in 1940, the political machine he crafted gradually fell into disrepair, since no leader emerged with either Gunter's personal appeal or political skills. Even had Gunter lived, his leadership would have been sorely tested by the potent mix of demographic and economic changes that his successors in office proved so unsuccessful in mastering. While Gunter was mayor, for example, the proportion of whites to blacks in the city remained stable, with about 61% white and 39% black. Migration patterns associated with World War II altered this relationship; whites moved from rural to urban Alabama and blacks to northern, industrial cities. By 1960, Montgomery's population of 134,000 was some 28,000 greater than a decade before, with almost all of that growth coming among lower middle-class whites. In that year, about 65% of the population was white and 35% black.

The new white voters owed little to the old Gunter machine. Moreover, as was true of most Sun Belt cities, Montgomery became more segregated, by both race and wealth. Developers in the late 1940s and through the 1950s began dozens of new housing developments in the city targeted to specific income groups. These projects increasingly concentrated the white, lower middle-class on the East side of the city; the upper classes more and more settled in the city's southern sections. The black population, on the other hand, remained settled where it had been—principally on the north side of Montgomery.

These demographic changes eroded the network of personal acquaintances and family alliances upon which Gunter's machine depended. The new mixture of voters added a new element of uncertainty to the political process. Once the behavior of the electorate became unstable, the ability of politicians to conduct business as usual diminished as well. Moreover, the introduction of civil service reform in 1949 denied Gunter's successors in city hall the all-important patronage base upon which the mayor had previously rested power. With no favors to give, the machine had increasing difficulty binding the voters. The surging ranks of lower middle-class whites were susceptible to appeal from politicians who played heavily on what had historically been the silent issue in city politics—race.

The ranks of black voters in Montgomery actually increased during the 1950s, even though the black population grew at a slower rate and became a smaller percentage of the total population. The Supreme Court's decision in *Smith v. Allright*[8] granted blacks through-

---

[8]321 U.S. 649 (1944).

out the South the right to participate in the previously all-white Democratic primary. The justices concluded that the historic exclusion of blacks from primary elections was a form of "state action" prohibited by the Fourteenth and Fifteenth amendments. Following the decision, the ranks of black voters slowly rose. By 1960, about 10% of the city's 25,000 registered voters were black, up from only 3.5% in 1950. Even though small in number, black voters were nonetheless important. The increasingly sharp divisions in the white electorate between the rivals from the East and South sides of the city heightened black voters' influence in municipal elections.

For a brief period in the 1950s, control of the black vote became one of the chief objects of Montgomery politics. In 1953, David Birmingham successfully campaigned to fill an unexpired term on the city commission by combining black voters with eastside segregationists resentful over the domination of the white business and professional classes from the southside. Once in office, Birmingham set about rewarding his black supporters, calling for the integration of the city's police force and public parks, something that the two other commissioners, both machine supporters, reluctantly embraced. Only two weeks before the Supreme Court handed down its decision in *Brown* v. *Board of Education*[9] in 1954, the Montgomery City Council voted to hire its first black policeman. The policy stirred a backlash among eastside segregationists, who felt betrayed—by Birmingham and by the machine.

At the same time, black leaders boldly pressed their new political advantage. High on the list of their demands was the adoption by the city council of the so-called "Mobile Plan" for seating on public buses. The Mobile Plan appealed to Montgomery blacks because, unlike in Montgomery, it did not require drivers to unseat black passengers. Instead, whites took seats at the front; blacks took seats in the back. The line separating them shifted back and forth; no person was ever required to give up a seat.

Birmingham's coalition proved short lived, as it collapsed under the weight of a white population unprepared for either the Mobile Plan or significant black political participation. The initial result was the election in 1955 of Clyde Sellers, a termite exterminator, former highway patrol director and ardent segregationist, to replace Birmingham as police commissioner. Sellers campaigned against Birmingham based on opposition to the Mobile Plan and to any further concessions to the increasingly active black community in Montgomery.

---

[9]374 U. S. 483 (1954).

Sellers' victory alerted black leaders that they would have to seek change outside the commission in order to make the city's public transportation system better accommodate black needs. When Rosa Parks boarded the Cleveland Avenue bus of the Montgomery City Lines at City Square on December 1, 1955, she took a seat in a white section. A few stops later the bus driver ordered her to surrender her place in favor of a white rider. She refused; within days the Montgomery bus boycott began.[10]

The bus boycott thoroughly polarized Montgomery. Blacks immediately organized the Montgomery Improvement Association (MIA) to run the boycott and named 26-year-old Martin Luther King, Jr., its president. Joining King on the group's board were close friend Ralph David Abernathy and S. S. Seay, Sr., another black minister. The MIA quickly recognized that direct action alone would not win the day; it's executive board, after some delay in the hope that compromise might ensue, decided to follow the recommendation of its attorney, Fred Gray. On February 1, 1956, two days after King's home was bombed by unknown persons, Gray filed a law suit in federal district court seeking an end to bus segregation.[11]

The bus boycott had a legacy of many lessons, not the least of which was the recourse to the law by all of those involved. Local state courts, of course, had never been friendly forums for blacks, let alone for blacks engaged in civil rights protests. Hence, Gray sought the protection of the federal courts. The white business community and the white segregationists associated with Sellers turned instead to the local state courts, where their influence was greater and their understanding of the law most likely to be appreciated. Sellers successfully pressed for the indictment of the boycott leaders under the Alabama Anti-Boycott Act of 1921. On February 21, 1956, the Montgomery County grand jury returned indictments against eighty-nine blacks, twenty-four of whom were ministers, for the misdemeanor of conspiring to boycott a lawful business.

The bus boycott was especially embarrassing for the fading Gunter machine. It eroded some of the machine's most cherished assumptions about the nature of the social order at the same time that political influence slipped into the hands of persons the machine had historically disdained—white, populist, race-baiting, lower class, religious fundamentalists. With the collapse of the machine, went the

---

[10]*See* BRANCH, *supra* note 4, at 289.

[11] *See* MARTIN LUTHER KING, JR., STRIDE TOWARD FREEDOM: THE MONTGOMERY STORY (1958); Randall Kennedy, *Martin Luther King's Constitution: A Legal History of the Montgomery Bus Boycott*, 98 YALE L.J. 999 (1989).

traditional vehicle for distributing political power, conducting public debate and adjusting race relations. This institutional dislocation fueled tension in the white community between moderates seeking accommodation and ardent segregationists, and it also heightened the already frayed relationships between lower-class whites and blacks.

The boycott drew to it an aggressive northern news media, the presence of which made the events surrounding the boycott all the more galling to moderate white leaders. What the northern press reported was not the paternalism and civility ostensibly associated with the Gunter machine's relations with the black community, but the ugly violence of the Klan and lower middle-class segregationists. The increasing attention paid by the northern press to the boycott spurred the segregationists to seek victory over black agitators, while white moderates from the city's southside searched for a compromise, all the while damning the interference of the northern liberal press.

Through the aegis of the federal courts, the MIA prevailed. On November 13, 1956, the Supreme Court, in *Gayle* v. *Browder*,[12] mandated that the city stop enforcing segregation on the buses. The decision was a stunning victory for the MIA, and it offered a means by which white moderates could bring about accommodation based on the rule of law. It was, however, also a significant blow to ardent segregationists, who were already fuming over the interference of the federal courts in the day-to-day lives of the South following the Supreme Court's decision in *Brown*.

As J. Mills Thornton has observed, the segregationists responded to this legal defeat by turning to extra-legal institutions. For example, the largest organization in Montgomery by early 1958 was the White Citizen's Council, which demanded absolute subservience by whites to the segregationist line and which had its strength on the city's eastside.[13] When, for example, a group of white women in 1958 organized a series of weekly inter-racial prayer meetings at a black Roman Catholic hospital, the council singled them out for public ridicule. In November, under threats that their husbands' business would be destroyed, most of the white women publicly recanted their racially moderate beliefs, although one of them, librarian Juliette Morgan, committed suicide rather than do so.[14]

In early 1960, therefore, a regime of total segregation seemed within the grasp of eastside political forces at the same time that the

---

[12]352 U. S. 903 (1956).
[13]Thornton, The Montgomery Bus Boycott, *supra* note 7, at 20.
[14] Kennedy, *supra* note 11, at 1067.

leaders of the once formidable Gunter machine, who disdained this new political force, wanted to set the public record straight—they and not the Klan embodied the South's real traditions. The demagogic exploitation of race, they asserted, violated the machine's tradition of political deference based on class, paternalism toward blacks, and habits and manners of civility in public discourse.

The lower middle-class segregationists were scoring impressive political and legal victories, both in the state and in Montgomery. Former Attorney General John Patterson won election to the Alabama governor's mansion in 1958 by conducting a political campaign of unalloyed racism that handed George C. Wallace a surprising defeat. In the wake of Patterson's victory, Wallace declared that he would "never be out-niggered again."[15] Patterson also won an order from Circuit Judge Walter Burwyn Jones, who would later preside over the Sullivan trail, that outlawed the NAACP in Alabama.[16] Finally, Montgomery city officials in January 1959 made clear that they were not going to retreat from their hard line, ordering that all thirteen city parks and the city zoo be sold as a way of evading a federal court order mandating their integration.[17]

In March 1959, the power of eastside segregationists surfaced again in the municipal elections. Earl James, another eastside leader, had won the mayor's post over incumbent William A. "Tacky" Gayle, a machine supporter, the son of a distinguished Alabama family, and generally a moderate on the race issue. James had successfully charged Gayle with being soft on the segregation issue because he had lost the bus boycott. An even more portentous political event for segregationists was the election of Lester Bruce Sullivan over incumbent *segregationist* police commissioner Clyde Sellers.[18]

THE PLAINTIFF: LESTER BRUCE SULLIVAN

Lester Bruce Sullivan, better know today by the initials L.B., was a highly visible public figure in Alabama politics from the early 1950s until his death in 1977.[19] Sullivan was born March 5, 1921, in Re-

---

[15] NUMAN V. BARTLEY & HUGH D. GRAHAM, SOUTHERN POLITICS AND THE SECOND RECONSTRUCTION 69 (1975).

[16] *See* NAACP v. Button, 371 U. S. 415 (1963). *But see,* the Court's earlier treatment in NAACP v. Alabama, 357 U. S. 449 (1958).

[17] Thornton, The Montgomery Bus Boycott, *supra* note 7, at 20–21.

[18] *Id.* at 21–22.

[19] The material on Sullivan comes from obituaries in the ALABAMA J., June 13, 1977, at 10; the MONTGOMERY ADVERTISER, June 13, 1977, at 2; and from interviews with M. Roland Nachman, Jr., lawyer, Montgomery, Ala. (Mar. 24, 1989); Ray

cords, Kentucky, the son of Henry Sullivan, a farmer and a sheriff, and Pauline Sullivan, a school teacher. He grew up in Vanceburg, Kentucky, and graduated in 1937 from Lewis County High School. He went to work with his brother, first in a drug store and then in the construction business. In 1941, Sullivan joined the Army Air Corps and, following in the law enforcement footsteps of his father, became a military police officer. He left the service as a staff sergeant in 1945 at Maxwell Air Force Base in Montgomery, Alabama, and became, first, a bread delivery person for the Colonial Bread Company and then a low-level administrator in the Office of Federal Price Administration, where he served until early 1947.

Except for a few brief periods, for the rest of his life Sullivan was involved in public service and politics. In 1947, he joined the Alabama Public Service Commission (PSC), where he served until 1951, first as an inspector and then as chief inspector. During these years, he established a close relationship with Gordon Person, the head of the PSC, who was elected governor in 1950. He joined Person's administration, serving for three months in 1951 as an investigator assigned to the governor's office. Person was impressed with the round-faced, stocky, quiet-spoken and hardworking Sullivan, whom he appointed Director of Public Safety in April. Sullivan remained in this important position, which included direction of the Alabama State Police, until early 1956.

In 1954, Sullivan's career took a decisive turn. As the state's chief law enforcement officer, he played an instrumental role in cleaning up Phenix City, Alabama. Phenix City was close to Ft. Benning military reservation; it was known in the 1950s as the most corrupt city in America.[20] Events reached a climax in June 1954 with the assassination of Senator Albert Patterson, a candidate for Attorney General of Alabama and the father of John M. Patterson, who was Attorney General of Alabama from 1955 until 1959, and then governor, from 1959 to 1963. Sullivan and the junior Patterson were joined in their crusade by Judge Walter Burwyn Jones, the longest-serving circuit court judge in Alabama history. Sullivan provided the investigative and police muscle; Patterson pursued the prosecutions of the criminal elements in Phenix City; and Jones presided over the trials. The trio freed Phenix City from much of the corruption into which it had sunk. Through the experience, a bond was forged among them, one

---

Jenkins, editor, *Baltimore Evening Sun*, Baltimore, Md. (Mar. 23, 1990); and William McDonald, media consultant, Montgomery, Ala. (June 26, 1990).

[20]*See* ALAN GRADY, WHEN GOOD MEN DO NOTHING: THE ASSASSINATION OF ALBERT PATTERSON 91–92 (2003).

that carried over into Montgomery, the state capital where Sullivan resided.

Sullivan spun through his personal life a web of political contacts among the middle and lower middle-classes of the city's east side. He was an active club worker, holding membership in the Alcazar Shrine, the American Legion, the Elks, the Eagles and the Andrew Jackson Lodge of the Masonic Order, and was president of the Davis Elementary School parent-teacher group. His religious fundamentalism complemented and reinforced his racism; he was at once a Baptist and a member of the Ku Klux Klan. In his 1959 campaign against Clyde Sellers, Sullivan promised voters, on the one hand, "the continuation of Southern traditions and customs," and, at the same time that, declared his intention to promote "industrial growth and development for our city, county, and state."[21]

There Sullivan became involved in police and public affairs as well as with the Ku Klux Klan. He is described by those who knew him as "smooth, polished, relatively sophisticated for Montgomery. He had read a few books."[22]

Sullivan drew national attention because of his success in bringing law and order to Phenix City. In 1955 he became police consultant with the International Association of Chiefs of Police, covering fourteen southern states, a position he held until 1957. In this role, Sullivan traveled throughout the South, dispensed advice on police practices and established a reputation for his tough-on-crime tactics. His success won him, in July 1957, the position of safety director for the P. C. White Truck Line in Montgomery. He subsequently attended the FBI Police Academy, the Northwestern University Traffic Institute and the Motor Vehicle Fleet Administrator's court at the University of Alabama. In all, Sullivan forged an impressive resume as a police and public safety official and a reputation for being a hands-on, no-nonsense administrator.

Sullivan's prominence increased as the civil rights movement began to roil the racial waters of Montgomery. In 1958 his political opportunity came when incumbent police commissioner Clyde Sellers decided to pay a fine for Martin Luther King, Jr., rather than have him jailed as a martyr. In the 1959 commission race, Sullivan effectively exploited this incident, charging that incumbent police commissioner Sellers with using kid gloves to handle social agitators.[23]

---

[21]Campaign Card, L. B. Sullivan File, Alabama Department of History and Archives, Montgomery, Ala.

[22]Interview with M. Roland Nachman, *supra* note 19.

[23]*L.B. Sullivan Likely City Race Candidate*, ALABAMA J., Aug. 4, 1958, at 1.

Sullivan's campaign also stressed his commitment to traditional Southern customs, opposition to tax increases, the elimination of special interests from government, the development of city-wide police patrols and the economic development of Montgomery.[24] Indeed, Sullivan mixed New South economic ambition with segregationist beliefs. As he explained during the election and throughout his time in office, the economic development of Montgomery depended on stable social relations and a predictable set of economic opportunities for both races without disturbing the historical pattern of race relations.[25]

From the outset of his tenure as commissioner of police, Sullivan had a rocky relationship with the media, one that had been troubled long before he came to office. One of Sullivan's first acts was to call a meeting between media representatives and police officials, at which he pledged cooperation. The truce was short lived. In the early 1960s, media attention on Sullivan grew even more intense, not just from the local papers but from the national press covering the civil rights movement. The press increasingly printed stories indicating that Sullivan had failed in his duties to protect black activists from the direct physical assault of white segregationists. The northern press quickly turned him and his counterpart in Birmingham, Eugene "Bull" Connor, into caricatures of southern police officials and extreme racists.[26] The Reverend Joseph Lowery, one of the ministers Sullivan sued, concluded, "He represents the Old South, the Old South with all the venom and vitriol and oppression."[27]

Sullivan's first major crisis occurred in February 1960, when the sit-in movement reached Montgomery. At 4 p.m. on February 1 of that year, the first black sit-in began at the F. W. Woolworth lunch counter in Greensboro, North Carolina. Within days, the protest spread through the rest of the non-cotton South, moving to Charlotte, Raleigh, then Rock Hill, South Carolina, Orangeburg, South Carolina and on to Nashville, Tennessee. The movement was unique,

---

[24]*Id.*

[25]MONTGOMERY ADVERTISER, *supra* note 19.

[26]Both men suffered from intense opposition by black political and civic leaders. As has been the case with many former segregationists, Sullivan has been the subject of some effort to rehabilitate his reputation by suggesting that he merely reflected his times, especially in his role as commissioner of public saftey. It is worth noting, however, that blacks who lived through the turbulent Sullivan years had a different view. As Frank Bray, the President of the Montgomery NAACP, noted in 1989: "L. B. Sullivan was a famous racist and a hater of black people and anything they stood for." Associated Press, *Honors for Montgomery Chief Stir Bad Memories*, BERGEN RECORD, Oct. 12, 1989, at A7

[27]*Move To Name Alabama Prison For White Ex-Police Exec Angers Blacks*, JET, Apr. 13, 1998, at 19

and in its novelty lay a source of profound concern for the white South. Until the sit-in movement began, whites had largely inspired and lead most of the major civil rights battles. There were, of course, the exceptions, of which the bus boycott in Montgomery was the most notable. But in the sit-ins, young blacks took an aggressive role that captured the attention of the national media, including the *New York Times*, whose editors dispatched, as they had done during the bus boycott, additional correspondents to cover breaking civil rights developments.

On February 25, thirty-five students from all-black Alabama State College sought service at the snack bar in the basement of the Montgomery County Courthouse. The students were rebuffed and arrested. The following day, Governor John Patterson, who was the *ex officio* chairman of the State Board of Education, demanded the expulsion of the students. On February 27, most of the 800 students at Alabama State marched to the State Capitol to protest Patterson's actions. Governor Patterson and Commissioner Sullivan decided to apply officially sanctioned force and intimidation against the students. While state and Montgomery police stood idly by, baseball wielding Klansman waded into the black students. The attack went unpunished, even though the *Montgomery Advertiser* ran pictures of the incident, with several of the mob clearly identified. The *Adverstiser*'s editor, Grover Hall, Jr., condemned the attack and rebuked Sullivan for failing to bring it to a halt and to seek arrests against those who had perpetrated it. At the same time, the extremist press praised the incident. The Montgomery *Home News* observed that "the crisp crack of a hickory bat on a Negro head snapped the people out of their apathy into the realization that the steady, cold siege against their way of life was now breaking out in ... obviously Communist-inspired racial strife." It served, the editor said, as "a signal for the white Christian race to stand up and be counted."[28]

These events formed the immediate background of the *Sullivan* case. Segregationists controlled the White Citizens Council and the police force; they used both to cow white moderates and black civil rights protestors. The political culture of Montgomery associated with the Gunter machine—its values of paternalism, deference and civility—was in disarray. Its once-influential leaders were not only driven from office but they had suffered the ironic fate of being attacked at home by segregationists while being held up to national ridicule by a northern liberal press that equated all white citizens of

---

[28]Quoted in Thornton, The Montgomery Freedom Rider Riots, *supra* note 7, at 5a.

Montgomery as segregationists. Such a characterization distressed the traditional white leadership class because it projected on them values that they associated with their lower middle-class eastside opponents. Taken together, lower-class segregationists and northern journalists threatened to rob the once-powerful leaders of the Gunter machine of not just their political fortunes but their sacred honor. The civic culture of Montgomery, as a result, was already under considerable stress when a full-page ad titled "Heed Their Rising Voices," appeared in the March 29 issue of the *New York Times*.[29]

THE ADVERTISEMENT

State authorities in the South mounted a full-scale legal attack on the nascent civil rights movement, seeking to outlaw the NAACP and other organizations and discredit individual leaders. In Alabama, for example, Governor John Patterson in early 1960 directed state revenue authorities to charge Martin Luther King, Jr., with tax evasion and perjury in completing his Alabama state income tax returns. The charges against King, who had already moved his ministry from the Dexter Street Church in Montgomery to his father's church in Atlanta, specified that he had diverted money raised for the Southern Christian Leadership Conference (SCLC) into his own pockets without ever reporting it as income. King had founded the group of southern, black ministers as a vehicle for pressing his desegregation initiatives specifically and social change in the South generally.[30]

Prominent northern civil rights leaders made a virtue out of the necessity of raising money to defend King. Bayard Rustin, a political and civil rights organizer in New York City, founded the "Committee to Defend Martin Luther King and the Struggle for Freedom in the South" and served as it executive director. Its chairman was A. Phillip Randolph, a pioneer in the black civil rights movement and the president of the Sleeping Car Porters Union. The board included such notable figures as the Reverend Harry Emerson Fosdick and labor leader Morris Iushewitz. At Rustin's prodding, the committee determined to bring attention to King's plight through a full-page ad in the *New York Times* that would also call attention to the sit-in movement generally and events in Montgomery specifically.

Rustin selected John Murray—a tall, thin, white man of great style and humor—to create the ad. A writer by trade, Murray was the son in a prominent Irish-Catholic family, whose history included an-

---

[29]N.Y. TIMES, Mar. 29, 1960, at L25.
[30]*See* GARROW, *supra* note 4, at 85–87, 89.

cestors that had strongly supported the abolition of slavery before the Civil War. A 1948 graduate of Yale University, Murray's credits included everything from off-Broadway plays to training films on sexual hygiene for the U.S. Army. The ad was principally Murray's work, although he had modest assistance from two other New York writers, William Branch and John Killens. The ad was based on an earlier memorandum prepared by Rustin that outlined the sit-in movement and stressed how events at the Alabama state capitol might be exploited for fund-raising purposes. The memo also listed the names of more than two dozen prominent entertainers, theologians and educators. Murray attempted to project the ad "in the most appealing forum ... to rev it up a little bit to get money."[31]

Late in the afternoon of March 23, 1960, Murray entered the second-floor offices of the national advertising department of the *Times* on West 43rd Street in New York City. The writer presented two items to Gershon T. Aronson, a twenty-five-year veteran of selling advertising space for the newspaper. The first item was Murray's typewritten manuscript of the advertisement, now headed "Heed Their Rising Voices"; the second was a letter from Randolph. The latter requested the *Times* to run the advertisement and vouched for the authenticity of the persons who endorsed it.

Aronson immediately sent the ad forward to the *Times'* Advertisers Services Department to consult about the size and style of the type arrangement. The ad itself was laid out by the Union Advertising Agency, a respected New York City firm that served as an intermediary between newspapers and advertisers.

As a matter of standard operating procedure, Aronson also had a copy of the typescript of the ad sent to the Advertising Acceptability Department. There, D. Vincent Redding, a six-year employee of the *Times* and manager of the department, was responsible for screening the acceptability of all advertisements before they were published. This particular kind of editorial ad had to conform to the *Times's* Advertising Acceptability Standards contained in a small booklet. Redding read and approved the ad based mostly on the fact that it "was endorsed by a number of people who are well known and whose reputation I had no reason to question."[32] He made no attempt to check, as the guidelines required, the accuracy of the most powerful assertions contained in the ad. His approval signaled the newspaper's Production Department to proceed to publication.

---

[31] Record, New York Times v. Sullivan, 254 U.S. 376 (1964) (Nos. 39 & 40), Vol. 2, at 815 (hereafter Record).

[32] *Id.*, Vol. 2, at 758.

After Redding had given his endorsement but before the ad could go to press, Bayard Rustin changed his mind. He decided that Murray's version lacked sufficient appeal. On March 28, Rustin asked Murray and the two other writers to attend a meeting in his office, but only Murray was available. Rustin informed the writer that the ad lacked sufficient emotional appeal, so much so that the civil rights leader worried that it would not generate enough of a response to cover the $4,552 charged by the *Times* to run it. After an extended discussion, Rustin pulled open a file drawer from which he took a list of black ministers associated with the SCLC. Rustin and Murray then proceeded to alter the approved proof, inserting two new items. The first was a single sentence that read, "We in the South who are struggling daily for dignity and freedom warmly endorse this appeal." The second was a list of twenty new names, including four Alabama ministers: Ralph D. Abernathy and S. S. Seay, Sr., of Montgomery; Fred L. Shuttlesworth, of Birmingham; and Joseph E. Lowery, of Mobile.

Murray cautioned Rustin not to use the ministers' names as endorsees without first seeking their approval, but the civil rights organizer replied that there was insufficient time to do so since the ad was scheduled to run the following day. Rustin also insisted that since SCLC was King's organization in the first place, there was no need to consult with the individual ministers. Hubris and impatience prevailed; Rustin had the ad altered. Since the business day was over by the time the ad was rewritten, Rustin called his personal contact at the Union Advertising Agency to obtain a promise that the ad would be promptly revised the following morning and sent to the *Times* immediately. D. Vincent Redding, having already given his approval based on the Randloph letter, never knew of Rustin's changes, nor did the twenty new endorsees whom Rustin added. On March 29, 1960, the full-page advertisement appeared on page L25.

Murray had taken the ad's heading, "Heed Their Rising Voices," from an editorial printed in the *Times* on March 19, 1960. Like so much else in the case of *Times v. Sullivan*, the choice had an ironic twist. Its author was Turner Catledge, the newspaper's managing executive editor since 1951 and a native of a farm near New Prospect, Mississippi, who, like the paper's publisher, Adolph Ochs, had moved north to pursue a career in journalism. Catledge grew up in a South dominated by separate-but-equal, a custom that he embraced until joining the staff of the *The Tunica Times* in 1922. In the course of his duties with that small weekly Mississippi paper, Catledge wrote a series of articles denouncing the Ku Klux Klan. "I thought very little about the plight of blacks," Catledge wrote years later, but "I realized that they [Supreme Court decisions outlawing segregation] were right, that segregation in public institutions and facilities cannot be tolerated."[33] Catledge was determined that the *Times* should play a vital role in what the former described as the "Great Revolution"—the series of events involving race relations that flowed from the Supreme Court's controversial decisions in *Brown v. Board of Education*.[34] In *Brown I*, Chief Justice Earl Warren, writing for a unanimous Court, had decreed an end to the practice of separate-but-equal in public education specifically and in all public places generally;[35] in *Brown II* the Court ordered that these changes be made "with all deliberate speed."[36] Catledge's own experience with race relations in Mississippi motivated him to ensure that the *Times* adequately covered the story of the budding civil rights movement there, including detailed reporting on the Montgomery bus boycott.[37] Catledge and Ochs also recognized that as the nation's newspaper of record, such coverage was essential and, given the paper's readership, economically sound.

The *Times* covered the civil rights movement in the South through several correspondents, the most notable of which was Atlanta-based Claude Sitton, and stringers in all of the major cities, including Montgomery and Birmingham, Alabama. The sit-in movement quickly captured the attention of the *Times*, whose editors dispatched Sitton and other correspondents to cover the breaking news throughout the South.

The editorial that Catledge penned for the paper's March 19 edition also reflected the newspaper's editorial policy of supporting the strategy of peaceful civil disobedience adopted by King during the Montgomery bus boycott and of urging Congress to enact civil rights legislation. The full sentence from which the advertisement's heading was taken read: "Let Congress heed their rising voice, for they will be heard."[38]

The first four of the ten paragraphs of the ad dealt specifically with the sit-in movement that Sullivan had sought to squelch. Appealing to the Constitution and the Bill of Rights, Murray's words recited how "thousands of Southern Negro students ... engaged in wide-

---

[33]*Turner Catledge Dies at 82; Former Editor of the Times,* N.Y.TIMES, Apr. 28, 1983, at A1.

[34] 347 U. S. 483 (1954); 349 U. S. 294 (1955).

[35]347 U. S. at 495.

[36]349 U.S. at 301.

[37]HARRISON SALISBURY, WITHOUT FEAR OR FAVOR: THE NEW YORK TIMES AND ITS TIMES 390 (1980).

[38]Editorial, *Amendment XV,* N.Y. TIMES, Mar. 19, 1960, at A20.

spread non-violent demonstrations ... had boldly stepped forth as the protagonists of democracy." The third paragraph dealt specifically with events in Montgomery. It reported that the 800 students from Alabama State College who marched to the State Capitol and on its steps had sung "My Country, 'Tis of Thee" after which their student leaders were expelled. Moreover, the third paragraph also claimed that "truckloads of police armed with shotguns and tear-gas" then "ringed the Alabama State College campus." When the students protested these actions by refusing to re-register for classes, the ad continued, "[T]heir dining hall was padlocked in an attempt to starve them into submission." The fifth and sixth paragraphs turned attention to the plight of Martin Luther King, Jr., identifying so-called "Southern violators of the Constitution" who were determined to destroy King and to answer his "peaceful protests with intimidation and violence." The sixth paragraph, in particular, claimed that these "Southern violators"had "bombed his home almost killing his wife and child," that they had "assaulted his person," and that they "have arrested him seven times—for 'speeding,' 'loitering,' and similar 'offenses.'" The grand design of these "Southern violators" was to "behead this affirmative movement, and thus to demoralize Negro Americans and to weaken their will to struggle." The remaining four paragraphs pleaded not just for moral support "but material help so urgently needed by those who are taking the risks, facing jail, and even death in a glorious re-affirmation of our Constitution and its Bill of Rights."[39]

Below these paragraphs were two blocks of endorsements. The first contained sixty-four names, including such prominent figures as Eleanor Roosevelt, Norman Thomas, Marlon Brando, Harry Belafonte, Sidney Portier, Shelly Winters, Van Heflin, Nat Hentoff, Ertha Kitt, Nat King Cole and Frank Sinatra. A second block listed the SCLC ministers, including the four from Alabama. To the right was a coupon to be clipped and returned with a contribution.

"Heed Their Rising Voices" was just what its creator John Murray said it was—a piece of propaganda designed to attract sympathy, and money.[40] It was an "editorial-type ad," one that pushed a particular point of view; it was neither news reporting nor an editorial. While Murray had considerable experience as a writer, "Heed Their Rising Voices" was his first effort at creating paid political advertising.

The Committee's decision to place the ad in the *Times* stemmed directly from the paper's prestige and political sympathies. Founded

---

[39] N.Y. TIMES, Mar. 29, 1960, at L25.
[40] See LEWIS, *supra* note 4, at 5–7, 32.

by Henry Jarvis Raymond in 1851, the paper became the political organ of the Republican Party and the respectable, stable and conservative antislavery groups that supported it before the Civil War. The *Times'* chief competitor during these early years was Horace Greeley's *Tribune* that urged social reforms sufficiently radical, such as the abolition of slavery, that it alienated much of the middle and upper class market in New York City. Over the next century, Raymond's newspaper won great distinction by balancing a progressive view of many social issues with a dignified approach to reporting the news. During the first half of the twentieth century, the *Times* leadership had steadily built up the paper's reputation, garnering an impressive list of Pulitzer Prizes that in the process made it America's most influential daily newspaper.

The *Times* daily circulation was about 650,000, a number that doubled on Sundays. Most of these papers were sold, of course, in the New York City area and the northeast corridor stretching from Washington, D. C., to Boston. Elsewhere circulation dropped markedly, with most copies sold to libraries, educational institutions, and a few individuals. On an average day in Alabama, for example, the *Times* sold about 390 papers with about 2,500 on Sunday. Of the Alabama circulation, approximately 35 copies were distributed in Montgomery County.

These numbers leave no doubt that Rustin directed his ad not at the population of Dixie, but at the sympathetic, white, progressive and intellectual leadership of the liberal North, where its non-New York City circulation was largest. The ad's invocation of "Southern violators" echoed prevailing stereotypes of the South as a racist, backward and violent place. The ad named no individuals and it made no specific reference to any public officeholder, but it did offer a damaging picture of police forces in the South, who were quickly earning a well-deserved reputation for brutality in dealing with the non-violent civil rights movement, and created a less than flattering impression of the public officials responsible for overseeing the police. Neither Murray nor Rustin had any idea that the ad would have any effect in the South. Clearly they miscalculated.

THE DISCOVERY

Early in the week of April 3, 1960, William H. MacDonald, the assistant editor in charge of the editorial page of the *Montgomery Advertiser*, was rummaging through the "exchanges" on his desk. Exchanges were other newspapers; MacDonald read them to find out what other papers considered newsworthy. The *New York Times* was one of the most important of these exchange papers because of its coverage of international events and foreign affairs. The editorial staff of the *Advertiser* and its sister afternoon paper, the *Alabama Journal*, also read the *Times* for other matters, most especially its reporting and editorial commentary on what was then the most important issue in the region—the growing civil rights movement. MacDonald and other southern journalists viewed the *Times* with a mixture of awe and contempt. It was at once the epitome of the modern newspaper and the mouthpiece for the Northeastern liberal establishment. What MacDonald was doing as he read through the *Times* that day was what he had been doing for the previous twelve years, ever since he had started work on the paper as a summer job between his law studies at the University of Alabama. What began as a summer job turned into a career; MacDonald never returned to law school.

As MacDonald scanned the March 29 issue of the paper, his eye stopped on page 25, which contained an impressive full-page ad headlined "Heed Their Rising Voices." He read the ad and "kind of chuckled," thinking to himself that "it had some foundation in fact," but that he "was not greatly distressed by it."[41] He was sufficiently impressed by the ad to show it to his immediate superior, Grover C. Hall, Jr., the editor and vice president of the *Advertiser*. Hall gave it slight attention: He "sorta of umphed" and walked on by.[42]

A short time later, MacDonald broke from his duties and walked to the Capitol Book Company, a distance of about six blocks. The ad was still on his mind when, in the course of browsing through the book and magazine racks, he came upon Calvin Whitesell, the new city attorney for Montgomery. Whitesell was a thirty-one-year-old graduate of the University of Alabama Law School and an aspiring political figure who had aligned himself with the new, strongly segregationist regime in city hall, headed by L. B. Sullivan. MacDonald, in an off-handed fashion ("The same way you would ask: 'What did you think of the football game?'"), asked Whitesell if he had read the ad. Whitesell, who never read the *Times*, had not, but his political antenna immediately perked-up.[43] He asked to see the ad; both men then walked the six or so blocks back to the *Advertiser* offices. There Whitesell quickly scanned the ad and took the paper back to his office, where he shared it with Sullivan and the two other city commissioners, Earl James and Franklin "Frank" Parks. A day later,

---

[41]Interview with William H. MacDonald, *supra* note 19.
[42]*Id.*
[43]*Id.*

Whitesell returned the paper to MacDonald, who then sent it on to other members of the editorial staff.[44]

On April 4, Ray Jenkins, the city editor of the *Journal*, came across the ad as he worked his way through the March 29 issue of the *Times*. Jenkins was born and raised on a farm in south Georgia and graduated from the journalism school at the University of Alabama. His first job in 1954 was as a reporter for the *Columbus Ledger* in Columbus, Georgia. Jenkins was assigned to cover Phenix City, a city with which he established a "unique relationship ... in that I participated in the vice by night and exposed it by day."[45] Jenkins covered both the assassination of Attorney General Albert Patterson and the sensational trials that followed. The *Ledger* won the Pulitzer Prize in 1955 for that coverage, and Jenkins basked in the glow of success.

Four years later, Jenkins moved his career forward another notch, this time joining the staff of the larger and more prestigious *Alabama Journal* at the behest of Grover Hall, Jr. His first assignment as city editor on January 15, 1959, was to cover the inauguration of John Patterson, the son of the martyred attorney general.

Jenkins immediately grasped the newsworthiness of the ad. He understood that King was a figure at once revered and hated in Montgomery. The ad, both among blacks and whites, was bound to be of interest—King's tax evasion and perjury trial was set to begin in only a few weeks.

Jenkins immediately set about checking as many of the assertions as possible and then composed a seven-paragraph story on his typewriter. That story listed some of the signers of the advertisement and quoted parts of the text that dealt with assertions that the civil rights movement had been subjected to "an unprecedented wave of terror."[46] Jenkins then noted certain discrepancies in the ad and suggested that there might be others, although he was unable to confirm them in the time available. The one error that Jenkins noted was a statement that "Negro student leaders from Alabama State College

---

[44]As is often the case, memories of the principal actors either fade with time, are reconstructed to suit new political realities or both. Whitesell, for example, provided information to Lindsley A. Smith that suggested he had originally discovered the ad and had taken a leading role in pressing Sullivan and the other commissioners to bring the lawsuit. The story, however, based on the memories of MacDonald seems more complex. In any event, it is also apparent that Ray Jenkins played an important although heretofore unreported role in moving the litigation forward. *See* Lindsley Armstrong Smith, From Casual Conversation to Constitutional Confrontation: Historical Origins of *New York Times v. Sullivan* (Jan. 12–16, 2003) (paper presented at the Hawaii International Conference on Arts and Humanities).

[45]Interview with Ray Jenkins, *supra* note 19.

[46]MONTGOMERY J., Apr. 5, 1960, at 1.

were expelled 'after students sang "My Country 'Tis of Thee" on the State Capitol steps.'" Actually, Jenkins's story continued, "[T]the students were expelled for leading a sitdown strike at the courthouse grill."[47]

Jenkins also reported that the ad had erred in another way. Its authors had claimed that "when the entire student body protested [the expulsion] to state authorities by refusing to re-register, their dining hall was padlocked in an attempt to starve them into submission." Jenkins informed his readers that officials at all-black Alabama State had said that "there is not a modicum of truth in the statement."[48] These same officials assured him that "our registration for the spring quarter was only slightly below normal" and they "deny that the dining hall was padlocked."[49] When Jenkins finished the story, he threw the newspaper in the wastebasket, since he was the last of the editorial staff to review the exchanges. Jenkins thought the advertisement more newsworthy than did MacDonald, but both journalists concluded that it was little more than another round in the sparing between King's civil rights followers and segregationist officials.

Much has been made of the role played by Jenkins in the events leading up to the law suit, perhaps too much. McDonald, of course, had already called the ad to the attention of the city attorney and to Grover Hall before Jenkins's article appeared. Yet, neither Jenkins nor McDonald played a decisive role in the events that followed. Instead, that honor clearly belongs to Merton Roland Nachman, the attorney who eventually argued the case for Sullivan before the Supreme Court.

Nachman was thirty-seven years old in 1960. After graduating from Harvard University and then the law school, he returned to his home state of Alabama, serving as assistant attorney general from 1949 to 1954. Almost immediately, Nachman established himself as a successful advocate, for his role in *Alabama Public Service Commission* v. *Southern Railway*.[50] The United States Supreme Court held that federal courts should ordinarily abstain from deciding constitutional claims when a state administrative proceeding has begun on the issue and it can be reviewed by state courts. Nachman's first victory came at age twenty-seven and with less than the three years of prior practice required for admission to the Supreme Court bar.

---

[47]*Id.*
[48]*Liberals Appeal for Funds to Defend M.L. King,* ALABAMA J., Apr. 5, 1960, at 1.
[49]*Id.*
[50]341 U. S. 341 (1951).

The Court waived the rule, although Justice Felix Frankfurter complained, "I don't know why we have these rules if we aren't going to enforce them."[51] In 1954, Nachman entered private practice in Montgomery with Walter Knabe, a future city attorney for Montgomery, remaining there until 1959 when he joined the firm of Steiner, Crum & Baker. The Steiner firm included among its clients the city's two newspapers, the *Advertiser* and the *Journal*.

In politics, Nachman was a moderate, southern Democrat, who sought to distance himself from the excesses of the states' rights wing of the Democratic Party in the South. He supported Harry Truman in 1948 against the insurgency of Senator Strom Thurmond and the Dixiecrats, and in 1956 he worked for several weeks in the Washington office of presidential candidate Adali Stevenson. When Stevenson lost the election, Nachman returned to private practice.

Perhaps nowhere was Nachman's sense of toleration more evident than in his decision in 1958 to represent in a civil suit for libel against Johnson Publishing Company[52] a black man who had assailed the Reverend Ralph David Abernathy for purportedly having an affair with his wife. A criminal jury had acquitted Edward Davis of charges of assault and attempted murder, but *Jet* magazine, on September 18, 1958, published a patently false expose of Davis. The magazine reported that the charge of a sexual liaison between Davis's wife and the Reverend Mr. Abernathy were false, and that Davis "was the pawn of persons seeking to embarrass Reverends Abernathy and King."[53] The story went on to explain that Davis had been discharged from his teaching position in Greenville, Alabama, a small town just south of Montgomery, because he had sexual relations with his grade school students. "It was an outrageous falsehood," Nachman complained, one that called out for help.[54] Nachman took the case, along with Truman Hobbs, a future federal district court judge who played a critical role in desegregating public facilities in Alabama. They secured a judgment in Judge Walter B. Jones's circuit court in Montgomery of $67,000 in damages, which the Alabama Supreme Court subsequently reduced to $45,000 on appeal.[55]

Three years before, Nachman had also represented three city commissioners—Gayle, Sellers and Parks—in a $750,000 libel suit

[51]Interview, M. Roland Nachman, *supra* note 19.

[52]Johnson Publishing Co., Inc. v. Davis, 124 So. 2d 441 (Ala. 1960).

[53]*Id.* at 446.

[54] Interview, M. Roland Nachman, Jr., lawyer, Montgomery, Alabama (Mar. 20, 1989).

[55]*Johnson Publishing Co.*, 124 So. 2d at 453.

against *Ken* magazine, a pulp publication based in New York City.[56]
The magazine had run a feature story entitled "Kimono Girls Check
in Again" that purported to expose rampant prostitution and gambling in Montgomery. During the Gunter era, the after-hours life of
the city had been tawdry, but following World War II city authorities
had mounted an extensive anti-vice campaign. Such actions appealed
to the fundamentalists among the east-siders and also presented to
northern businesses thinking of investing in the city a sense of moral
order and progressive efficiency, qualities that were particularly important in attracting business in the wake of the bus boycott.
Nachman made quick work of the case in federal district court in
Montgomery. He showed that the author of the essay had never visited Montgomery, that he had fabricated his lurid tales about the
city's moral bankruptcy, and that the magazine had published them
knowing that they were false. *Ken* settled the suit, paying $15,000 in
damages to the commissioners and issuing a public apology.[57]

By the spring of 1960, Nachman had established himself as the pre-
eminent libel lawyer in Montgomery and one of the best in the state.
He had fashioned political moderation, a keen intellect and impressive
lawyering skills into an increasingly successful law practice. Perhaps
as a result of his years at Harvard, Nachman held a far more cosmopoli-
tan vision of the world than did most of Montgomery's public officials.
For Nachman, one window on that world came from his daily reading
of the *New York Times*, to which he subscribed.

Nachman discovered "Heed Their Rising Voices" at about the
same time that McDonald and Jenkins were reading their exchanges.
Because of his experience as a libel lawyer, however, Nachman saw
something far different than the two journalists. He immediately
recognized that the falsity of the statements in the ad might make
them libelous *per se* under Alabama law. His success against *Ken*
magazine was only the most recent manifestation of the common law
rule in Alabama that persons making libelous statement about public officials that were false were subject to damages. "Heed Their Rising Voices," at least in Alabama, was no ordinary newspaper ad; it
was an actionable insult. More than the lawyer's mind was at work,
however. Like many moderates, Nachman was frustrated by the excesses of the burgeoning civil rights movement and its white segregationist tormentors. The ad was not just wrong, it was mean spirited,
at least in the eyes of Nachman, and it promised to do nothing more

---

[56]William A. Gayle et al. v. Magazine Mgmt. Co., 153 F. Supp. 861 (M.D. Ala.
1957).

[57]Record, *supra* note 31, Vol. 2, at 2005.

than contribute even more to an already high level of misunderstanding and distrust. When Nachman opened the page to the ad, he was, in his own words, "outraged by it and knew that some of the things were absolutely false and some of the charges were grossly exaggerated to the point of bullshit."[58] At that point, Nachman became the prime moving force in what would become the lawsuit brought against the *Times*.

Nachman clipped the page from the newspaper and delivered it to the three city commissioners. He indicated to Police Commissioner Sullivan that, even though he was not directly named in the ad, there could be little doubt that he could bring an action against the *Times*. The ad cast aspersions on Sullivan because it attributed to the police force he led complicity in bombing the home of Martin Luther King, Jr., and, more generally, in fomenting police-state terrorism. Nachman pointed out to Sullivan that the ad discredited his administration because it essentially concluded that his efforts to make the police force more progressive, better trained, more efficient, and more responsive to citizens had failed. Calvin Whitesell almost simultaneously brought the ad to the commissioners' attention. In short, Nachman and Whitesell told the commissioners that, based on existing Alabama law, they could sue the *Times* for libel and that they were almost certain to win.

THE REACTION

When MacDonald had shown Hall the advertisement, the editor had expressed little interest. But when the copy of Jenkins's story crossed his desk on the afternoon of April 5, Hall reacted entirely differently. "Grover Hall read the story," Ray Jenkins reported years later, "and came running out there and wanted to see that ad. So I fished the thing out of the trash can and gave it to him."[59] Hall had apparently not paid sufficient attention when MacDonald first showed him the ad. Jenkins's story, however, left little doubt in Hall's mind that something was amiss.

Grover Hall was a deeply complex figure, who attempted to walk a line between fidelity to the South he loved and, with it, the system of racial control that made it so distinctive, and the emerging liberalism

---

[58]Interview with M. Roland Nachman, Jr., *supra* note 51.

[59]Interview with Ray Jenkins, *supra* note 19. Anthony Lewis reports that Hall read Jenkins's story in the *Advertiser* and then sought the paper. *See* LEWIS, *supra* note 4, at 9–10. Jenkins reports, however, that it was the typescript of the story, not the printed version, that drew Hall's attention.

on race matters and economic development that ground against such ideas. Hall was a bachelor who reveled in his reputation as a dandy; a white newspaper editor who was not a knee-jerk segregationist; and a son who never quite lived up to his father's success in winning a Pulitzer Prize. The younger Hall had earned a reputation for professional reporting on civil rights matters; he had once served on the national board of the American Civil Liberties Union; and he had urged a moderate course during the bus boycott.[60] Yet, Hall was also a southerner and Alabamian.[61] Like his father, he disdained lower-class, white segregationists, such as Sullivan, whom he disliked, and the Klan because they mocked the South's historic position on the race issue.[62] He viewed the *Times* as a model of modern newspaper reporting, but he also believed that its editors and reporters had affronted his and his paper's honor by giving far too much attention to white extremists, which the *Advertiser* railed against, and discounting the South's ability to evolve gradual solutions to the race issue.[63]

The contradictions in Hall's position had brought him under substantial personal and professional pressure. His paper had lost advertising and subscription revenues as a result of its moderate position during the bus boycott.[64] Hall attempted in 1957 to recoup his financial loss by dispatching reporters to investigate race relations in the heart of the liberal North. The so-called "Ascalon" series revealed racial injustices, discrimination and de facto segregation in the big cities of the North.[65] Hall was proud of his efforts; he believed he would win the Pulitzer Prize for investigative journalism in 1957. When he did not, he bitterly chalked up his failure to liberal northerners.

---

[60]*See* BRANCH, *supra* note 4, at 152.

[61]Interview with Ray Jenkins, editor, *Baltimore Evening Sun*, Baltimore, Maryland (Mar. 25, 1990).

[62]Interview with William McDonald, *supra* note 19.

[63]*Id.*; interview with Ray Jenkins, *supra* note 61. As Jenkins points out, blacks gradually became critical of both the upper-class paternalism and lower-class violence directed at them. Leaders like Martin Luther King, Jr., eventually concluded that moderates offered little hope for real change, and that strategy simply left white moderates isolated.

[64]*See* BRANCH, *supra* note 4, at 183–84. *See also* interview with Joe Azbell, political consultant, Montgomery, Ala. (June 25, 1990).

[65]Interview with William McDonald, *supra* note 19. Ascalon was one of the five chief cities of the Philistines on the seacoast between Gaza and Jamnia. In 1099, the crusaders routed the Egyptians camped near the city and then returned to Jerusalem triumphant. Hall adopted the title for his series on race relations in the north with the same goal of exposing what he saw as hypocrisy. Today, the ruins of the city of Ascalon present a sense of mournful desolation.

On April 7, 1960, Hall reacted directly to the ad. In a blistering editorial, written in the space of about forty minutes, he denounced the *Times* and the author of the ad, John Murray. Hall wrote that "[t]he Republic paid a dear price once for the hysteria and mendacity of abolitionist agitators. The author of this ad is a lineal descendant of those abolitionists and the breed runs true."[66] Hall took particular exception to those portions of the ad describing the behavior of the student protestors, the supposed response of Alabama state officials in, among other things, attempting to starve the students into submission, and the role of the police in dealing with the disturbances. "Lies, Lies, Lies," Hall stridently proclaimed, "and possibly willful ones on the part of the fund-raising novelist who wrote those lines to prey on the credulity, self-righteousness and misinformation of northern citizens."[67]

A newspaper editor as egocentric and energetic as Hall should have wanted to enhance the right of the press to comment critically on public figures. Hall took the opposite position; he complained that the *Times* ad fostered a climate of disrespect for authority by holding the South up to national ridicule. Lingering below the surface of Hall's slashing editorials was a sense of inferiority that had long plagued the region.[68] Hence, an Alabama newspaper editor, and a liberal one at that, cast his journalistic fate with segregationists that he neither liked nor respected in an attempt to protect the honor of his section and his class.

On April 9, Nachman gave instructions to Sullivan, James and Parks to write identical letters—not only to the *Times* but to each of the four Alabama preachers—demanding that they prepare a full retraction.[69] The latter were joined as parties in order to keep the litigation in the Alabama courts and to block removal to the potentially more sympathetic federal courts.[70]

The events in Montgomery were given additional momentum by developments in Birmingham to the North. Turner Catledge had dispatched Harrison Salisbury, who had previously served in the prestigious post of Moscow correspondent, to investigate racial conditions in the South. Salisbury left on April 1, two days after "Heed Their Rising Voices" appeared. His first stop was Birmingham, where the

---

[66] Grover Hall, *Lies, Lies, Lies,* MONTGOMERY ADVERTISER, Apr. 17, 1960, at 3.
[67] *Id.*
[68] Interview with Ray Jenkins, *supra* note 61.
[69] The *Times* did publish a retraction with regard to Governor Patterson, but refused to do so in the case of Sullivan. See LEWIS, *supra* note 4, at 13.
[70] Interview with N. Roland Nachman, Jr., lawyer, Montgomery, Ala. (Apr. 25, 1989).

sit-in movement was about to begin. Salisbury interviewed blacks and whites, and he concluded that something approaching a reign of terror existed. In a two-part story that appeared April 8 and 9, Salisbury described Birmingham as a city where telephones were tapped, mail intercepted and opened, and where the "eavesdropper, the informer, the spy have become a fact of life."[71] Salisbury dubbed Birmingham the "Johannesburg of America," words that particularly insulted the white leadership of the self-proclaimed "Magic City" of the South. The city's chief of police, Eugene "Bull" Conner, took exception to Salisbury's story, since it equated the behavior of the police there with the same state terror tactics that had characterized Hitler's Germany and that the "Heed Their Rising Voices" ad had attributed to law enforcement officials in Montgomery. As was true in Montgomery, the Birmingham press immediately attacked the *Times*. John Temple Graves, the editorial columnist for the *Birmingham News*, described Salisbury as a "tooth-and-claw hate ... purveyor of prejudgment, malice and hate" and the *Times* as engaged in fomenting "[h]atred of the South, engendered by racial emotions" that amounted to "almost a total lie."[72]

Grover Hall, in an April 17 editorial, joined the Birmingham and Montgomery events. He denounced those at the *Times* as "abolitionist hellmouths" who propagated "the big lie" about the city's racial conditions and, in doing so, were "misleading the United States and much of the civilized world."[73] Hall charged the *Times* with "dereliction and emotionalism" and observed that "[i]t seems incredible that men of honor could be challenged by a famous Southern newspaper to check the facts and ignore that challenge."[74]

Although there is no evidence to suggest any direct connection, there was, nonetheless, an almost simultaneous movement in the two cities to bring lawsuits against the *Times*. At Nachman's direction, on April 19, Sullivan and commissioners Earl James and Frank Parks individually filed suits in the Montgomery County Circuit Court against the *Times* and the four ministers, seeking damages of $500,000 against each of the defendants. On May 6, the three city commissioners of Birmingham, Connor, James Morgan and J. T. Waggoner filed suit for libel against the *Times* and against Harrison Salisbury. In each case damages of $500,000 was asked, a total of $1,500,000 in each city; a total of $3,000,000 from the commissioners

---

[71] Transcript, *supra* note 31, at 2011.
[72] *See* SALISBURY, *supra* note 37, at 381.
[73] Hall, *supra* note 66, at 3.
[74] Record, *supra* note 31, vol. 2, at 2014.

alone. On May 31, the three city commissioners of the town of Besse-
mer, an industrial enclave where Birmingham's steel mills were located, filed identical libel suits, seeking another $1,500,000. On July
20, 1960, a Birmingham city detective named Joe Lindsey brought a
similar action asking for $150,000.

To this total must be added two other suits. The first was brought
on May 30 by Governor Patterson for $1,000,000. The previous day,
an all-white jury had found King not guilty of violating Alabama income tax laws. Patterson wrote to the *Times* May 9 demanding, as
had Sullivan, Parks and James, that the newspaper retract the ad.
Patterson claimed that he had been specifically maligned because in
his capacity as governor he also served as "ex-officio chairman of the
State Board of Education." Attorney General MacDonald Gallion
urged this course of action on the governor as did the members of the
Board of Education. A week later, the *Times* retracted the ad, noting
that since it was an advertisement it did not reflect "the judgment or
the opinion of the editors of The Times."[75] Orvil Dryfoos, the president of the *Times,* wrote to Governor Patterson on the same day and
apologized.[76]

Patterson did nothing for two weeks, waiting until King's trial
ended. When the all-white jury acquitted the civil rights leader,
Patterson filed his own suit, not only against the *Times* and the four
ministers, but against King as well.

Finally, Clyde Sellers, a former commissioner who had overseen
the police, also brought suit against the *Times* and the four ministers. Together, therefore, by early June 1960, the *New York Times*
and the four ministers faced suits amounting to $3,000,000 in Mont-
gomery. In addition, the *Times* was facing another $3,150,000 in
damages in Birmingham and Salisbury $1,500,000 in Birmingham.

Those in Montgomery today who were involved in the case insist
that all of these actions occurred independently.[77] Perhaps, but
Montgomery in 1960s was still a small community, one in which ties
of family, friends, neighborhoods and clubs bound persons together.
Law suits, moreover, often make for strange bedfellows. Hall and
Nachman held Sullivan and the other city commissioners in contempt for their race demagoguery and their connections to
lower-class whites on the eastside. Yet, they all shared a common dis-
dain for an implacable northern press and an active black civil rights
movement.

---

[75] LEWIS, *supra* note 4, at 13.
[76]*Id.*
[77]Interview with M. Roland Nachman, *supra* note 19.

The stakes were high for all concerned. The plaintiffs saw not only their own honor and dignity impugned, but that of the region as a whole. The suit, Grover Hall proclaimed in an *Advertiser* editorial of May 22, 1960, promised that "the recent checkmating of the *Times* in Alabama will impose a restraint upon other publications."[78] For the management of the *Times*, the law suits represented a threat to the paper's balance sheet and, even more important, a chilling of its coverage of the civil rights movement. Only an infinitesimal portion of the Alabama public would have ever read the ad had not Ray Jenkins and Grover Hall decided to report it. Nachman and others, however, were not worried about the *Times* changing minds in Alabama; they worried, instead, about the fate of their reputations in the North.[79] Besides, Nachman was certain that, as had been the case with *Ken* magazine, the law was on his side and that he would make short work of the *Times* in the trail to follow. In the end, of course, Nachman, Hall and the commissioners succeeded in winning before a local trial court in Montgomery but losing on appeal. What they lost was not only the case but the sectionally bound cultural assumptions that those who litigated it had so desperately sought to preserve.

LIBEL LAW, CIVILITY AND THE IMPORTANCE OF *SULLIVAN*

When framed against this background, Justice William J. Brennan's opinion dripped with irony for the supporters of the old Gunter machine. Figures such as Hall, Nachman and even Judge Jones liked to think of themselves as models for and agents of habits and manners of civility. They represented, from their perspective, a moderating influence on the racism of lower-class southern whites and a restraint on what they viewed as hypocritical northern liberalism and its egalitarian ethos.

Upper class and moderate southerners championed ideas of local control, state sovereignty, and habits and manners of civility. Their ideal was to draw the best men into public life and, in order to do so, they sought a law of libel that would foster a climate of respect for governmental authority and the persons who exercised it. Of course, as the evolving history of Montgomery made clear, such a perspective was something of a will-o'-the-wisp, but the vision behind it stood in stark contrast to the prevailing northern ideology of liberal legalism with its uncompromising commitment to rights consciousness, total

---

[78]Grover Hall, *Checkmate*, MONTGOMERY ADVERTISER, May 22, 1960, at 15.
[79]Interview with N. Roland Nachman, lawyer, Montgomery, Ala. (Apr. 24, 1989).

justice and, ultimately, suspicion of political authority. That is why southerners like Nachman and Hall condemned Brennan's opinion in *Sullivan* not just for being bad law but for bringing about the decay of community values associated with First Amendment law since the 1930s.

The background of the *Sullivan* case is notable, then, for the sectionally bound social and legal assumptions that animated it. Justice Brennan and his colleagues exploded both by adopting a modern, essentially northern conception of libel law that depended on an intellectual marketplace characterized by a robust exchange of ideas. They rejected the competing vision of libel law espoused by Nachman and his clients, one anchored in habits and manners of civility and deference to authority. They also rejected the social perspective that white moderate Alabamians such as Nachman brought to the cse. As a result, they lost not only the struggle over segregation but, just as important, their genteel approach to political discourse, their skewed understanding of the social bases of politics, and their noble but naïve belief that those who govern should do so secure in the knowledge that falsehoods could never be protected.

NEW YORK TIMES CO. V. SULLIVAN: A FIRST AMENDMENT LAWYER'S RETROSPECTIVE

Robert M. O'Neil*

Forty years after it was delivered, New York Times Co. v. Sullivan *remains one of the Supreme Court's most important opinions. This essay explores three questions about the opinion: How novel was it? How significant was it? How beneficial was it? The answers to these questions focus on the expanded protection for the criticism of public officials, recognizing that robust public debate is highly important, even in the face of possible abuse by critics. Part of the import of the opinion, however, lies not in what was decided, but in what was not decided.*

As the principal eulogist at Justice William Brennan's funeral in the summer of 1997, President Bill Clinton recalled some of the late justice's judicial milestones. "Thanks to him," noted the president, "a person's property may not be seized without a hearing." The eulogy, written by a staff member who must have sensed Clinton's admiration for Brennan, continued: "Thanks to him, a convicted prisoner may seek collateral review in a federal court. And thanks to him, a public official or public figure cannot recover for libel without proving actual malice." At that moment the president paused, looked up from his text for the first time, and added spontaneously, "[A]nd that's a decision that some of us in public life are less happy about than the others." Then, looking straight at the coffin directly before him, Clinton added: "And maybe, Mr. Justice, that's why you were right there as well."[1]

---

*Director, Thomas Jefferson Center for the Protection of Free Expression, University of Virginia; law clerk to Justice William J. Brennan, Jr., 1962–63 term.

[1]*See, generally, Clinton: Brennan A Defender of Justice and Equality,* CNN: US News, July 29, 1997, *available at* http://www.cnn.com/us/9707/29/brennan.funeral/.

The moment was as inspired as it was unexpected. The one public official who in recent times had probably suffered most at the hands of hostile media came face to face with the legal source of unfettered press commentary, covering everything from the *Washington Post* to the *Drudge Report*. In so doing, President Clinton accepted not only the inevitability, but the soundness of Justice Brennan's most memorable opinion. In the process, he seemed also to appreciate that the son of Newark's police commissioner, who had grown up in a world of urban ward politics, was unlikely to be naïve about the perils of politicians at the mercy of a hostile press.

As we mark the fortieth anniversary of Justice Brennan's opinion for the Court in *New York Times Co. v. Sullivan*,[2] the subject of this timely symposium, we may pose several related questions: First, how novel a decision was it? Second, how significant? And third, how beneficial? The answers to such questions could not easily have been framed at any time during the first decade or even two decades after the judgment. But we are now far enough from that time in the late winter of 1964 that we might usefully attempt such an inquiry.

First, we might ask how *novel* a decision this was. The answer turns out to be surprisingly complex. In one sense, the *New York Times* ruling was hardly a break with the past, while in other respects it was truly revolutionary. Both dimensions merit attention. The notion that suits for defamation (libel or slander) might be barred or at least diluted by certain legal "privileges" was surely not novel, for the applicable legal principles had recognized certain privileges almost since the earliest recognition of such a cause of action. For example, an employee has long enjoyed a privilege to report the transgressions of a fellow worker to a superior without incurring legal liability, even though the report may stray slightly from the truth. Reliance upon official documents or communications has also conferred a measure of license upon those who in good faith publish what turn out to be modestly inaccurate accounts. And, only a few years before it agreed to review the *Times* case, the Supreme Court had declared that federal officials enjoy a measure of privilege with respect to official statements that may give rise to lawsuits by aggrieved citizens.[3] In these and myriad other situations, the mitigating effect of well defined privileges upon potential liability for false statements injurious to reputation was indelibly established long before the winter of 1964.

---

[2]376 U.S. 254 (1963).
[3]*See* Barr v. Matteo, 360 U.S. 564 (1959).

For that matter, the very privilege that proved central to the *Times* case—latitude for fair comment on the public acts of a public official—was hardly novel. Such a privilege had first been recognized by the Supreme Court of Kansas as far back as 1908,[4] and was later adopted by ten or a dozen other states in the intervening years.[5] A federal court of appeals decision in 1942 had also embraced such a defense to public officials' libel suits against the news media.[6] Several legal scholars had urged broader recognition of such a privilege decades before the issue reached the Supreme Court.[7] Moreover, a privilege of fair comment was wholly in the spirit of this branch of tort law, which had long balanced the interests of those whose reputations had been harmed by false statements against the public interest in encouraging the free flow of beneficial or valuable information, without fear that a single lapse would open the floodgates of legal liability.

What, then, was so novel about this momentous ruling? If it was well settled that a state like Kansas could accord a privilege to fair comments about public officials, if it so chose, that was a far cry from imposing such a privilege on all states as a matter of federal First Amendment law. Indeed, such tort principles as defamation lend themselves especially well to variations among states and seem unlikely sectors for mandated federal uniformity. Yet, the *Times* Court quickly concluded that nothing less than a uniform federal privilege of fair comment would adequately protect vital interests both of the news media and of their readers, listeners and viewers to probe contentious public issues without excessive fear of liability for a slight exaggeration or misstatement.

Had the *Times* decision merely nationalized the Kansas privilege and made it mandatory, that would have been novel enough. But Justice Brennan's opinion went much further in making states subject to uniform rules and standards in the adjudication of libel claims—notably by establishing the "actual malice" standard [that false statements must have been made with actual knowledge of their falsity or reckless disregard or truth or falsehood] as the talisman of proof in such cases,[8] and by declaring that the proof the plain-

---

[4]*See* Coleman v. MacLennan, 98 P. 281 (Kan. 1908).

[5]*See, e.g.,* cases cited at *New York Times,* 376 U.S. at 279–80 n.20. *See also,* W. WAT HOPKINS, ACTUAL MALICE 52–67, 96–107 (1989).

[6]Sweeney v. Patterson, 128 F.2d 457 (D.C. Cir. 1942).

[7]*See, e.g.,* George Chase, *Criticism of Public Officers and Candidates for Office,* 23 AM. L. REV. 346, 367–71 (1889); John E. Hallen, *Fair Comment,* 8 TEXAS L. REV. 41, 61 (1929); Dix W. Noel, *Defamation of Public Officers and Candidates,* 49 COLUM. L. REV. 875, 891–95 (1949).

[8]376 U.S. 254, 279–80 (1964).

tiffs had advanced in the Alabama courts was constitutionally insufficient to meet that standard.[9] Equally novel was the Court's imposition on the states of a uniform federal standard for "innuendo"—the "of and concerning" nexus between plaintiff and publication—in the course of ruling that the Alabama commissioner did not qualify as a plaintiff since he was neither named in the *New York Times* civil rights ad that triggered the suit, nor had he even been identified with sufficient clarity to give him adequate legal interest to press such a lawsuit.[10]

Thus, it was not simply the fair-comment privilege itself that now acquired the full force of federal law under the First Amendment, but equally the heavy burden that must be met to overcome that privilege, and the degree to which a person must be identified (if not named) before being a proper party to pursue such a libel claim. The federalization of all these issues in one stroke of the judicial pen was truly extraordinary and, without more, entitled the *Times* decision to its singular niche in judicial history.

The novelty of the *Times* judgment went substantially further, however. Among its signal contributions was the declaration that civil lawsuits might abridge First Amendment freedoms as gravely as criminal prosecutions or administrative sanctions. It was not so much that earlier courts had reached a contrary view—but simply that the issue had never really been addressed. In 1940, Professor Zechariah Chaffee published the second edition of his massive treatise on *Free Speech in the United States*. Within some 597 pages of dense legal analysis, the potential harm to free expression posed by civil lawsuits received but a single paragraph. The balance of the book concerned threats from governmental sources—prosecutors, grand juries, legislative committees, movie censors and other administrative agencies. Thus, not surprisingly, the Alabama plaintiff argued that "the Fourteenth Amendment [including the First] is directed against State action and not against private action."[11]

Such a claim, replied Justice Brennan, could be briefly put to rest:

> [T]he Alabama courts have applied a state rule of law which [the defendants] claim to impose invalid restrictions on their constitutional freedoms of speech and press. It matters not that the [defamation] law has been applied in a civil action and that it is common law only ... . [T]he

---

[9]*Id.* at 284–88.
[10]*Id.* at 289–91.
[11]*Id.* at 265.

test is not the form in which state power has been applied but, whatever the form, whether such power has in fact been exercised.[12]

Thus, with a single, almost cursory, stroke of the judicial pen, the focus of First Amendment freedoms expanded to encompass a host of potential threats posed by private parties suing other private parties—the degree of government involvement limited to enforcement by the courts of remedies derived from the common law. That was a truly remarkable break with the past and created almost casually a doctrine which, to this day, remains contentious among constitutional scholars, some of whom continue to insist that only government sanctions can abridge expressive freedoms.[13]

Though much more could be said about the novelty of the *New York Times* decision, we turn now to the second question—how *significant* was the ruling? Its immediate import was obvious, and most especially in freeing the news media to comment far more openly on the business of government. But the media were not the only beneficiaries; we easily forget that the individual defendants—civil rights leaders who had sponsored the ad that gave rise to the libel suit—were equally entitled to such a privilege of fair comment.[14] Well beyond simply creating the privilege as a First Amendment right, Justice Brennan established vital principles of press freedom that transcended the immediate issue, important though that issue surely was. His persistent emphasis upon such core values as the contribution of "robust debate" to the public arena, the vitality of "breathing space" and even the need to tolerate "some degree of abuse" in media comment on public affairs carried its import far beyond the immediate judgment and that judgment's obvious implications.

Yet, at the same time, the opinion was notable for what it did not decide. Many important issues were deliberately left for a later day. No definition was offered of a "public official"—nor for that matter has the Court ever given guidance on how far down into government service the reach of this privilege extends.[15] To what extent the privilege might extend beyond "official acts" also remained open at first; Justice Arthur Goldberg expressed his view that a public official's

---

[12]*Id.*

[13]*See, generally,* Ashley Poyle-leach, Note: *Golden Gateway Center v. Golden Gateway Tenants Ass'n: Is the California Supreme Court stripping California's Citizens of Their Constitutional Right to Free Speech,* 32 Sw. U. L. Rev. 383 (2003).

[14]Individual defendants in the case were the Rev. Ralph D. Abernathy, the Rev. J.E. Lowery, the Rev. S.S. Seay and the Rev. Fred L. Shuttlesworth.

[15]Indeed, the Court has eschewed drawing precise lines. *See* 376 U.S. at 283 n.23; Rosenblatt v. Baer, 383 U.S. 75, 85 (1966).

private life remained off limits,[16] though the Court was soon to bury any such line and make at least high ranking office-holders fair game for media scrutiny twenty-four hours a day.

What happens to a libel plaintiff who is a prominent and highly visible person but does not hold public office, also remained open for another day. Three years later the Court would, quite uncritically and with minimal analysis, extend the same privilege of fair comment to defamation claims brought by non-office holding "public figures."[17] In an equally offhand manner, the Court would soon extend the privilege to the barely analogous context of "false light privacy" claims[18] and some two decades later to cases of intentional infliction of emotional distress.[19] The *Times* decision offered no hint as to how far back in time the privilege might reach. Here also the Court would soon take an expansive view and would declare the boundaries of the privilege essentially coextensive with potential public interest in the activities of a prominent person, even concerning events two decades earlier.[20] Lower courts were also left to decide for themselves whether and to what extent the privilege applied to non-media defendants, and at least one state supreme court would flatly reject the claim that a commercial credit-rating firm could seek refuge under the doctrine of fair comment.[21]

On a host of such questions, Justice Brennan deliberately resisted the temptation to pronounce more broadly than the occasion required—even though his later opinions gave clear evidence that he would have favored a broader privilege than his *Times* opinion announced. Indeed, he would eventually argue that the privilege should cover all matters of public concern, even without either a public official or public figure as plaintiff.[22] Brennan was not able to garner a majority for his proposition.[23] The majority would eventually limit the full privilege to public officials and public figures, requiring proof of "actual malice" only for punitive damages in "public concern"

---

[16]376 U.S. at 301 (Goldberg, J., concurring in the result).

[17]*See* Curtis Publ'g Co. v. Butts, 388 U.S. 130 (1967).

[18]*See* Time, Inc. v. Hill, 385 U.S. 374 (1967).

[19]*See* Hustler Magazine v. Falwell, 485 U.S. 46, 55–56 (1988).

[20]*See* Wolston v. Reader's Digest Ass'n, 443 U.S. 157 (1979).

[21]*See* Greenmoss Builders, Inc. v. Dun & Bradstreet, 461 A.2d 414, 417–18 (Vt. 1983), *rev'd on other grounds,* 472 U.S. 749 (1985).

[22]*See* Rosenbloom v. Metromedia, 403 U.S. 29, 52 (1971) (plurality); Gertz v. Robert Welch, Inc., 418 U.S. 323, 361–69 (1974) (Brennan, J., dissenting).

[23]*See id.*

cases,[24] and demanding nothing stronger than proof of "fault" in cases containing no such issue or person.[25]

The significance of the *Times* ruling relates closely to its rationale, and here again conventional wisdom slightly distorts what actually happened in 1964. In addition to the values that Justice Brennan stressed—the need for "robust debate" and "breathing space" in the public arena—we often identify two other interests. Recalling President Harry Truman's famous maxim, we equate the *Times* ruling with the injunction that "if you don't like the heat, stay out of the kitchen." We also associate the *Times* judgment with the notion that a libeled public official has uncommon ways of defending injured reputation, as in "if you call a press conference, they will come." Curiously, neither rationale appears in Justice Brennan's opinion.

It was, in fact, Justice Goldberg who contributed both notions in his concurring opinion, suggesting that one who assumes public office "must expect that his official acts will be commented upon and criticized,"[26] and later that public officials have "equal if not greater access than most private citizens to media of communication."[27] The key point is that Justice Brennan, though undoubtedly sensitive to such related values, wished not to confuse the occasion by casting too broad a net, perhaps fearing such multiplicity of rationales might well dilute or devalue the central First Amendment principles to which his opinion was devoted. To that extent, our natural tendency to read back into the opinion such consistent explanations as facing the heat if you enter the kitchen represents a plausible if unauthorized expansion of an originally and preeminently First Amendment rationale for the *Times* ruling.

Finally, it may be useful to ask, on balance, how beneficial the *New York Times* libel judgment has proved over these past four decades. For the news media, there can be little doubt of such benefit, though the scope and locus of the protection the *Times* privilege afforded the media deserves closer scrutiny. Clearly the ultimate beneficiary was not the *New York Times*, whose vast resources could easily have satisfied this and a host of other libel judgments brought by aggrieved public officials. The real parties in interest were small, struggling newspapers and magazines for whom a single major libel judgment would have effected a death sentence and brought silence. Such lesser media could simply not have covered civil rights issues in ways

---

[24]*Gertz*, 418 U.S. at 349.

[25]*Id.* at 347.

[26]376 U.S. 254, 299 (1964) (Goldberg, J., concurring in the result).

[27]*Id.* at 304–05 (Goldberg, J., concurring in the result).

that would risk potential liability even in six figures, let alone seven or eight. Indeed, the Mississippi paper edited by the crusader Hodding Carter had already experienced the chilling effect of such a suit—a circumstance of which the Court was keenly aware, and could have (but chose not to) take judicial notice.[28] Thus both the immediate and the long-term benefits of the *Times* ruling for the news media, especially the lesser media, can hardly be exaggerated.

The issue on which the jury is still out is a very different one—how beneficial has the decision been to the quality of public service in the United States? Justice Brennan's major concerns were for the quality of public *discourse*, and not necessarily for the public *service*. Indeed, some have argued that helping the former may inadvertently have harmed the latter.[29] Within the Supreme Court, the most consistently skeptical voice was that of Justice Byron White, no stranger to public life or its controversies. In a later case, White insisted that

> the New York Times rule ... countenances two evils: first, the stream of information about public officials and public affairs is polluted and often remains polluted by false information; and second, the reputation and professional life of the defeated plaintiff may be destroyed by falsehoods that might have been avoided with a reasonable effort to investigate the facts.[30]

Thus, concluded Justice White, "[I]n terms of the First Amendment and reputational interests at stake, these seem grossly perverse results."[31] For him, the solution was clear: "The necessary breathing room for speakers can be ensured by limitations on recoverable damages; it does not also require depriving many public figures of any room to vindicate their reputations sullied by false statements of fact."[32]

In the end, neither Justice White's cramped concept of the *Times* privilege nor Justice Brennan's expansive view prevailed. The majority of their colleagues and successors have settled somewhere in the middle—preserving the full privilege for fair comment on public offi-

---

[28]*See, e.g.,* Edmonds v. Delta Democrat Publ'g Co., 93 So. 2d 171 (Miss. 1957).

[29]*See,* for one lament about the potential effect of freer media scrutiny of public figures and officials, Statement of President George Bush on the Failure of the Senate to Approve the Nomination of John Tower as Secretary of Defense, Mar. 9, 1989.

[30]Dun & Bradstreet v. Greenmoss Builders, Inc., 472 U.S. 749, 769 (1985) (White, J., concurring in judgment).

[31]*Id.* (White, J., concurring in judgment).

[32]*Id.* at 771 (White, J., concurring in judgment).

cials and public figures, with a partial privilege for matters of public concern, but limiting libel actions brought by purely private individuals to a fault requirement, thus ensuring that defamation could never become a strict liability or *per se* cause of action.

Such a compromise is neither surprising nor unusual in the annals of Supreme Court litigation. Indeed, given Justice Brennan's pragmatism, and his own politically savvy perspective, he might well have anticipated that he would eventually lose the fight for a "public concern" privilege, but would leave as his most durable constitutional legacy the basic principle of press freedom to comment fairly and freely on the conduct of government and the lives of those who seek public attention.

NO PLACE IN THE LAW:
THE IGNOMINY OF CRIMINAL LIBEL
IN AMERICAN JURISPRUDENCE

GREGORY C. LISBY*

The application of the Sullivan *standard to the crime of libel was a mistake. There is no common law affiliation with or legal justification for the existence of criminal libel in a democracy. Its existence is antithetical to the First Amendment's guarantees of equality of speech, as well as to the broader constitutional guarantees of equality of speaker. The crime has become almost completely indistinguishable from the tort of libel, both in form and function, as a result of its evolution in America—from the importance of truth as a defense to the audience's responsibility for its own reaction to the speech, violent or not. And the American experience demonstrates clearly and ignominiously that the abuse of prosecutorial discretion, and even the mere threat of prosecution, results in the suppression of constitutionally protected speech.*

The decision of the Supreme Court of the United States in *New York Times Co. v. Sullivan*[1] forty years ago for the first time in this nation's history provided constitutional protection to some falsehoods—that is, honest, inadvertent falsehoods about public officials which are not knowingly or recklessly false.[2] In so doing, the Court has come the closest to fulfilling the libertarian ideal of self-government and its prerequisite of an informed electorate—or at

---

*Professor, Department of Communication, Georgia State University; member, State Bar of Georgia.

[1]376 U.S. 254 (1964).

[2]The *Sullivan* rule "prohibits a public official from recovering damages for a defamatory falsehood relating to his official conduct unless he proves that the statement was made with 'actual malice'—that is, with knowledge that it was false or with reckless disregard of whether it was false or not." *Id.* at 279–280.

least Justice Oliver Wendell Holmes's characterization of it as a marketplace of ideas where truth, or the best of available options, should always prevail.[3] And the Court acknowledged that "speech concerning public affairs is more than self-expression; it is the essence of self-government."[4] The Court subsequently applied the *Sullivan* rule to criticism of public officials under the First Amendment's petition clause[5] and determined that they should be given the same protection from libelous criticism as they were in *Sullivan*.[6] Even though the Court accepted the requirement that such plaintiffs must establish "express malice" to state an actionable claim,[7] it also required them to meet the *Sullivan* "actual malice" standard to collect damages.[8] These decisions reflect America's "profound national commitment to the principle that debate on public issues should be uninhibited, robust and wide-open, and that it may well include vehement, caustic, and sometimes unpleasantly sharp attacks on government and public officials."[9]

Yet the Court also failed the ideals of the First Amendment miserably forty years ago in *Garrison v. Louisiana*[10] when it applied the *Sullivan* rule to the crime of libel.[11] The reason for this may be found

---

[3]"The best test of truth is the power of the thought to get itself accepted in the competition of the market." Abrams v. United States, 250 U.S. 616, 630 (1919) (Holmes, J., dissenting). *See also* W. Wat Hopkins, *The Supreme Court Defines the Marketplace of Ideas*, 73 JOURNALISM & MASS COMM. Q. 40 (1996). John Stuart Mill first applied Jeremy Bentham's social philosophy of utilitarianism to John Milton's conception of public deliberation when he wrote:

> The peculiar evil of silencing the expression of an opinion is that it is robbing the human race, posterity as well as the existing generation—those who dissent from the opinion, still more than those who hold it. If the opinion is right, they are deprived of the opportunity of exchanging error for truth; if wrong, they lose, what is almost as great a benefit, the clearer perception and livelier impression of truth produced by its collision with error.... Complete liberty of contradicting and disproving [an] opinion is the very condition which justifies us in assuming its truth for purposes of action.

JOHN STUART MILL, ON LIBERTY 16, 18 (Elizabeth Rapaport ed., Hackett Pub. Co. 1978) (1859). *See also* JEREMY BENTHAM, AN INTRODUCTION TO THE PRINCIPLES OF MORALS AND LEGISLATION (James Burns & Herbert Hart eds., Athlone Press 1970) (1789); JOHN MILTON, AREOPAGITICA—A SPEECH FOR THE LIBERTY OF UNLICENSED PRINTING (John W. Hales ed., Oxford University Press 1961) (1644).

[4]Garrison v. Louisiana, 379 U.S. 64, 74–75 (1964).

[5]*See* MacDonald v. Smith, 472 U.S. 479 (1985).

[6]*Sullivan* dealt with the First Amendment's free speech and press clauses. 376 U.S. at 254.

[7]*MacDonald*, 472 U.S. at 484. *See also* White v. Nicholls, 3 How. 266, 291 (1845).

[8]*Id.* at 485.

[9]*Sullivan,* 376 U.S. 254, 270 (1964).

[10]379 U.S. 64 (1964).

[11]"Only those false statements made with the high degree of awareness of their probable falsity demanded by [the *Sullivan* rule] may be the subject of either civil or criminal sanctions." *Id.* at 74.

in the differences between civil libel and criminal or seditious libel.[12] Civil libel is a tort; as an alleged private wrong, the opposing parties are equal before the law. Criminal libel, on the other hand, is an alleged public wrong, and the state is one of the opposing parties;[13] it is always the more dominant of the two. The prosecution of a criminal libel thus involves the misuse and abuse of power.[14] It could be blatant;[15] or it could be as subtle as a prosecutor's choice of whether criminal charges should be brought and, if so, what they should be.[16] This is the "ignominious history of the law surrounding criminal libel."[17] The purpose of the crime is not to promote or provide "breathing space" for free expression.[18] Its purpose is to chill speech. It does not promote the equality of persons or of ideas. It has no place in a democratic society.

Consider the following recent example: David Carson and Edward Powers were each convicted of seven counts of misdemeanor criminal libel on July 17, 2002, for—among other things—accusing the mayor of Kansas City, Kansas, and her husband, a county judge, of

---

[12]While sedition is an action whose tendency is to cause violence against the state, seditious libel is speech whose tendency is to cause violence against the state or its officials, or to bring them into disrepute. The argument developed herein focuses on the latter, modern purpose of seditious libel—today subsumed in the crime of libel. The law of criminal libel today "consists of a curious meld of two dissimilar factual situations. One, known as seditious libel, is based on a criticism of government or public officials. The other involves an uncomplimentary statement about a nongovernmental individual that can best be described as name calling." LOIS G. FORER, A CHILLING EFFECT: THE MOUNTING THREAT OF LIBEL AND INVASION OF PRIVACY ACTIONS TO THE FIRST AMENDMENT 51 (1987).

[13]For a discussion of the distinctions between crimes and torts, see JOHN C. KLOTTER, CRIMINAL LAW 16 (3d ed. 1990). For the purposes of this discussion, the most important distinctions are who sues and on whose behalf a suit is filed.

[14]See Morrison v. Olson, 487 U.S. 654, 727 (1988) (Scalia, J., dissenting) ("Only someone who has worked in the field of law enforcement can fully appreciate the vast power and the immense discretion that are placed in the hands of a prosecutor with respect to the objects of his investigation.").

[15]Jim Fitts, for example, was arrested on charges of criminal libel Friday, May 20, 1988, after he published allegedly offending remarks three days earlier. At the end of the business day, bond was set at $40,000. By the time Fitts had raised the money, the court clerk had left for the weekend. Fitts remained jailed until the following Monday, without having been or ever subsequently being convicted of any crime whatsoever. See Politicians Have Columnist Jailed on Criminal Libel Charges, EDITOR & PUBLISHER, June 18, 1988, at 19.

[16]This is known as prosecutorial discretion. The decision to prosecute Ian Lake, a 16-year-old juvenile, for criminal libel in Utah, for example, was made a month after his arrest on May 18, 2000, for posting offensive comments about school officials on his personal Internet Web site. See Joe Baird, Libel Case Against Teen To Proceed, SALT LAKE TRIBUNE, Dec. 6, 2000, at C1.

[17]Tollett v. U.S., 485 F.2d 1087, 1094 (8th Cir. 1973).

[18]Sullivan, 376 U.S. 254, 272 (1964).

not maintaining their legal residence in Wyandotte County, as required by law as a prerequisite to holding their respective political offices.[19] Carson and Powers were fined $3,500 each, of which all but $700 was suspended for each defendant, and sentenced to one year of unsupervised probation.[20] Yet each man could have been sentenced to pay a maximum fine of $17,500 and to serve a jail term of up to seven years.[21]

A cursory examination of the free-circulation, monthly tabloid, the *New Observer*, leaves no doubt that the newspaper's policy is—as the adage goes—"to afflict the comfortable."[22] In its November 2000 issue, it asked: "Is gossip that [the Kansas City mayor] lives in Johnson County true?"[23] After the publisher and editor's indictments on charges of criminal libel, the newspaper described the Wyandotte County district attorney and the mayor as "two vicious, self-interested politicians, for whom holding public office is more important than basic principles of democracy," and called the prosecutor the mayor's "protector," perpetually blind to increasing public corruption, and "frequently wrong but never in doubt."[24] Yet neither the mayor nor the prosecutor ever filed a claim for civil libel, and the *New Observer* claimed that if its accusations were "wrong or libelous, [the mayor] would have filed endless numbers of lawsuits over the last two years."[25] Instead, Carson and Powers were accused, indicted and convicted of criminal libel, despite—or, perhaps, because of or without regard to—the fact that the Kansas legislature revised the

---

[19]*Newspaper Execs Convicted of Libel*, QUILL, Sept. 2002, at 7.

[20]Newspaper Editor, Publisher Get Fines and Probation for Criminal Libel (Dec. 4, 2002), Reporters Committee for Freedom of the Press, *at* http://www.rcfp.org/news/2002/1204kansas.html (last visited Jan. 30, 2004). An appeal is pending.

[21]Each count carried "a maximum fine of $2,500 and a jail term of up to a year." *Jury Delivers Rare Criminal Libel Conviction*, NEWS MEDIA & THE LAW, Summer 2002, at 48.

[22]This adage is variously attributed to New York publisher Joseph Pulitzer and Chicago humorist Finley Peter Dunne. The Reader (January 1, 2004), *at* http://www.booksandbrainfood.com/thereader/index.shtml (last visited Jan. 30, 2004); The Watchdog Misunderstood (2004), ¶ 1, Journalism.org, Project for Excellence in Journalism, *at* http://www.journalism.org/resources/tools/reporting/watchdog/misundestood.asp (last visited Jan. 30, 2004).

[23]Quoted in Extra! Extra! Kansas City Newspaper Convicted of Criminal Defamation (Aug. 1, 2002), ¶ 1, Center for Individual Freedom, *at* http://www.cfif.org/htdocs/freedomline/current/in_our_opinion/criminal_defamation.html (last visited Oct. 3, 2002).

[24]D.A. Nick Tomasic Stabs First Amendment in the Back, Files 10 Counts of Criminal Libel Charges Against New Observer Publisher, Editor, The New Observer (March 1, 2001), ¶¶ 13, 3, 1, *at* http://www.thenewobserver.com/observerreports/criminal%20liable.htm (last visited Jan. 30, 2004).

[25]*Id.* at ¶ 19.

state's criminal libel statute in 1995 to meet the heightened constitutional requirement of actual malice mandated in *Garrison*.[26] Remarking on the unique style of political debate in the area—which includes language "imbued with a heavy dose of rhetoric and hyperbole," "exclamations," and "inflammatory entreaties"[27]—the *New York Times* wrote: "Politics in Kansas City, Kan., is to standard Kansas politics what the XFL was to the National Football League—meaner and rowdier, and proud of it."[28]

Almost every time an event such as this occurs, journalists and legal commentators will note that criminal libel is "obsolete in most states."[29] Libel as a crime,[30] whether in Kansas or in any other state, is wholly unconstitutional and should be completely erased from America's legal lexicon by the Supreme Court. It is contrary to the rights guaranteed by the First Amendment to the Constitution,[31] it is inimical to the free expression of ideas in the United States,[32] and it is antithetical to any and every form of representative government for the following reasons: First, it is a historical "throwback to pre-Magna Carta England and to the common-law principles the monarchy used to justify keeping its heel on critics' necks" and, therefore, contrary to the principles of free expression enshrined in the First Amendment.[33] Second, its authoritarian philosophical and political foundations cannot be reconciled with the democratic, liber-

---

[26]Kan. Stat. Ann. § 21–4004 (2000).

[27]Dan Bischof, *Criminal Libel as Political Tactic*, NEWS MEDIA & THE LAW, Spring 2001, at 17.

[28]Felicity Barringer, *A Criminal Defamation Verdict Roils Politics in Kansas City, Kan.*, N.Y. TIMES, July 29, 2002, at C7. For one season, 1999–2000, the eXtreme Football League played "football the way it is supposed to be played," which included much more physical contact and other rules promoting the extreme blending of spectacle and sport. Official XFL.com (2000), *at* http://www.officialxfl.com/index.asp (last visited March 5, 2004).

[29]*Newspaper Execs, supra* note 19, at 7.

[30]As this research focuses on the differences and similarities between the crime of libel and the tort of libel, it is not concerned with the distinction between libel and slander, and includes both in the term "libel." Generally, however, "[W]ritten defamation is libel; spoken defamation is slander. Libel is a crime as well as a tort; slander of a private individual may be a tort, but is no crime." Van Vechten Veeder, *The History and Theory of the Law of Defamation (I)*, 3 COLUM. L. REV. 546, 571 (1903).

[31]"Congress shall make no law respecting an establishment of religion, or prohibiting the free exercise thereof; or abridging the freedom of speech, or of the press; or the right of the people peaceably to assemble for the redress of grievances." U.S. Const. amend. I.

[32]*See* J. Philip Bahn, *Constitutionality of the Law of Criminal Libel*, 52 COLUM. L. REV. 521, 533 (1952).

[33]*See* Timothy Smith, *Criminal Libel Case, a Legal Throwback, Divides Community*, WALL ST. J., June 29, 1988, 1, at 17. *See infra* text accompanying notes 79–129.

tarian ideals on which the America was founded.[34] Third, it functionally serves the same purpose as civil libel, as American courts have now allowed truth to be a defense for the crime.[35] Fourth, its "breach of the peace" rationale has been discarded by American courts, making its purpose no different from that of civil libel.[36] Fifth, the American experience with criminal libel and its concomitant abuse of prosecutorial discretion is humiliating, embarrassing, shameful and reprehensible.[37]

ORIGINS OF CRIMINAL LIBEL

If the purpose of civil libel is to restore one's reputation through the payment of damages, the first function of criminal libel has always been social order and control.[38] More accurately, its purpose historically has been to protect power and privilege. Its philosophical and political foundations may be traced to the Middle Ages and beyond, where it originated as a rationale for government.[39]

The relationship of government with those who are governed may be described in one of two basic ways: either the governors are the people's superiors or they are the people's servants. It was, and still is, an issue of fealty: the allegiance to another, either to the state itself or to the people themselves. The philosophy under which criminal libel developed—authoritarian theory—assumes that the governors are the people's "betters," "and therefore must not be subjected to censure that would tend to diminish their authority."[40] In order to maintain this circumstance, the governors—with the active assistance of Christian religious authorities—maintained that the nation-state "derived its power ... through a process not generally capable of complete human analysis ... divine guidance,"[41] also known as the divine right of kings.

---

[34]*See infra* text accompanying notes 142–154.

[35]*See infra* text accompanying notes 163–193.

[36]*See infra* text accompanying notes 195–226.

[37]*See infra* text accompanying notes 260–391.

[38]*See* Thomas Emerson, *Toward a General Theory of the First Amendment*, 72 YALE L. J. 877, 923 (1963).

[39]This period, between the fall of the Roman Empire and the Renaissance (circa 476–1450 C.E.), was a time of extreme political, economic and religious oppression and subjugation of those without power or privilege. Some would go so far as to argue that "the history of any civilization is a history of oppression." WALTER M. BRASCH & DANA R. ULLOTH, THE PRESS AND THE STATE: SOCIOHISTORICAL AND CONTEMPORARY INTERPRETATIONS 3 (1986).

[40]ZECHARIAH CHAFEE, JR., FREE SPEECH IN THE UNITED STATES 18–19 (1941).

[41]Fred S. Siebert, *The Authoritarian Theory of the Press*, in FRED S. SIEBERT ET AL., FOUR THEORIES OF THE PRESS 11 (1956).

Control of expression, then, could be justified to protect both the ruler's power and his exercise of it through the interpretation of divine commands.[42] For example, the *Bible* declares that God cannot lie or do wrong;[43] it affirms that God has ordained all governments and rulers.[44] Therefore, the ruler cannot lie or do wrong, because God made him sovereign.[45] As God is righteous and just,[46] so the monarch is "the fountainhead of justice and law."[47] Thus, to criticize the ruler or the actions of his ministers or to question the ruler's power or privileges "was to threaten the stability of the state."[48] What power "the church [had] in the spiritual world, a monarch [had] in temporal affairs."[49] Punishment for criticism of the government "was originally designed ... to suppress sedition and, later, to prevent breaches of the peace provoked by the defendant's speech."[50] Because of this—and the monarch's inability to make mistakes—the truth of the matter made no difference whatsoever. If anything, it "exacerbated the situation," because of its threat to social order and stability.[51]

Criminal libel, which could conceivably include any expression, usually took one of four forms:[52] (1) libels tending to impact the administration of government—this could include words defaming the ruler, the government or its officials (such as, seditious and treasonable words); words defaming the constitution and the laws generally; and words defaming the courts or their judges, or tending to obstruct the administration of justice generally, such as, contempt of court;[53] (2) libels tending to corrupt public morals and to injure society gener-

---

[42]*See* BRASCH & ULLOTH, *supra* note 39, at 4.

[43]*See Titus* 1:2; *Hebrews* 6:18.

[44]*See Romans* 13:1–2.

[45]In the words of King James I of England (1603–1625 C.E.), "[A]s to dispute what God may do is blasphemy ... so it is sedition in subjects to dispute what a King may do in the height of his power." James Stuart, The State of Monarchy and the Divine Right of Kings, Speech in Whitehall (Mar. 21, 1609), *in* BRITISH ORATIONS FROM ETHELBERT TO CHURCHILL 20–21 (1915).

[46]*See Daniel* 9:14.

[47]2 JAMES STEPHEN, HISTORY OF THE CRIMINAL LAW OF ENGLAND 299 (1883). By extension, the king's ministers and agents also can do no wrong.

[48]Siebert, *Authoritarian Theory*, in SIEBERT ET AL., *supra* note 41, at 23.

[49]*Id.* at 17.

[50]ROBERT SACK, LIBEL, SLANDER AND RELATED PROBLEMS 130 (2d ed. 1980).

[51]*Id.*

[52]*See* MARTIN L. NEWELL, THE LAW OF SLANDER AND LIBEL IN CIVIL AND CRIMINAL CASES 1126 (3d ed. by Mason H. Newell) (1914). Another commonly accepted division also sorts all libels into four categories: defamatory libel, obscene libel, blasphemous libel and seditious libel. *See* J.R. Spencer, *Criminal Libel—A Skeleton in the Cupboard*, 1977 CRIM. L. REV. 383. On the other hand, William Blackstone categorized libels as blasphemous, immoral, treasonable, schismatic, seditious and scandalous. 4 WILLIAM BLACKSTONE, COMMENTARIES *151 (1769).

[53]*See* W. BLAKE ODGERS, THE LAW OF LIBEL AND SLANDER 513–514 (5th ed. 1912).

ally—this could include obscene libels,[54] blasphemy[55] and profanity;[56] (3) libels tending to harm the reputation of the living "and expose [them] to hatred, contempt, or ridicule"[57]—this could include group libel, fighting words and specific instances of injury, such as, damage to a woman's reputation for being chaste;[58] and (4) libels tending to blacken the memory of the dead and to expose "his family and posterity ... to contempt and disgrace."[59] As the historical purpose of criminal libel was to protect the public peace from disruption by violence, it was unnecessary for the state to show that the particular words in question had been communicated or published "to some third person other than the person defamed," as long as there was an "obvious tendency" to provoke anyone, including the subject of the words himself, and incite him to violence.[60] Because of this, all of these types of libel could be controlled by the ruler, either because his power comes from God or—according to Samuel Johnson's modern theory of authoritarianism—because "every society has a right to preserve public peace and order, and therefore has a good right to prohibit the propagation of opinions which have a dangerous tendency."[61] Thus, in contemporary times, criminal libel is widely associated with all autocratic and tyrannical systems of government,

---

[54]Obscene libels may be defined as "vicious and immoral words ... uttered publicly in the hearing of many persons." *Id*. at 506. *See also* Colin Manchester, *A History of the Crime of Obscene Libel*, 12 J. LEGAL HIST. 36 (May 1991).

[55]Blasphemy may be defined as "any profane words vilifying or ridiculing God, Jesus Christ, the Holy Ghost, the Old or New Testament, or Christianity in general, with intent to shock and insult believers, or to pervert or mislead the ignorant and unwary." *Id*. at 477. To be criminal, the "words must be truly irreverent and designed to bring Things or Persons Divine into contempt." FRANK THAYER, LEGAL CONTROL OF THE PRESS 365 (4th ed. 1962).

[56]Profanity may be defined as "any words [uttered] in a public place and [to the] annoyance [of] the public ... importing an imprecation of future Divine vengeance." NEWELL, *supra* note 52, at 1148–1149. *See also* THAYER, *supra* note 55, at 366.

[57]NEWELL, *supra* note 52, at 1153.

[58]*See* Lisa R. Pruitt, *"On the Chastity of Women All Property in the World Depends": Injury from Sexual Slander in the Nineteenth Century*, 78 INDIANA L. J. 965 (Fall 2003).

[59]NEWELL, *supra* note 52, at 1151. Though a person's reputation is supposed to die with the person and may not be the basis for a civil suit, libel of the dead is a crime, because "all publications tending to defame the memory of deceased persons might have the tendency to excite some persons to breaches of the peace, whether they be relatives or friends of the deceased or others who may have a high regard for the deceased, though such regard rest only upon traditional or historical knowledge." State v. Haffer, 162 P. 45, 47 (Wash. 1916). *See also* THAYER, *supra* note 55, at 327.

[60]NEWELL, *supra* note 52, at 1158.

[61]2 JAMES BOSWELL, BOSWELL'S LIFE OF JOHNSON 249 (G.B. Hill, ed.; rev. & ed. by L.F. Powell) (1934). Johnson (1709–1784) was an English lexicographer, poet and man of letters.

which use the crime to preserve the existence of the nation-state.[62] For example, many modern "dictatorships [have] criminal [libel] statutes,"[63] which are "a threat to human rights."[64]

While the ignominious history of the law of criminal libel largely may be attributed to the excesses of the English Court of the Star Chamber,[65] certain characteristics of the crime may be found in much older legal codes. To preserve the public peace, the Babylonian Code of Hammurabi, for example, protected women from insult,[66] and set death as the appropriate punishment for one convicted of accusing another of a capital crime without proof.[67] In addition, the Jewish Mosaic law contained an express prohibition against false statements and reports—calumniations—though no specific penalty was attached to its violation.[68] However, penalties were set for a man's false attacks on his wife's reputation or chastity prior to their marriage.[69] The Greek laws

---

[62]Under both the authoritarian and totalitarian systems of government, the people exist to serve the state. Yet totalitarian systems claim their right and power to govern comes from the people themselves, instead of any deity. Also, totalitarian systems generally do not allow for private ownership of property, while authoritarian systems do. *See* Wilbur Schramm, *The Soviet Communist Theory of the Press*, in SIEBERT ET AL., *supra* note 41, at 105. It is not uncommon for modern scholars to group the two systems under the general rubric of authoritarianism, which "views society as a hierarchical organization with a specific chain of command under the leadership of one ruler or group ... ." R.L. CORD ET AL., POLITICAL SCIENCE: AN INTRODUCTION 119 (1974). *See also* Warren Hoge, *Latin America Losing Hope in Democracy, Report Says*, N.Y. TIMES, Apr. 22, 2004, at A3. The modern theory of authoritarianism has never been better explained than by Louis XIV, who ruled France 1643–1715, when he declared, *"L'etat, c'est moi"*—"I am the state." BARTLETT'S FAMILIAR QUOTATIONS (10th ed. 1919), *available at* http://www.bartleby.com/100/772.15.html. In such a system, the "ruler decides what shall be published because truth is essentially a monopoly of those in authority.... [D]issent [is] an annoying nuisance and often subversive." WILLIAM A. HACHTEN, THE WORLD NEWS PRISM 62–63 (1981).

[63]Lucy Dalglish, executive director of the Reporters Committee for Freedom of the Press, *quoted in*, U.S. Ready To Jail Its Journalists, Index on Censorship (July 17, 2002), ¶ 11, *at* http://www.indexonline.org/news/20020719_unitedstates.shtml (last visited Sept. 5, 2002).

[64]*Id.* at ¶ 3.

[65]*See* Tollett v. United States, 485 F.2d 1087 (8th Cir. 1973).

[66]"If a man has caused the finger to be pointed against a votary, or a man's wife, and has not justified himself, that man they shall throw down before the judge and brand his forehead." THE OLDEST CODE OF LAWS IN THE WORLD: THE CODE OF LAWS PROMULGATED BY HAMMURABI, KING OF BABYLON B.C. 2285–2242 127 (C.H.W. Johns, trans., The Lawbook Exch. 2000). *See also* George E. Stevens, *Criminal Libel After Garrison*, 68 JOURNALISM Q. 522 (1991).

[67]*See* NEWELL, *supra* note 52, at 4. The code dates from about 2250 B.C.E.

[68]*See Exodus* 20:16, 23:1. This is known as the Ninth Commandment. Historically, of course, the Jewish people were a unique group in that it was the only one which claimed to be "chosen," guided and governed by direct revelation from God. The Ten Commandments and subsequent laws date from about 1500 B.C.E.

[69]Penalties included corporal punishment, payment of a fine to the woman's family—"the highest fine imposed by the Mosaic law"—and forfeiture of his right to di-

of Solon contained the first prohibition against libeling the dead, "not on account of injury to the dead, but in respect to the quiet of families" and "the peace and honor of Athens."[70]

Laws against libel multiplied during the period of the Roman Republic, "their main object the preservation of the public peace."[71] Their aim was not to restrict expression, for—as the historian Tacitus wrote—"deeds only were liable to accusation; words went unpunished."[72] This state of affairs generally continued beyond the end of the republic and throughout the lives of the first emperors.[73] However, following the deaths of Augustus and Tiberius—and their subsequent deification—later emperors became ever more closely identified with the state itself, in some cases claiming divinity during their own lifetimes, and criticism of them or their appointees became to be seen as a threat to national stability.[74] By the time Theodosius II collected the statutes of previous emperors into what is known as the Theodosian Code, at least four distinct criminal laws prohibiting libel existed,[75] authorized as early as the reign of Constantine the

---

vorce. *See* NEWELL, *supra* note 52, at 3; *Deuteronomy* 22:13–19. It should be noted, however, that truth was considered a defense. Proof of the accusations would result in the woman being stoned to death. *See Deuteronomy* 22:20–21.

[70]NEWELL, *supra* note 52, at 5–6. Solon's laws date from about 600 B.C.E. They also contained the first codification of monetary damages, payable to the person whose reputation was injured.

[71]*Id.* at 6. The laws of the Roman Republic date from about 200 B.C.E.

[72]THE COMPLETE WORKS OF TACITUS 48 (trans. by Alfred J. Church & William J. Brodribb, Modern Library 1942) (c. 116 C.E.). The Emperor Augustus (27 B.C.E.–14 C.E.) "first ... applied legal inquiry to libelous writings, provoked, as he had been, by the licentious freedom with which Cassius Severus had defamed men and women of distinction in his insulting satires." *Id.*

[73]On one occasion, when Aemilius Aelianus was accused of "vilifying Caesar," Emperor "Augustus pretended to lose his temper and told the counsel for the prosecution: 'I wish you could prove that charge! I'll show Aelianus that I have a nasty tongue, too, and vilify him even worse!' He then dropped the whole inquiry." SUETONIUS, THE TWELVE CAESARS 80 (trans. by Robert Graves, Penguin Books 1957) (c. 117 C.E.). In a letter to his nephew (and future emperor) Tiberius, Augustus asked the young man not to "take it to heart if anyone speaks ill of me; let us be satisfied if we can make people stop short at unkind words." *Id.* Tiberius, who reigned as emperor from 14–37 C.E., remained "quite unperturbed by abuse, slander, or lampoons on himself and his family, and would often say that liberty to speak and think as one pleases is the test of a free country." *Id.* at 125. He once explained his position stating: "If So-and-so challenges me, I shall lay before [the Senate] a careful account of what I have said and done; if that does not satisfy him, I shall reciprocate his dislike of me." *Id.*

[74]*See* BRASCH & ULLOTH, *supra* note 39, at 12.

[75]The *Quattuor Constitutiones Constantini de Famosis Libellis* provided that:

- First Constitution: "If at any time libels are found, let those concerning whose acts or names they make mention suffer no false accusations therefrom, but rather let the one who instigated the writer be found, and, when found, let him be compelled with

Great.[76] These decrees later were introduced into the English Court of the Star Chamber by Edward Coke, "and declared by him to be the resolutions of the judges of that court, and to have descended to us from that period as the language and rule of the common law."[77]

DEVELOPMENT OF CRIMINAL LIBEL IN THE COMMON LAW

Though the English common law, upon which the American system of jurisprudence is largely based, cannot be traced directly back to "the ruins of the civil law and the Roman system,"[78] links clearly exist. The nuances of the modern law of criminal libel are the direct consequence of the unifying authority of Christianity throughout the Middle Ages,[79] the slow decline of the power of local lords and govern-

---

all rigor to give proof concerning those things which he has thought fit to set forth; nor yet let him be released from punishment even if he shall show anything."
- Second Decree of Constantine: "Although copies of libels which have circulated in Africa are preserved in your office and in that of your deputy, nevertheless you will permit those whose names they contain to enjoy peace and freedom from fear, and you will only admonish them that they hasten to be free not only from crime but also from the appearance of it. For he who has the confidence to make an accusation ought to establish it and not conceal what he knows, since with merit about to fall into the act of public prescription, he will be praiseworthy."
- Third Decree in January: "As patience is to be shown to accusers if they desire to prosecute any one in court, so no credit must be given to libels; nor should they be brought to our knowledge, since he may cause such libels, of which no other appears, to be immediately destroyed by fire."
- Fourth Decree: "A defamatory writing which does not have the name of the accuser must not be examined at all, but must be wholly destroyed; for he who trusts in the motive of his accusation ought to call another's life into judgment rather by an outspoken charge than by an insidious and secret writing."

NEWELL, *supra* note 52, at 9–10.

The phrase, *"famosis libellis,"* "was almost exclusively given to that species of libel which affected the credit or tranquility" of the nation. *Id.* at 14.

[76]Emperor Theodosius (408–450 C.E.) completed the *Codex Theodosianus* in 438 C.E. Emperor Constantine ruled 312–337 C.E. Other criminal libel statutes included in Theodosius's collection required that defamatory writings be destroyed and not publicized, that anonymous defamatory remarks not be admitted into evidence by a court of law, and that one who circulates a defamatory writing be as guilty as its author. Fifth Decree, to the Africans; Sixth Decree, to the People; and Ninth Decree. *Id.* at 11–12. The purpose of these laws was, in essence, "to prevent secret and ambiguous accusation." *Id.* at 12. As in the Greek system, the injured individual could be awarded "damages according to the quality of the injury and [his] dignity ... ; and, unless the charge were of that kind which the State had an interest in publishing, the truth was no vindication." *Id.* at 17.

[77]*Id.* at 8. Coke's "mediaeval learning had such an air of finality about it that further recourse to mediaeval law was not so necessary, and it became more and more the tendency to take Coke's words on matters of ... learning." THEODORE F.T. PLUCKNETT, A CONCISE HISTORY OF THE COMMON LAW 232 (4th ed. 1948).

[78]NEWELL, *supra* note 52, at 18.

[79]Christianity, it has been said, was "part of the common law of England." Quotation attributed to Sir Edward Coke (1552–1634 C.E.). *Id.* Stuart Banner calls it

ments,[80] the evolution of a national monarchy with absolute power,[81] the nationalization of justice, the low literacy rate, early movement toward social equality and representative government, and the invention of moveable type.[82] Yet the difficulties in application were exacerbated by the problem of legal jurisdiction in England.[83]

Church courts—also known as, ecclesiastical courts—"were the first legal bodies to effectively prosecute libel,"[84] acting not only to protect the morals of the community but also for "the correction of the sinner [and] his soul's health."[85] The church, then, "being an-

---

"part and parcel of the common law of England." Stewart Banner, *When Christianity Was Part of the Common Law*, 16 LAW & HIST. REV. 27, 30 (1998) (quoting Rex v. Woolston, 64 Eng. Rep. 655, 656 (1729)).

[80]Until the twelfth century, law and justice were

> administered mainly by feudal and shire courts, courts of hundreds, etc.... The court and justice of the king was but one among many.... The monarchs wished, however, to increase their revenues and expand their power and prestige. Various devices were invented and fictions set up by means of which the jurisdiction of kingly courts was extended. The method was to allege that various offenses, formerly attended to by local courts, were infractions of the king's peace. The centralizing movement went on till the king's justice had a monopoly.

JOHN DEWEY, THE PUBLIC & ITS PROBLEMS 48 (1927).

[81]Throughout

> the fifteenth century, disorder and oppression by local magistrates constantly becomes more common; petitioners are continually complaining of the lawlessness of their great neighbors, and it is perfectly evident that the courts of common law are helpless in the face of this situation. Their procedure was too slow and too mild; juries and sometimes judges were intimidated by large forces of retainers who constituted the private armies of unruly subjects. With such grave matters, the [King's] Council alone was powerful enough

to deal with matters. PLUCKNETT, *supra* note 77, at 172.

[82]*See* ELIZABETH L. EISENSTEIN, THE PRINTING PRESS AS AN AGENT OF CHANGE (1979).

[83]*See* Veeder, *supra* note 30, at 555.

[84]At that time, "[S]tate justice ... was very feeble—men were judged by their lords, by their fellow burghers, by their priests, but they were seldom judged by the state." John Kelly, *Criminal Libel and Free Speech*, 6 KANSAS L. REV. 295, 296 (1958). The efforts of early churches to persuade parishioners to take their differences to their pastors evolved into a "universal spiritual jurisdiction" with canons enforced by church councils. Veeder, *supra* note 30, at 550. The *Bible*, in fact, warns Christians against having disputes settled in secular courts:

> Dare any of you, having a matter against another, go to law before the unjust, and not before the saints? Do ye not know that the saints shall judge the world? And if the world shall be judged by you, are ye unworthy to judge the smallest matters? Know ye not that we shall judge angels? How much more things that pertain to this life? ... Is it so, that there is not among you one wise man who will be able to decide between his brethren, but brother goes to law with brother, and that before unbelievers? Actually, then, it is already a defeat for you, that you have lawsuits with one another. Why not rather be wronged? Why not rather be defrauded?

I *Corinthians* 6:1–7 (King James).

[85]Veeder, *supra* note 30, at 550.

swerable for the cleanliness of men's lives," forbade defamation, as well as sexual immorality, blasphemy, perjury, obscenity and usury.[86] Malice—which would come to have a place in all common law definitions of defamation—was understood to be part of the sin of defamation, because bad intent or malevolent motive was an essential element of all sin.[87]

Feudal courts—also known as manorial, baronial or seigniorial courts—were also hearing criminal libel cases before the Norman conquest of England in 1066. Feudal lords and kings enforced the crime of defamation harshly as a means of social stability, in an attempt to substitute public justice for private revenge.[88] Alfred the Great, for example, "commanded that the forger of slander should have his tongue cut out, unless he redeemed it by the price of his head."[89] However, as a result of the Norman conquest came a rapid increase in royal power, accompanied by the establishment of the king's council as a royal court—in which "a single wrong might be redressed by a combination of civil and criminal remedies"[90]—and a steady decline of the feudal court system.[91]

---

[86]*Id.* at 551. The "usual penance" for defamation "was an acknowledgment of the baselessness of the imputation, in the vestry room in the presence of the clergyman and church wardens of the parish, and an apology to the person defamed." *Id.* Later, punishment was as extreme as excommunication. *See* S.F.C. MILSOM, HISTORICAL FOUNDATIONS OF THE COMMON LAW 380 (2d ed. 1981).

[87]*See* Van Vechten Veeder, *The History and Theory of the Law of Defamation (II)*, 4 COLUM. L. REV. 33, 35–36 (1904).

[88]John Kelly refers to this as the substitution of "legal process for the drawn sword." *Supra* note 84, at 295. This was "a motivation for much of the original criminal law." *Id.* at 297. *See also* Robert C. Post, *The Social Foundations of Defamation Law: Reputation and the Constitution*, 74 CAL. L. REV. 691, 704 (1986). As a result, "the vague authority of the law of God [was] gradually replaced by the alternative theory that libels are punishable because they disturb the state (if directed against magnates and magistrates), or because they provoke a breach of the peace (if directed against private individuals)." PLUCKNETT, *supra* note 77, at 460.

[89]NEWELL, *supra* note 52, at 18. Alfred ruled 871–899 C.E. *See* Colin R. Lovell, *The "Reception" of Defamation by the Common Law*, 15 VAND. L. REV. 1051, 1053 (1962).

[90]A.K.R. KIRALFY, THE ENGLISH LEGAL SYSTEM 5 (1990). *See also* GEORGE CRABB, A HISTORY OF ENGLISH LAW (1839).

[91]Though William the Conqueror (1066–1087) did not question ecclesiastical jurisdiction—many of his judges were members of the clergy—he did forbid clergy who were also judges from hearing ecclesiastical matters in his royal courts, which began "the rivalry between the secular and spiritual jurisdictions." Veeder, *supra* note 30, at 551. Following the signing of the Magna Carta in 1215, by which King John (1199–1216) agreed that his power was subject to the law and in which the beginnings of the English common law and representative government may be found—through its guarantee of rights and liberties to the king's barons—the feudal court system disappeared altogether and the king's royal courts, originally open only to a limited aristocracy, continued to gain power and prestige in their "aggressive" pursuit of justice.

Then, in 1275, Edward I promulgated the first libel statute, *de Scandalis Magnatum*, which punished defamatory "news or tales" about the king "and great men of the realm" without any proof of special damage.[92] The statute would become "the doctrinal core of the law of criminal libel until the fifteenth century."[93] Richard II subsequently statutorily defined the "great men" as including, "Prelates, Dukes, Earls, Barons, and great men of the realm, and also of the Chancellor, Treasurer, Clerk of the Privy Seal, Steward of the King's House, Justices of the one bench or the other, and of other great officers of the realm."[94] The statutes, then, were "not only to punish such things as import a great scandal in themselves, or such for which an action lay at common law, but also such reports as were anywise contemptuous towards the persons of peers and the great men of the realm, and brought them into disgrace" with the common people.[95] They intended to preserve the people's allegiance to their ruler, by recognizing "the importance of the control of the communication of ideas in the maintenance of the control of the ruling group as well as in the policing of the populace to keep down private fights."[96] Their significance was in their anti-democratic tendencies; they separated nobles from all others in the eyes of the law:

Kelly, *supra* note 84, at 297. Though "the most autocratic monarch of Western Europe would not have dreamed of denying the authority of the canon law" before the second millennium, successive kings acted to limit the church courts' power. Veeder, *supra* note 30, at 550. One of the first limits "was the requirement that if the sin was also an offense which the temporal courts could punish [or in which money was demanded as damages, as in modern civil law], the spiritual judges were not to meddle with it." *Id.* at 551. With this act, coupled with the creation of the Court of Common Pleas—designed to try cases brought by commoners against other commoners—the gradual separation of civil law from criminal law began.

[92]The Statute of Westminster I provided:

Whereasmuch as there have been aforetimes found in the country devisers of tales ... whereby discord or occasion of discord hath arisen between the king and his people or great men of this realm ... it is commanded that none be so hardy as to tell or publish any false news or tales whereby discord or occasion of discord or slander may grow between the king and his people or the great men of the realm; he that doth so shall be taken and kept in prison until he hath brought him into the court which was the first author of the tale.

Veeder, *supra* note 30, at 553.

Edward ruled 1272–1307. *See* John C. Lassiter, *Defamation of Peers: The Rise and Decline of the Action for Scandalum Magnatum, 1497–1773*, 22 AM. J. LEGAL HIST. 216 (July 1978).

[93]Kelly, *supra* note 84, at 298.

[94]Veeder, *supra* note 30, at 553 n.3. Richard ruled 1377–1399.

[95]NEWELL, *supra* note 52, at 21.

[96]Kelly, *supra* note 84, at 298. Lois Forer writes that "libelous statements [were thought to stir] up the people and [endanger] the stability of government. Significantly, there was no evidence that the people were stirred up or that the stability of the government was endangered." *Supra* note 12, at 54.

Protecting none but the great men of the realm who, on account of their noble birth or official dignity, could not or would not demean themselves either by personal encounter or by resort to any other jurisdiction than that of their sovereign, these statutes are hardly to be taken as a recognition by the royal authority of the right to reputation. They were in fact directed rather against sedition and turbulence than against ordinary defamation.[97]

The administration of criminal justice, it was said, did not "concern itself with trifling offenses."[98] The "substantive effect was to allow 'magistrates' to recover for words which their lesser neighbors would have to swallow."[99] With the continued decline of ecclesiastical courts and the slow transformation of baronial courts into the king's courts of common law,[100] the only court in the mid-sixteenth century left with any power in the area of criminal libel was the king's council "sitting in the starred chamber."[101]

Though the English Court of the Star Chamber would eventually assume "jurisdiction of cases of ordinary or non-political defamation, which it decided in the way of criminal proceedings," it was originally "directed against political scandal,"[102] involving "the authority and connections of the nobles [who] were too powerful for the ordinary course of the law."[103] These individuals were far more concerned "with protecting their own interests, including their reputation," than they were with issues of equality and freedom of expression.[104] The public's growing "preference for the civil remedy, which enabled the frustrated victim to trade chivalrous satisfaction for damages, had substantially eroded the breach of the peace justification for criminal libel laws."[105] Yet English nobles and peers were not com-

---

[97]Veeder, *supra* note 30, at 554.

[98]THAYER, *supra* note 55, at 321.

[99]MILSOM, *supra* note 86, at 388.

[100]The decline of the ecclesiastical courts was a result of "the increasing tyranny and corruption of the church," as well as of their "inquisitorial procedure." Kelly, *supra* note 84, at 298. *See also* Veeder, *supra* note 30, at 552. They survived for centuries before the church's jurisdiction was abolished during Victoria's reign (1837–1901). The lengthy struggle "ended in the complete victory of the secular jurisdiction." Veeder, *supra* note 30, at 557.

[101]Veeder, *supra* note 30, at 554. Prior to the reign of Elizabeth I (1558–1603), the kings' courts of common law "practically gave no remedy for defamation." *Id*. at 555.

[102]*Id*. at 554–55.

[103]NEWELL, *supra* note 52, at 22.

[104]Robert Leflar, *The Social Utility of the Criminal Law of Defamation*, 34 TEXAS L. REV. 984, 1017 (1956).

[105]Garrison v. Louisiana, 379 U.S. 64, 69 (1964). The civil remedy for libel "was extremely popular ... and except for a few political offenses, the civil action usurped the field of defamation." Kelly, *supra* note 84, at 299.

pletely satisfied. Their positions, they felt, required state criminal sanctions for libelous remarks. Thus, although the Star Chamber claimed "all its right and authority [to be grounded] in the common law,"[106] criminal libel owes its modern origins "to an innovation in [the] Star Chamber whereby elements of Roman law were employed as the basis for prosecuting the publishers of defamatory statements," because of their tendency "to cause breaches of the peace."[107] Whether the statement was true was considered immaterial.[108] In fact, "[T]hat a disagreeable bit of printed matter was true made it all the more objectionable to the powerful lord about whom it was written," which gave rise to the maxim, "the greater the truth the greater the libel."[109]

Punishments included "imprisonment, pillory, fine, whipping, loss of ears, and brands in the face"[110]—including, "excision of the tongue" or the "loss ... of the right hand for writings"[111]—as well as, "frequently mutilation."[112] It was not difficult to see, then, why the Star Chamber's reputation, especially in the United States, has always been "unsavory" and its methods viewed as "odious."[113] It is

---

[106]NEWELL, *supra* note 52, at 23.

[107]Bahn, *supra* note 32, at 522. Ella Thomas notes that

the English Star Chamber conceived a wholly new idea of this offense, by making it a crime to utter seditious words against the government or its officials, or to make defamatory statements against private persons which might lead to a breach of the peace. The law of seditious libel, which included any publication criticizing the legality or policy of any act of the government was ruthlessly applied.

ELLA THOMAS, THE LAW OF LIBEL AND SLANDER AND RELATED ACTIONS 2 (1973).

[108]*See* Bahn, *supra* note 32, at 522.

[109]Leflar, *supra* note 104, at 1017.

[110]NEWELL, *supra* note 52, at 23.

[111]PLUCKNETT, *supra* note 77, at 454, 457.

[112]Spencer, *supra* note 52, at 385. In one instance in which an individual, after being tortured, refused to reveal the author of an objectionable statement, Star Chamber justices ordered that he be "drawn" and then

you shall be hanged by the neck, and being alive, shall be cut down, and your privy members shall be cut off, your entrails shall be taken out of your body, the same to be burnt before your eyes; your head to be cut off, your body to be divided into four quarters, and your head and quarters to be disposed of at the pleasure of the King's Majesty.

Wayne Terry, *Past Punishments: Life—and Death—Before the First Amendment,* QUILL, January 1982, at 9.

The Star Chamber's legal rationale for its actions was to draw "an analogy with poisoning: harm easily done in secret must be severely punished when brought to light." MILSOM, *supra* note 86, at 390.

[113]NEWELL, *supra* note 52, at 23. Justice usually was not the result of a Star Chamber trial:

In various ways the government contrived to stack the cards against the accused. The Attorney-General himself usually prosecuted. The prosecution was nearly always be-

also not therefore surprising that those tried in the Star Chamber were usually found guilty, and that the court's methods have not been sanctioned by the verdict of history.[114]

The court—an "arbitrary and high-handed tribunal which sat without a jury"[115]—took on added responsibilities with the invention of moveable type.[116] The church and ecclesiastical courts had historically suppressed ideas which they deemed to be heretical or blasphemous.[117] The monarchy viewed printed defamation with a renewed sense of alarm as a threat to "the public peace and security of the crown,"[118] based on its permanence and its ability to be duplicated quickly, and required all printed works to be either licensed or censored. The Star Chamber assumed jurisdiction over this new form of communication because the court was composed of leaders of both church and state and because it "exercised practically unlimited authority."[119]

Its most famous policy statement establishing criminal libel as a common law crime—"the starting point of the modern law of criminal libel"[120]—may be found in its 1605 *de Libellis Famosis* decision.[121] As a

---

gun on the Attorney-General's *ex officio* information—a procedure which short-circuited the preliminary stages through which prosecutions ordinarily had to go, and so obviated the risk of an independently-minded jury refusing to find a true bill against the accused. And, latterly at any rate, the trial was further stage-managed in that a special jury was usually summoned to hear it—on the usually correct hypothesis that rich men have little sympathy with radicals. In the early days ... the court was virtually an arm of the government.

Spencer, *supra* note 52, at 384.

However, Martin Newell asks if there might "not have been some period of the history of the human race in which the superior learning of the high officers of church and state, and the collected authority and splendor of the nobles immediately attached to the court of a king, were a better safeguard for the public peace than the juries of a barbarous age, or their independence at a time when every peer was the sovereign of his vicinage?" *Supra* note 52, at 23.

[114]Irving Brant calls it "the most iniquitous tribunal in English history." Irving Brant, *Seditious Libel: Myth and Reality*, 39 N.Y.U. L. REV. 1, 5 (1964).

[115]FORER, *supra* note 12, at 55.

[116]William Caxton set up the first printing press in England in 1476, which quickly "aroused the absolute monarchy to a keen sense of the danger of this new method of diffusion of ideas." Veeder, *supra* note 30, at 561.

[117]*See* Philip Hamburger, *The Development of the Law of Seditious Libel and the Control of the Press*, 37 STAN. L. REV. 661, 671–672 (1985).

[118]Kelly, *supra* note 84, at 300.

[119]Veeder, *supra* note 30, at 562. The court "disregarded forms; it was bound by no rules of evidence; it sat in vacation as well as in term time; it appointed and heard only its own counsel, thereby not being troubled with silly or ignorant barristers, or such as were idle and full of words." *Id.* at 563.

[120]Kelly, *supra* note 84, at 300. The crime could be punished in either the king's courts or in the Star Chamber.

[121]The ruling states:

result, the two primary elements of criminal libel were established as law: first, truth was not a defense; and, second, libel could be prohibited if it tended to cause a breach of the peace.[122] As a result, elements of the Roman civil law were introduced into the common law of criminal libel—though, arguably, they were misapplied by the court without regard to Roman limitations.[123] However, criminal libel's "newer and vaguer" common law foundations were not established by Edward Coke and the justices of the Star Chamber in 1605.[124] Twenty-two years later, in his *Institutes of the Laws of England*, Coke would report that he had discovered two libel prosecutions in 1336 and 1344 that demonstrated and established criminal libel's English common law origins.[125] Coke's evidence was accepted without question through the Tudor and Stuart reigns of the sixteenth and seventeenth centuries, and even after the Star Chamber was finally abolished in 1641. The English government continued its licensing system and gave the

---

Every libel is made either against a private man, or against a magistrate or public person. If it be against a private man it deserves a severe punishment, for although the libel be made against one, yet it incites all those of the same family, kindred, or society to revenge, and so tends *per consequens* to quarrels and breach of the peace, and may be the cause of the shedding of blood and great inconvenience; if it be against a magistrate, or other public person, it is a greater offense; for it concerns not only the breach of the peace, but also the scandal of Government; for what greater scandal of Government can there be than to have corrupt and wicked magistrates to be appointed and constituted by the King to govern his subjects under him.

5 Co. Rep. 125a–125b, 77 Eng. Rep. 250–251 (1605).

[122]If the libel concerned a public official, it was punished as seditious libel as it was deemed "a threat to the security of the state;" if it concerned a private individual, it was punished as criminal libel as it was a "risk [to] a breach of the peace." William Holdsworth, *Defamation in the Sixteenth and Seventeenth Centuries*, 40 LAW Q. REV. 302, 305 (1924). The prevention of violence, as well as the promotion of social order, was the purpose of both, "for ... two motives were at work: the general threat to good order inherent in insult, and the particular threat to authority inherent in sedition." MILSOM, *supra* note 86, at 379.

[123]*See* Veeder, *supra* note 87, at 44.

[124]PLUCKNETT, *supra* note 77, at 461.

[125]In the two cases:

Adam de Ravensworth was indicted in the King's Bench for the making of a Libel in writing, in the French tongue, against Richard of Snowshill, calling him therein, Roy de Raveners, etc. Whereupon he being arraigned, pleaded thereunto not guilty, and was found guilty, as by the Record appeareth. So as a Libeller, or a publisher of a Libel committeth a publick offence, and may be indicted therefore at the Common Law. John de Northampton an Attorney of the King's Bench, wrote a Letter to John Ferrers, one of the King's Council, that neither Sir William Scot, Chiefe Justice [of Common Pleas], nor his fellows the King's Justices, nor their Clerks, any great thing would do by the commandment of our Lord the King, nor of Queen Philip[pa], in that place, more than any other of the Realme; which said John being called, confessed the said Letter by him to be written with his own proper hand.

EDWARD COKE, THE THIRD PART OF THE INSTITUTES OF THE LAWS OF ENGLAND 174 (repr., Garland Pub. Co. 1979) (1628).

power to punish those violating the Star Chamber doctrine of criminal libel to the common law courts, which also provided a civil remedy for claims of defamation.[126]

Finally, based on Coke's evidence, William Blackstone, in 1769, incorporated the common law of criminal libel into his own *Commentaries on the Laws of England*,[127] clothing it "in the flowing robes of State and Church, God and the King—a system of regulation and repression which he thought essential to the maintenance of an orthodox and orderly monarchic society."[128] Freedom of expression, Blackstone wrote, "is indeed essential to the nature of a free state; but this consists in laying no *previous* restraint upon publications, and not in freedom from censure for criminal matter when published."[129] This summarized the eighteenth century's position of free expression—which at the time was considered quite liberal—concisely: Licensing and prior restraints were improper but speakers could be held criminally liable for their expression.

Yet Coke was wrong; Blackstone was wrong. The Anglo-American legal origins of criminal libel are not to be found in the English common law. The two cases Coke cited were not libel cases at all. One was treason, the other contempt of court.[130] Thus, the common law should not have been used to justify prosecution of anyone for the crime of libel. The common law of criminal libel—"the major obstacle to literal acceptance of the words of the First Amendment"[131]—is a sham.[132] Although common law courts assumed jurisdiction over

---

[126]KIRALFY, *supra* note 90, at 52. Thus,

the Star Chamber's law of libel was henceforth to be administered by the same court as had developed the common law of slander; inevitably the two bodies of law were bound to influence each other, and tended to become more coherently combined into something approaching a systematic law of defamation.

PLUCKNETT, *supra* note 77, at 467.

[127]BLACKSTONE, *supra* note 52, at *151–*152.

[128]Brant, *supra* note 114, at 19. To make this more palatable, "Blackstone dropped the Star Chamber completely out of the picture, except for historical beginnings. He described the restraint of the press through prosecutions for criminal libel as if this were entirely an emanation from the common law." *Id*. It is thus easy to see why Blackstone as a legal scholar "has fallen into deep discredit." *Id*. at 14.

[129]BLACKSTONE, *supra* note 52, at *151–*152 (emphasis in original). Yet the then widely accepted practice of licensing could not help but operate as a form of prior restraint on expression. As governmental licensing declined, it was replaced by seditious libel prosecutions. *See* William T. Mayton, *Seditious Libel and the Lost Guarantee of a Freedom of Expression*, 84 COLUM. L. REV. 91, 98 (1984).

[130]*See* Brant, *supra* note 114, at 8. Brant's research and conclusions were cited with approval in *Garrison v. Louisiana*, 379 U.S. 64, 83 (1964) (Black, J., concurring).

[131]Brant, *supra* note 114, at 3.

[132]Irving Brant's "straightening of the record leaves *civil damage suits* for libel within the scope of the common law, a jurisdiction growing naturally out of its cogni-

criminal libel after the abolition of the Star Chamber, as a legal concept it was still "cut from ... poisonous wood."[133] American jurisprudence for more than two-and-a-half centuries has thus been misled.

CRIMINAL LIBEL'S TRANSITION TO THE UNITED STATES

The question remaining and the basic issue of criminal libel in the United States is this: "To what extent does the First Amendment cut across and limit the law of criminal libel?"[134] Arguably, of course, "the Declaration of Independence ... was the most monumental seditious libel in British history."[135] But how well did the English concept of criminal libel migrate to America? Irving Brant contends that

> nowhere in the world was the legal groundwork laid for complete recognition and permanent enforcement of freedom of speech, press, and religion until written constitutions came into existence in the United States .... To reach a conclusion that the First Amendment was intended to embody the *practices* of eighteenth century England, it is necessary to believe that the framers intended to sanction the state of affairs described by [the statement]: "To speak ill of the government [is] a crime."[136]

No such plausible argument can be made, especially given "the abandonment of ... authoritarian principles in government, the rise of political parties, and the spread of democratic doctrines" throughout Europe[137] and "in the increasingly dissatisfied [American] colonies" of the eighteenth century.[138]

---

zance of similar private actions for slander. It makes *criminal libel* entirely the creation of the Star Chamber." *Id.* at 11 (emphasis in original).

[133]*Id.* at 12. The effect of this "mistake" on the development of American law "has been to put the full weight of eighteenth-century British jurisprudence behind a dogmatic remark by Coke about common-law jurisdiction as an alternative to trial in the Star Chamber—a remark that had no supporting evidence when he made it, and in support of which, twenty-two years later, he cited two ancient cases that evaporate completely upon examination." *Id.* at 19.

[134]Kelly, *supra* note 84, at 321.

[135]CHARLES A. MILLER, THE SUPREME COURT AND THE USES OF HISTORY 83 (1969).

[136]Brant, *supra* note 114, at 18 (emphasis in original). At that time in England, of course, "any publication which reflected upon the Government was criminal." PLUCKNETT, *supra* note 77, at 470. However, Brant argues that "if seditious libel has any genuine common-law affiliation, it is by illegitimate descent from constructive treason and heresy, both of which are totally repugnant to the Constitution of the United States." *Supra* note 114, at 5.

[137]Siebert, *Authoritarian Theory*, in SIEBERT ET AL., *supra* note 41, at 24.

[138]Kelly, *supra* note 84, at 305.

In addition, the civil remedy for libel—which "filled an important gap in the earlier law"[139]—continued its growth in popularity, for in America the civil remedy, coupled with "the immeasurable importance of political writing in an age of revolution," began redefining and limiting criminal libel to its "most important aspect"—seditious libel.[140] Criminal sanctions, like the ecclesiastical penalties of earlier centuries, "punished the defamer but did not make his victim whole."[141] The increasing use of the civil remedy, therefore, may also be seen as an expression of that most important egalitarian principle—the significance and equality of all persons in the eyes of the law.

A Philosophical and Political Shift

Equality was and still is the defining ideal of America. This concept represents a philosophical shift away from the authoritarian view that the governors are the peoples' "betters" to one in which government generally is viewed as the peoples' servant. This trend viewed seditious libel especially as "unnecessary and evil, because criticism of the rulers of the state was desirable as a method of keeping them responsive to the will of the public, their masters."[142] Factors which influenced this development during what has become known as the "Age of Enlightenment," which postulated humans as rational beings, included a developing individualistic temperament, a growing literacy rate, the emergence of a social middle class, the economic and legal freedom to make contracts, and a belief in the value of free discussion and competition among ideas for acceptance[143]—a "marketplace of ideas," identified by Justice Oliver Wendell Holmes in *Abrams v. United States*,[144] though first articulated by John Milton.[145] Although "the path of truth might lie

---

[139]*Id.* at 299.

[140]*Id.* at 305.

[141]*Id.* at 299.

[142]*Id.* at 303.

[143]The utilitarian jurisprudence of Jeremy Bentham, thus, "cast a long shadow" over American law. LAWRENCE M. FRIEDMAN, A HISTORY OF AMERICAN LAW 123 (1979).

[144]250 U.S. 616, 630 (1919) (Holmes, J., dissenting). *See also* BERNARD SCHWARTZ, MAIN CURRENTS IN AMERICAN LEGAL THOUGHT 383–86 (1993).

[145]In what has become to be understood as "the beginnings of [the] underlying theme of First Amendment theory." DONALD GILLMOR & JEROME BARRON, MASS COMMUNICATIONS LAW: CASES AND COMMENT 3 (3d ed. 1979), John Milton wrote:

> And though all the windes of doctrin[e] were let loose to play upon the earth, so Truth be in the field, we do injuriously by licensing and prohibiting to misdoubt her strength. Let her and Falsehood grapple; who ever knew truth put to the wors[e], in a free and open encounter?

through a morass of argument and dispute,"[146] popular sovereignty, the free exchange of ideas, and a self-righting marketplace would guarantee achievement of the "ultimate goal" of society—"the fulfillment of the individual."[147] Though widely debated and critiqued,[148]

MILTON, *supra* note 3, at 51–52.

Similarly, John Locke wrote:

> The business of laws is not to provide for the truth of opinions, but for the safety and security of the commonwealth, and of every particular man's goods and person. And so it ought to be. For the truth certainly would do well enough if she were once left to shift for herself. She seldom has received, and I fear never will receive, much assistance from the power of great men, to whom she is but rarely known, and more rarely welcome. She is not taught by laws, nor has she any need of force to procure her entrance into the minds of men. Errors indeed prevail by the assistance of foreign and borrowed succours. But if Truth makes not her way into the understanding by her own light, she will be but the weaker for any borrowed force violence can add to her.

JOHN LOCKE, TREATISE OF CIVIL GOVERNMENT AND LETTER CONCERNING

TOLERATION 205 (Charles L. Sherman ed., Appleton-Century-Crofts 1937) (1689). On the other hand, Steven H. Shiffrin and Jesse H. Choper question whether Milton envisioned his "free and open encounter" occurring in a commercial marketplace. *See* STEVEN H. SHRIFFIN & JESSE H. CHOPER, THE FIRST AMENDMENT: CASES—COMMENTS—QUESTIONS 16 (2d ed. 1996).

[146]Siebert, *The Libertarian Theory of the Press*, in SIEBERT ET AL., *supra* note 41, at 41.

[147]*Id.* at 40. Libertarians would

> let the public at large be subjected to a barrage of information and opinion, some of it possibly true, some of it possibly false, and some of it containing elements of both. Ultimately the public could be trusted to digest the whole, to discard that not in the public interest and to accept that which served the needs of the individual and of the society of which he is a part.

Id. at 51.

[148]*See, e.g.*, C. EDWIN BAKER, HUMAN LIBERTY AND FREEDOM OF SPEECH (1989); LAURENCE H. TRIBE, AMERICAN CONSTITUTIONAL LAW 786 (2d ed. 1988); Jerome Barron, *Access to the Press—A New First Amendment Right*, 80 HARV. L. REV. 1641 (1967); Stanley Ingber, *The Marketplace of Ideas: A Legitimizing Myth*, 1984 DUKE L. J. 1. It is beyond the scope of this discussion whether this marketplace should more properly be analogized as a government-regulated "town meeting." *See* ALEXANDER MEIKLEJOHN, POLITICAL FREEDOM: THE CONSTITUTIONAL POWERS OF THE PEOPLE 24 (1960); William J. Brennan, Jr., *The Supreme Court and the Meiklejohn Interpretation of the First Amendment*, 79 HARV. L. REV. 1 (Nov. 1965). On the other hand,

> the metaphor that there is a "marketplace of ideas" does ... apply.... The metaphor is honored; Milton's *Aeropagitica* and John Stewart Mill's *On Liberty* defend freedom of speech on the ground that the truth will prevail, and many of the most important cases under the First Amendment recite this position. The Framers undoubtedly believed it. As a general matter it is true.

American Booksellers v. Hudnut, 771 F. 2d 323, 330 (7th Cir. 1985). *See also supra* note 3.

this is still a central tenet of all libertarian/democratic societies and certainly "a central American theme."[149]

The libertarian theory, upon which the United States was founded, thus assumes that "the prime function of society is to advance the interests of its individual members," not of any ruling elite.[150] Because humans are rational beings, the purpose of government is thus to help every person achieve his or her fullest potential and "truth [is] a definite discoverable entity capable of demonstration to all thinking men."[151] Under the libertarian theory, then, "[T]he free flow of ideas about matters of public importance [is necessary] for the attainment of truth and responsive government."[152] Therefore,

> let all with something to say be free to express themselves. The true and sound will survive; the false and unsound will be vanquished. Government should keep out of the battle and not weigh the odds in favor of one side or the other. And even though the false may gain a temporary victory, that which is true, by drawing to its defense additional forces, will through the self-righting process ultimately survive.[153]

As a consequence, the libertarian theory created "an economic and social environment which made libel actions of all types unwanted and unneeded in the United States [and] of less significance [here] than in any other country under the civil or the common law."[154]

At least, that was the presumption. Yet the move "from authoritarian to libertarian principles ... was not accomplished overnight,"[155] nor has it even now been fully attained. First, the imposition of the English common law of criminal libel upon the American colonies "bottled up popular criticism [and] made armed revolution the only course open to aggrieved Americans."[156] In his history of American jurisprudence, Charles Warren points out that "it is probable that no one thing contributed more to enflame the public mind against the common law than did the insistence of the American [co-

---

[149]Aviam Soifer, *Freedom of Speech in the United States*, in PNINA LAHAV, PRESS LAW IN MODERN DEMOCRACIES: A COMPARATIVE STUDY 80 (1985).

[150]Siebert, *Libertarian Theory*, in SIEBERT ET AL., *supra* note 41, at 40.

[151]*Id.* at 41.

[152]Kelly, *supra* note 84, at 307.

[153]Siebert, *Libertarian Theory*, in SIEBERT ET AL., *supra* note 41, at 45. Inherent in this marketplace of expression is not only the speaker's freedom to speak but also the audience's implicit legal responsibility for its own reactions to that speech.

[154]Kelly, *supra* note 84, at 317.

[155]Siebert, *Libertarian Theory*, in SIEBERT ET AL., *supra* note 41, at 47.

[156]Kelly, *supra* note 84, at 306. *See also* Siebert, *Libertarian Theory*, in SIEBERT ET AL., *supra* note 41, at 48.

lonial] courts on enforcing the harsh doctrines of the English law of criminal libel—that truth is no defense, and that the jury could pass only on the fact of publication."[157] Second, even if citizens of the new country believed that censorship and the crime of libel had been eliminated by the American revolution, "[t]he judges of the young nation unanimously disagreed" and "took the view that the constitutional provisions were only declaratory of the English common law as set down" by Coke and Blackstone,[158] leaving "intact the common law of criminal libel which was felt to be a necessary limitation" on the freedom of speech.[159] "Unchallenged by the legal profession,"[160] criminal libel thus became "kind of a national crime" in what was supposed to be a libertarian society.[161] This state of affairs lasted well into the twentieth century and "stands today as the major obstacle to literal acceptance of the words of the First Amendment."[162]

Truth as a Defense in Criminal Libel

Under "the harsh English criminal rule,"[163] truth was not allowed as a defense in criminal libel cases, because the purpose of the prosecution of the crime was to prevent violence—either against public of-

---

[157]CHARLES WARREN, A HISTORY OF THE AMERICAN BAR 236 (1911).

[158]Kelly, *supra* note 84, at 310–311. *See also* Warren, *supra* note 157, at 237.

[159]*Id.* at 310. Charles Miller states:

In American history the most important broad topic in legal history dealt with by the courts has been the extent to which the English common law was "received" as the law of the colonies and, later, of the states. Like many issues in legal history, the nineteenth-century argument over the reception of the common law was not a legal issue alone but was embroiled in politics. Like other legal receptions it was conditioned by cultural attitudes towards the home country of the system—in the American case the attitude toward England—but the issue was argued in terms of law.... Ultimately the country succumbed to [its] Anglo-Saxon heritage, but with the qualification that the law adopted would have to measure up to the "civil and political condition" of America.

Supra note 135, at 21–22 (quoting Murray's Lesee v. Hoboken, 18 How. 272, 277 (1855)). *See also* Ford W. Hall, *The Common Law: An Account of Its Reception in the United States*, 4 VAND. L. REV. 791 (1951).

[160]Brant, *supra* note 114, at 3.

[161]Chief Justice Thomas McKean of the Pennsylvania Supreme Court, *quoted in* WARREN, *supra* note 157, at 238.

[162]Brant, *supra* note 114, at 3. In 1931, in *Near v. Minnesota*, Chief Justice Charles Evans Hughes stated:

But it is recognized that punishment for the abuse of the liberty accorded to the press is essential to the protection of the public, and that the common law rules that subject the libeler to responsibility for the public offense, as well as for the private injury, are not abolished by the protection extended in our constitutions. The law of criminal libel rests upon that secure foundation.

283 U.S. 697, 715 (1931) (citations omitted).

[163]Leflar, *supra* note 104, at 1017.

ficials and prosecuted as seditious libel, or against private persons and prosecuted as criminal libel.[164] As a result, it made no difference whether the matter was true or false, because the greater the truth the more likely violence would result.[165] English common law judges would allow "the question of actual publication to go to the jury"—to determine the fact of the matter—but treated the libelous character of the expression, its truthfulness, as "a question of 'law' for the judge."[166] However, in American law "truth seems from the first to have been viewed as admissible."[167]

That divergence between English and American law was evident as early as 1735 when John Peter Zenger was acquitted of seditious libel by appealing to "principles of elementary justice"—in other words, by "pleading the truth"—based on the legal argument "that for any statement to be a libel, it had to be both false and injurious."[168] Zenger was indicted for his frequent published attacks on government ministers, especially as they reflected on the royal governor of New York.[169] His newspaper's "manifesto on the freedom of the press" included the following statement about the governor:

> For if such an overgrown criminal, or an impudent monster in iniquity, cannot immediately be come at by ordinary justice, let him yet receive the lash of satire, let the glaring truths of his ill administration, if possible, awaken his conscience, and if he has no conscience, rouse his fear, by showing him his deserts, sting him with shame, and render his actions odious to all honest minds.[170]

Another time, Zenger's newspaper suggested that the governor's actions threatened New Yorkers with slavery.[171] After eight months in prison, Zenger was acquitted when his attorney "argued politics

---

[164]*See* Holdsworth, *supra* note 122, at 305.

[165]*See* SACK, *supra* note 50, at 130; WARREN, *supra* note 157, at 236; Leflar, *supra* note 104, at 1017.

[166]Kelly, *supra* note 84, at 299. Thus, in the early history of the American colonies "a royally appointed judge became the *ex post facto* arbiter of the extent of ... freedom of speech." *Id*. at 302.

[167]Bahn, supra note 32, at 523.

[168]WILLIAM L. PUTNAM, JOHN PETER ZENGER AND THE FUNDAMENTAL FREEDOM 104 (1997).

[169]*See* STEPHEN B. PRESSER & JAMIL S. ZAINALDIN, LAW AND AMERICAN HISTORY 31–59 (1980); Frederic B. Farrar, *A Printer, a Lawyer and the Free Press*, EDITOR & PUBLISHER, Aug. 3, 1985, at 31.

[170]JAMES ALEXANDER, A BRIEF NARRATIVE OF THE CASE AND TRIAL OF JOHN PETER ZENGER, PRINTER OF THE NEW YORK WEEKLY JOURNAL 11 (Stanley N. Katz ed., The Belknap Press of Harvard University Press 1972) (1736).

[171]*Id*. at 16. *See also* NEWELL, *supra* note 52, at 26.

rather than law"[172] and after the jury disregarded the court's instructions not to consider the truth or falsity of the statements.[173] Though it could be argued that the result was little more than an early instance of jury nullification,[174] the decision has generally been accepted as "the first chapter in the epic of American liberty," a precursor of the revolution "which was to make an ideal of 1735 an American reality," serving "repeatedly to remind Americans of the debt free men owe to free speech."[175] It also "helped snap the leading strings that bound the American Colonies to the mother country" and stood as "the morning star of that liberty which subsequently revolutionized America."[176]

The Zenger verdict was so influential that one argument in favor of enactment of the Sedition Act of 1798[177]—which punished any expression contemptuous of the president, the government or Congress[178]—was that it allowed defendants to establish the truth of their accusations as a defense.[179] Though supposedly adopted in response to the threat of war with France, historians agree that the act was nothing more than a thinly disguised attempt to limit press criticism of John Adams's presidency, "part of a campaign of intimidation."[180] Yet it is also further proof that the law of criminal libel survived the American Revolution and ratification of the First Amendment to the Constitution.[181]

---

[172]*Id.* at 24.

[173]Zenger's attorney argued that the jury had "the right beyond all dispute to determine both the law and the fact[s]." *Id.* at 78. *See* NEWELL, *supra* note 52, at 26–27; Kelly, *supra* note 84, at 306–07.

[174]Instances of this occur when a jury reaches a verdict without regard to the weight of the evidence or the requirements of the law, as "ultimately, the factfinder in a criminal trial has the raw power irrevocably to acquit a defendant for any reason whatsoever." JOSHUA DRESSLER, CASES AND MATERIALS ON CRIMINAL LAW 15 (1994). *See also* PUTNAM, *supra* note 168, at 116.

[175]ALEXANDER, *supra* note 170, at 1, 35. *See also* Warren C. Price, *Reflections on the Trial of John Peter Zenger*, 32 JOURNALISM Q. 161 (1955); James R. Wiggins, *The Zenger Case Today*, EDITOR & PUBLISHER, Aug. 3, 1985, at 33.

[176]VINCENT BURANELLI (ED.), THE TRIAL OF PETER ZENGER 61, 63 (1957).

[177]1 Stat. at Large 596 (1798).

[178]Under the statute, to bring government and government officials "into disrepute tended to overthrow the state." CHAFEE, *supra* note 40, at 23.

[179]*See* FRANK L. MOTT, AMERICAN JOURNALISM 148 (3d ed. 1962).

[180]*Id.* at 149. *See also* JOHN C. MILLER, CRISIS IN FREEDOM: THE ALIEN AND SEDITION ACTS (1951). Criticism of Vice President Thomas Jefferson, for example, who was not a member of Adams's Federalist political party, was not prohibited. *See* ALLAN NEVINS & HENRY S. COMMAGER, A SHORT HISTORY OF THE UNITED STATES 151 (1968); Max Frankel, *Democracy in Infancy*, N.Y. TIMES MAGAZINE, Jan. 23, 2000, at 17. John Kelly, however, contends that it "was hardly the pernicious legislation it is usually made out." *Supra* note 84, at 313.

[181]*See* LEONARD LEVY, EMERGENCE OF A FREE PRESS 173–219 (1985); D. Jenkins, *The Sedition Act of 1798 and the Incorporation of Seditious Libel into First Amendment Jurisprudence*, 45 AM. J. LEGAL HIST. 154 (April 2001). Of course, "the Consti-

That the statute "led to widespread contemporary abuses" would be impossible to deny.[182] An individual offering truth as a defense was made to "prove every charge he has made to be true; he must prove it to the marrow. If he asserts three things and proves but two, he fails in his defense, for he must prove the whole of his assertions to be true."[183] At least twenty-four persons were arrested, fifteen indicted, and ten convicted under the provisions of the act.[184] Though its constitutionality was never challenged in court, the public's "manifest opposition" to the act "was an important indication that freedom of speech and the press had a much broader popular connotation than [Blackstone's] mere prohibition of prior restraint."[185] The convictions were also proof that the mere inclusion of a clause allowing truth as a defense was inadequate to protect the free and open discussion of public affairs. After the act's expiration in 1801, all those convicted were pardoned by President Thomas Jefferson and their fines repaid by Congress.[186] The law's "ultimate failure ... proved that Americans believed that they had an indestructible right of political criticism."[187] Its unconstitutionality was finally acknowledged by the Supreme Court in *New York Times v. Sullivan*: "The attack on its validity has carried the day in the court of history."[188]

The use of truth as a defense in criminal libel was finally established as American law in *People v. Croswell*.[189] There, Federalist edi-

---

tution of the United States, including the Bill of Rights, is above all else an anti-authoritarian document." Ruth Walden, A Government Action Approach to First Amendment Analysis 2 (paper presented at the annual convention of the Association for Education in Journalism and Mass Communication, Boston, Mass., Aug. 7–10, 1991).

[182]Eric M. Freedman, *American Libel Law—1825–1896: A Qualified Privilege for Public Affairs?* 30 CHITTY'S L. J. 113, 117 n.10 (April 1982).

[183]United States v. Cooper, 25 Fed. Cas. 631, 642–643 (C.C.D. Penn. 1800).

[184]*See* BERNARD WEISBERGER, AMERICA AFIRE 200–224 (2000); PRESSER & ZAINALDIN, *supra* note 169, at 210–234.

[185]Kelly, *supra* note 84, at 313. *See also supra* note 129.

[186]PUTNAM, *supra* note 168, at 124.

[187]Kelly, *supra* note 84, at 316.

[188]376 U.S. 254, 276 (1964). This conclusion, according to Justice William Brennan, writing for a unanimous Court, reflects "a broad consensus that the act, because of the restraint imposed upon criticism of government and public officials, was inconsistent with the First Amendment." *Id.* The statute "came to an ignominious end and by common consent has generally been treated as having been a wholly unjustifiable and much to be regretted violation of the First Amendment." *Id.* at 296 (Douglas, J., concurring). Yet, after its expiration in 1801, state statutes making libel a crime began to proliferate.

[189]3 Johns. Cas. 307 (N.Y. Sup. Ct. 1804). It has been called "the leading state case" in criminal libel law. Beauharnais v. Illinois, 343 U.S. 250, 295 (1952) (Jackson, J., dissenting). *See* Kyu H. Youm, *The Impact of People v. Croswell on Libel Law*, 113 JOURNALISM MONOGRAPHS (June 1989).

tor Harry Croswell had been convicted of criminal libel after being forbidden from using truth as his defense. Though a split New York appellate court upheld the conviction, the state legislature subsequently allowed truth, published "with good motives,"[190] to be used as a mitigating factor in such cases. The outcome was "the beginning of the end for the inadmissibility of truth."[191] This evolution culminated in 1964 with the Supreme Court's decision in *Garrison v. Louisiana*,[192] in which the Court not only acknowledged that truth may not be punished in criminal libel cases, but ruled that falsehood—published without "knowledge of its falsity or in reckless disregard of whether it was false or true"—is also protected by the First Amendment.[193] Yet that ruling was not enough, as "the mere threat of prosecution may operate as a gag" on all speech, without regard to whether it is true or false.[194]

Prevention of Violence as a Legal Rationale Underlying Criminal Libel

Despite the speed with which truth was adopted by American courts as a defense in actions for criminal libel in the eighteenth century, they "clung tenaciously" to its underlying legal justification of preventing breaches of the peace well into the twentieth century.[195] In part, this was as a result of their continued misplaced reliance on Blackstone;[196] more generally, it was a result of their common law understanding of historical precedent dating all the way back to the Babylonian empire.[197] This was also the essence of what distinguished the crime from the tort.[198] The historic purpose of criminal libel was the prevention of "tumult and disor-

---

[190]*Id.* at 353.

[191]Marc A. Franklin, *The Origins and Constitutionality of Limitations on Truth as a Defense in Tort Law*, 16 STAN. L. REV. 792, 792 (1964).

[192]379 U.S. 64 (1964).

[193]*Id.* at 74.

[194]MOTT, *supra* note 179, at 149.

[195]HAROLD L. NELSON & DWIGHT L. TEETER, JR., LAW OF MASS COMMUNICATIONS 51 (5th ed. 1986).

[196]In criminal libel, "the tendency which all libels have to create animosities and to disturb the public peace, is the whole that the law considers." BLACKSTONE, *supra* note 52, at *150–*151.

[197]*See supra* text accompanying notes 66–129.

[198]Insofar as libel

is merely an injury to the person, it comes within the category of private wrongs or torts and as such is cognizable by courts of civil law, but the bare fact that all libels are personal injuries, is a matter of indifference to the criminal law.... The criminal law ig-

der."[199] Though one who had been "falsely libeled might get satisfaction by proving that the statement was not true," the "only hope for satisfaction by one truly libeled was to cause harm to the defamer" by having him disciplined.[200] This interest in order and retribution—or justice—was taken so seriously that a criminal libel did not have to be communicated to a third party,[201] only directly to its intended recipient, as it might "move him to quick violence in reply."[202] Yet, as Zechariah Chafee points out, the "breach of the peace theory" is particularly susceptible to exploitation and abuse, especially in the case of unpopular expression: "It makes a man a criminal simply because his neighbors have no self-control and cannot refrain from violence."[203]

Increasing confidence in and reliance on the fledgling American court system in the nineteenth century, coupled with the growing preference for compensatory and punitive damages[204]—not available through criminal libel actions—meant a concomitant decreasing reliance on the prevention of violence as a rationale underlying the crime of libel. By the mid-twentieth century, "[T]he prime test [was] whether the defamation tend[ed] to disturb the public peace or, in more recent decisions, whether it [was] unlawful simply because it injure[d] another."[205] Yet that trend did not stop the Supreme Court from relying upon the rationale in situations involving seditious libel,[206] fighting words[207] and group libel.[208]

---

nores the private injury, leaving that to be remedied by a civil action, and exercises itself solely in the conservation of the public peace.

Frederick W. Brydon, *Criminal Libel*, 23 ALB. L. J. 46, 46 (1881).

[199]PLUCKNETT, *supra* note 77, at 471.

[200]ROLLIN M. PERKINS & RONALD N. BOYCE, CRIMINAL LAW 490 (3d ed. 1982).

[201]*See, e.g.*, State v. Avery, 7 Conn. 266, 18 Am. Dec. 105 (1828); People v. Spielman, 149 N.E. 466 (Ill. 1925).

[202]Leflar, *supra* note 104, at 1012.

[203]CHAFEE, *supra* note 40, at 151.

[204]Garrison v. Louisiana, 379 U.S. 64, 69 (1964). *See also* Kelly *supra* note 84, at 299.

[205]WILLIAM F. SWINDLER, PROBLEMS OF LAW IN JOURNALISM 156 (1955).

[206]*See* Schenck v. United States, 249 U.S. 47 (1919).

[207]Words which "have a direct tendency to cause acts of violence" could be prohibited. The test was "what men of common intelligence would understand would be words likely to cause an average addressee to fight." Chaplinsky v. New Hampshire, 315 U.S. 568, 573 (1942).

[208]Words which were "liable to cause violence and disorder" could be prohibited. Beauharnais v. Illinois, 343 U.S. 250, 254 (1952).

In evaluating the application of seditious libel statutes[209]—such as the Espionage Act of 1917,[210] "the first federal seditious libel legislation since 1798"[211]—the Supreme Court required some form of the clear and present danger test to be used to determine the proper balance between individual freedom and the government's need to protect security.[212] However, the Supreme Court's decision in *New York Times v. Sullivan* "soundly rejected" the law of seditious libel[213] and "has resulted in the apparently permanent establishment of the anti-seditious-libel doctrine as authentic constitutional history."[214] As a result, the only remaining viable analysis—the modern test—for determining when state governments may restrict speech based on the prevention of violence rationale is the "imminent lawless action" test from *Brandenburg v. Ohio*, applying a state criminal syndicalism statute.[215]

Though the Supreme Court in *Beauharnais v. Illinois*[216] accepted both "the public right to tranquility" and "the private right to enjoy integrity of reputation" as the two legal theories upon which "the criminality of the defamation is predicated,"[217] the prevention of violence rationale behind criminal sanctions against fighting words and group libel,[218] as well as libel of the dead,[219] appears to have been all

---

[209]The federal common law of seditious libel was expunged from American law by the Supreme Court in *United States v. Hudson and Goodwin*, 7 Cranch 32 (1812). However, "various state syndicalism acts and the federal act on espionage may be used to punished sedition, particularly in attempts to overthrow government or in time of war." THAYER, *supra* note 55, at 323. *See* Near v. Minnesota, 283 U.S. 697, 716 (1931).

[210]40 Stat. at Large 553 (1917).

[211]MILLER, *supra* note 135, at 87–88.

[212]*See* Schenck v. United States, 249 U.S. 47, 52 (1919). In *Abrams*, the test was defined as requiring "a clear and imminent danger." 250 U.S. 616, 627 (1919).

[213]Walden, *supra* note 181, at 36.

[214]MILLER, *supra* note 135, at 92. *See also Sullivan*, 376 U.S. 254, 273–277 (1964).

[215]395 U.S. 444, 447 (1969). *Brandenburg* was cited as holding seditious libel to be protected speech, "unless the danger is not only grave but also imminent." American Booksellers v. Hudnut, 771 F. 2d 323, 329 (7th Cir. 1985).

[216]343 U.S. 250 (1952).

[217]*Id.* at 294.

[218]Thomas Emerson argues that

[T]he major premise of *Beauharnais*—that libel laws are not within the coverage of the First Amendment—was overruled by *New York Times v. Sullivan* in 1964. A minor premise—that criminal laws are outside the First Amendment—was expressly repudiated a few months later in *Garrison v. Louisiana*. Hence little remains of the doctrinal structure of *Beauharnais*.

THOMAS EMERSON, THE SYSTEM OF FREE EXPRESSION 396 (1970) (citing New York Times Co. v. Sullivan, 376 U.S. 254 (1964); Garrison v. Louisiana, 379 U.S. 64 (1964); Beauharnais v. Illinois, 343 U.S. 250 (1952)).

[219]Because by definition the dead have no reputation to be harmed, libel of the dead appears wholly invalid today without the prevention of violence as an underlying legal rationale. *See* RODNEY A. SMOLLA, LAW OF DEFAMATION 4–118 (2d ed. 1999).

but eviscerated by the Court's subsequent rulings in *Garrison v. Louisiana*[220] and *Ashton v. Kentucky*.[221] This was first

> clearly evidenced in the wide recognition of truth as either a partial or complete defense. The departure [was] also pointed up by the fact that most of the present [state] statutes declare the nub of criminal libel, like that of civil libel, to be the publication of matter tending to injure reputation.[222]

This change was based in part on the First Amendment's freedom of speech guarantee, which generally requires audiences to avoid communication they do not wish to receive, as the nation's founders

> knew that order cannot be secured merely through fear of punishment for its infraction; that it is hazardous to discourage thought, hope, and imagination; that fear breeds repression; that repression breeds hate; that hate menaces stable government; that the path of safety lies in the opportunity to discuss freely supposed grievances and proposed remedies; and that the fitting remedy for evil counsels is good ones.[223]

It was also based in part on the basic impossibility of measuring "the degree of self-restraint necessary for an individual to maintain orderly conduct when humiliated by a ... libel to his character"[224]—not because the likelihood of violence is so high, but rather because it is so low.[225] Thus,

> [T]he dubious claim that violence will result from the publication of defamatory material, when contrasted with the real dangers of disorder

---

[220]The Supreme Court cited "changing mores and the virtual disappearance of criminal libel prosecutions" as evidence supporting its position. 379 U.S. at 69. According to the U.S. Court of Appeals for the Seventh Circuit (which includes Illinois, Indiana and Wisconsin), the "foundations of *Beauharnais*" have been "so washed away" that it can "not be considered authoritative" today. American Booksellers, 771 F. 2d at 331 n.3 (citing Collin v. Smith, 578 F. 2d 1197, 1204–1205 (7th Cir. 1978)).

[221]384 U.S. 195 (1966). In this decision, the Court determined the common law of libel to be unconstitutional.

[222]Bahn, *supra* note 32, at 525–526 ("But the historical foundation of criminal libel accounts for continued differences between the criminal and civil actions.").

[223]Whitney v. California, 274 U.S. 357, 375 (1927) (Brandeis, J., concurring).

[224]THAYER, *supra* note 55, at 321–322.

[225]As Zechariah Chafee explained: "Under modern law-abiding conditions, there is very small likelihood that anybody will be physically hurt." 1 ZECHARIAH CHAFEE, GOVERNMENT AND MASS COMMUNICATIONS: A REPORT FROM THE COMMISSION ON FREEDOM OF THE PRESS 57 (1947).

which have failed as a ground of conviction in the Supreme Court, compels the conclusion that the breach of the peace rationale will not support the constitutionality of the law of criminal libel."[226]

As a result, the only real distinction between civil and criminal libel is between those who seek to redress defamation through the awarding of compensatory damages to the one defamed and those who seek to redress defamation by punishing the defamer with a monetary fine or jail time—though the tort of libel can achieve this same end result through the awarding of punitive damages to the one defamed.

THE AMERICAN EXPERIENCE WITH CRIMINAL LIBEL

Though some could argue that "scant, if any, evidence exists that the First Amendment was intended to abolish the common law of libel,"[227] the trends are clear. During the twentieth century, America began the process of slowly freeing itself from the common law of criminal libel, in all its forms.[228] Blasphemy did not survive the trip to America, as the First Amendment also guarantees freedom of religious belief, freedom from religious belief, and freedom from state-imposed religion.[229] Obscene and profane libels evolved into separate areas of the criminal law altogether—obscenity and indecency.[230] Seditious libel as a threat to the public tranquility—including group libel and libel of the dead—appears to survive only through application of the imminent lawlessness test;[231] as for defamation of public officials, it has been subsumed into the statutory crime of libel.[232] Modern scholars have described prosecutions for libel as

---

[226]Bahn, *supra* note 32, at 528 (citing Terminiello v. Chicago, 337 U.S. 1 (1949); Cantwell v. Connecticut, 310 U.S. 296 (1940)).

[227]Gertz v. Robert Welch, Inc., 418 U.S. 323, 381 (1974) (White, J., dissenting). *See also* Beauharnais v. Illinois, 343 U.S. 250, 254–55 (1952).

[228]*See* MILLER, *supra* note 135, at 85.

[229]*See, e.g.*, Allegheny County v. ACLU, 492 U.S. 573 (1989); Larson v. Valente, 456 U.S. 228 (1982).

[230]Though obscenity has never been thought to be protected by the First Amendment, indecency is, at least to a degree. *See* FCC v. Pacifica Foundation, 438 U.S. 726 (1978); Miller v. California, 413 U.S. 15 (1973); Roth v. United States, 354 U.S. 476 (1957).

[231]*See supra* note 215.

[232]John D. Stevens et al., *Criminal Libel as Seditious Libel, 1916–1965*, 43 JOURNALISM Q. 110 (1966). If "the framers of the First Amendment sought to preserve the fruits of the ... victory abolishing ... censorship and to achieve a new victory abolishing sedition prosecutions," that has not been the historical result. CHAFEE, *supra* note 40, at 22. Donald Gillmor and Melanie Grant adopt an even more extreme position and contend that civil libel's

rare[233] and "now generally discouraged,"[234] and criminal libel statutes as "mostly dormant,"[235] "not a real problem,"[236] "no longer ... a serious risk,"[237] "obsolete legal action[s],"[238] which have "largely fallen into disuse,"[239] "relics of the past,"[240] "not yet buried,"[241] and "like the vampire legend [which] never quite seems to die out."[242] Yet more than a decade before the 1964 Supreme Court decision in *Garrison*, scholars also described criminal libel statutes as latent[243] and libel actions as "almost obsolete action,"[244] and prosecutions for the crime as rare[245] or unusual.[246] And one justice wrote that they are "so innocuous that chronicles of American journalism give them only passing reference."[247] In fact, one newspaper's in-house attorney is reported to have said fifty years ago that he "had not even bothered

---

complexity has created a vacuum in comprehension that has sustained sedition, but in a new form—the civil libel suit—in which an outraged public official ... asks for astronomical sums of money to compensate for alleged damage done to reputation by negative media exposure. Where public officials are concerned, this is punishment for sedition in a civil guise.

Donald Gilmoor & Malanie Grant, Sedition Redux: The Abuse of Libel Law in U.S. Courts 2, a working paper of the Freedom Forum Media Studies Center, Columbia University, New York, N.Y., 1991.

[233]*See* MAURICE R. CULLEN, JR., MASS MEDIA AND THE FIRST AMENDMENT 266 (1981); RONALD T. FARRAR, MASS COMMUNICATION: AN INTRODUCTION TO THE FIELD 375 (1988); RALPH L. HOLSINGER & JON P. DILTS, MEDIA LAW 114 (3d ed. 1994); W. WAT HOPKINS (ED.), COMMUNICATION AND THE LAW 98 (2004); KENT R. MIDDLETON ET AL., THE LAW OF PUBLIC COMMUNICATION 77 (2003); WAYNE OVERBECK, MAJOR PRINCIPLES OF MEDIA LAW 173 (2004); THOMAS L. TEDFORD & DALE A. HERBECK, FREEDOM OF SPEECH IN THE UNITED STATES 79 (4th ed. 2001); DWIGHT L. TEETER, JR., & BILL LOVING, LAW OF MASS COMMUNICATIONS 83 (10th ed. 2001). Others describe them as "extremely rare." DON R. PEMBER & CLAY CALVERT, MASS MEDIA LAW 240 (2005); JOHN D. ZELEZNY, COMMUNICATIONS LAW 116 (4th ed. 2004).

[234]DONALD M. GILLMOR ET AL., FUNDAMENTALS OF MASS COMMUNICATION LAW 50 (1996).

[235]BARBARA DILL, THE JOURNALIST'S HANDBOOK ON LIBEL AND PRIVACY 214 (1986).

[236]DON R. PEMBER, MASS MEDIA LAW 233 (2001).

[237]T. BARTON CARTER ET AL., THE FIRST AMENDMENT AND THE FOURTH ESTATE: THE LAW OF MASS MEDIA 125 (3d ed. 1985).

[238]OVERBECK, *supra* note 233, at 172.

[239]T. BARTON CARTER ET AL., MASS COMMUNICATION LAW IN A NUTSHELL 47 (5th ed. 2000).

[240]PEMBER, *supra* note 236, at 232.

[241]TEETER & LOVING, *supra* note 233, at 83.

[242]*Id.* at 79.

[243]SWINDLER, *supra* note 205, at 105.

[244]Bahn, *supra* note 32, at 533.

[245]SWINDLER, *supra* note 205, at 101.

[246]Kelly, *supra* note 84, at 317.

[247]Beauharnais v. Illinois, 343 U.S. 250, 298 (1952) (Jackson, J., dissenting).

to know just what the law of criminal libel is."[248] Based on these qualitative assessments, it is unclear what effect, if any, the *Garrison* ruling has had on prosecutions for the crime of libel. Because the crime "had already fallen into disuse" by 1964,[249] it has received even less scholarly attention since, especially with regard to the appropriateness of and alternatives to the *Garrison* ruling.[250]

The Quantitative Trend

Prosecutions for the crime of libel have been on the decline since the beginning of the twentieth century.[251] Studies by John Stevens[252] and Robert Leflar[253] confirm this trend. An extension of the reported data back to the earliest American criminal libel cases; a verification of the quantitative data reported by Stevens and Leflar; and an updating of the two studies through 1996 is shown in the table.

TABLE 1: Reported Criminal Libel Appellate Cases, 1797–1996[254]

1797 to 1806	1807 to 1816	1817 to 1826	1827 to 1836	1837 to 1846	1847 to 1856	1857 to 1866	1867 to 1876	1877 to 1886	1887 to 1896
7	7	8	11	14	14	1	15	60	99

1897 to 1906	1907 to 1916	1917 to 1926	1927 to 1936	1937 to 1946	1947 to 1956	1957 to 1966	1967 to 1976	1977 to 1986	1987 to 1996
98	93	52	50	20	19	19	19	10	5

---

[248]Kelly, *supra* note 84, at 318.

[249]CARTER ET AL., *supra* note 237, at 125.

[250]There is a dearth of legal scholarship on the issue, especially when compared to the plethora of legal research, commentary and analysis on the constitutional defense for civil libel developed in *Sullivan*.

[251]The data do not support the claim that "criminal libel actions were few throughout most of the Nineteenth Century." TEETER & LOVING, *supra* note 233, at 81.

[252]Stevens, *supra* note 232, at 111. The significance of the results of the study by Stevens and his colleagues is somewhat limited, as West's *Digest* system reports only appellate decisions, and not even necessarily all of them, exercising editorial discretion as to which to report. In an attempt to collect data which would be comparable, the study here employed the same research method.

[253]Leflar, *supra* note 104, at 985. The Leflar study counted criminal defamation case citations from 1920 through 1955. The beginning date "was selected ... not only because it gives a substantial 36-year period for study of the cases, but also because it roughly marks the beginning of a new national era in terms of social and economic attitudes that might have some bearing on the law and practice of defamation." *Id.* at n.1.

[254]This table is based upon a close examination of the hardcover West *Decennial Digest* system from 1658–2001: the *American Digest* (1658–1896), the *First Decennial Digest* (1897–1906), the *Second Decennial Digest* (1907–1916), the *Third Decennial Digest* (1916–1926), the *Fourth Decennial Digest* (1926–1936), the *Fifth Decennial Digest* (1936–1946), the *Sixth Decennial Digest* (1946–1956), the *Seventh*

No cases were reported from 1658 to 1796.[255] From 1997 to 2001, only two additional criminal libel cases have been reported in the West *Eleventh Decennial Digest* (Part I). None have been reported to date in the West *General Digest* (Tenth Series, 2001–2002).

Of the 595 reported cases examined here, 37.65% (224 of 595) clearly involved public officials or public figures.[256] All of the remaining cases dealt with fears for the maintenance of the public peace—as the Leflar study also found[257]—including, group libels (attacks on religious, racial or ethnic groups), false allegations and private disputes (including, criminal behavior or drunkenness, family quarrels, business or professional disagreements, and religious or labor arguments), and accusations of a woman's lack of chastity. For the period 1990 to 2002, Russell Hickey reports twenty-three criminal libel prosecutions and threatened prosecutions, of which 52.17% (12 of 23) involved "political prosecutions."[258] And, of the remaining eleven cases, at least eight appear to involve either public figures or issues of public controversy,[259] suggesting that the overwhelming majority of modern criminal libel cases—86.96% (20 of 23 cases)—involve public issues of one sort or another. Yet, though the overall quantitative trend is clear, the

---

Decennial Digest (1956–1966), the *Eighth Decennial Digest* (1966–1976), the *Ninth Decennial Digest* (1976–1986), *Tenth Decennial Digest* (1986–1996), and *Eleventh Decennial Digest* Part I (1996–2001)—and West's *General Digest* (Tenth Series, 2001–2002). (In the Tenth Series, volume 25 was the last and most recent volume available for examination for this study.) Duplicate citations were eliminated. Often, it was necessary to examine decisions in individual case reporters where the digests gave inadequate or incorrect information regarding the details of the case.

[255]The *American Digest* covers the period 1658–1896. The earliest reported criminal libel prosecution in America was *United States v. Lyon*. 15 Fed. Cas. 1183, No. 8,646 (C.C.D. Vt. 1798).

[256]This percentage is greater than the 20.95% (31 out of 148 cases, from 1916–1965) reported by Stevens. *See supra* note 232, at 110. This percentage is slightly less than the 40% (44 out of 110 cases, from 1920–1955) reported by Leflar. *See supra* note 104, at 985. One explanation for the difference is that the earlier studies—conducted as they were before the Supreme Court's ruling in *Butts v. Curtis Publishing Co.*, 388 U.S. 130 (1967)—did not count the number of criminal libel suits brought on behalf of public figures involved in issues of public interest. The two studies also examined different time periods. Between 1946 and 1960, according to the drafters of the Model Penal Code, "[T]he law reports of this country record[ed] only eleven criminal libel cases, nearly all involving defamation of officials, sometimes as candidates for reelection." Model Penal Code § 250.7 comment at 44 (Tentative Draft No. 13, 1961).

[257]Leflar, *supra* note 104, at 985. The Stevens study only examined criminal libel cases involving public officials. Stevens, *supra* note 232, at 110.

[258]Russell Hickey, *A Compendium of U.S. Criminal Libel Prosecutions: 1990–2002*, LIBEL DEFENSE RESOURCE CENTER BULL., Mar. 27, 2002, at 97.

[259]*Id.* at 105–06.

effect of the 1964 *Garrison* ruling on this trend is either unclear or nonexistent, depending how the data are interpreted.

Illustrative Incidents

Even though the trend in reported appellate decisions is declining, the use of criminal libel as a bludgeon against unpopular expression continues unchecked. Perhaps the case most paradigmatic of the American experience with criminal libel involved Jim Fitts, editor and publisher of *The Voice*, a weekly newspaper in Kingstree, S.C., who could not have known the consequences of his actions on Tuesday, May 17, 1988. That day, in a signed column with the headline, "My Vote Is Not for Sale," Fitts—without naming names—accused his community's legislative representatives of corruption and theft, figuratively if not literally.[260] As Fitts did not specify what he believe had been stolen, some contended that the statement was mere hyperbole.[261] The two Williamsburg County legislators up for re-election in the June 14 Democratic primary, state Senator Frank McGill and state Representative B.J. Gordon, however, believed their reputations had been damaged.

Rather than filing civil libel lawsuits, however, the two veteran legislators signed arrest warrants three days later charging Fitts with two counts of criminal libel.[262] Fitts was arrested at 11 a.m., Friday, May 20, and held in the Williamsburg County jail. At a 7 p.m. hearing, a local magistrate set a surety bond for Fitts in the amount

---

[260]Fitts wrote on his newspaper's editorial page:

> Ask yourself: What have they done for the people they represent? Everything they have done was for themselves. They have created so much fear in the hearts of the people who don't support their corrupt dealings until the citizens will not [exercise] their right to stand for justice and speak the truth. They would have you believe that blacks are drowning on the economic stabilities of our county. I will say to you without fear of contradiction, if every black in Williamsburg County would start stealing today and steal for every day for the rest of their lives, they could not steal as much as those two have stolen during their time in power.

Jim Fitts, *My Vote Is Not for Sale*, VOICE, May 17, 1988, at 2.

[261]Editorial, *Charges in Strange Libel Case Dismissed*, STATE, July 10, 1988, at 2B.

[262]The South Carolina criminal libel statute made it a crime for anyone "with malicious intent [to] originate, utter, circulate, or publish any false statement concerning another, the effect of which shall tend to injure such a person in his character or reputation" and provided that conviction be punished by a fine of up to $5,000 or imprisonment for not more than one year, or both. S.C. CODE ANN. § 16–7–150 (1976). This was clearly an instance in which the "rules for criminal cases appear ... to make it easier to secure criminal convictions than tort judgments in libel cases." Leflar, *supra* note 104, at 1016.

of $40,000—which was "eight times the maximum fine provided for in the statute"[263]—instead of a "more common" personal recognizance bond.[264] The judge then refused to hear a motion that he reduce the bond. Once Fitts had raised the $4,000 necessary to be released—10% of the amount in cash or property valued in the amount of the bond—he was told that the clerk of the court was off duty for the weekend and would not be available to receive his bond money until the coming Monday.[265]

Fitts remained in jail until his bond was changed to a $30,000 signature bond on Sunday, May 22, and he was released on his own recognizance after an emergency hearing before a circuit judge in Bishopville, approximately forty miles north in neighboring Lee County.[266] As a condition of his release, Fitts was ordered not to write or talk about his arrest or his disagreements with the two legislators.

Both McGill and Gordon won their Democratic primary races with ease on June 14.[267] On June 23, the Williamsburg County grand jury convened to consider whether Fitts should stand trial for criminal libel. Gordon told South Carolina journalists that the state's criminal libel statute was valid: "If it's outdated, then the Ten Commandments are outdated."[268] On June 27, Fitts was indicted on two misdemeanor counts of criminal libel and ordered to stand trial.[269]

Then, in a surprise move on Friday, July 1, McGill and Gordon asked that the charges against Fitts be dropped.[270] Fitts attempted to force the prosecution to go forward, arguing that otherwise he would

---

[263]Fitts v. Kolb, 779 F.Supp. 1502, 1505 (D. S.C. 1991).

[264]*See* Holly Gatling, *Writer Jailed on Criminal Libel Charges*, STATE, May 21, 1988, at 1A.

[265]*See* Will Moredock, *Columnist Spends Second Night in Jail*, STATE, May 22, 1988, at 1A.

[266]*See* Holly Gatling & Richard Chesley, *Columnist Released from Jail*, STATE, May 23, 1988, at 1A. Representatives from "the Third Circuit solicitor's office [were] expected to oppose the motion, but did not show up." *Id.*

[267]*See* Margaret O'Shea & Holly Gatling, *Grand Jury To Mull Editor's Criminal Libel Case*, STATE, June 22, 1988, at 1A.

[268]Margaret O'Shea & Maureen Shurr, *Editor Says He'd Like Day in Court*, STATE, June 24, 1988, at 1A.

[269]*See* Margaret O'Shea & Maureen Shurr, *Editor Indicted in Libel: Fitts Happy To Have Day in Court To 'Tell My Story'*, STATE, June 28, 1988, at 1A.

[270]In an undated letter, Gordon wrote:

I realize that vengeance is not mine but God's. God in his own time will rectify all situations. I, Rev. B.J. Gordon, Jr., feeling no malice in my heart for Mr. James Fitts, and finding that justice has prevailed by the grand jury's indictment, I hereby drop all charges against Mr. Fitts and forgive him of any malicious comments written or spoken against me.

Holly Gatling, *Charges of Libel Dropped*, STATE, July 2, 1988, at 1A; *See also Libel Charges Dropped Against Newspaper Editor*, WALL ST. J., July 5, 1988, at 26.

be subjected to double jeopardy, but was told by Third Circuit Solicitor Wade Kolb, Jr., that a defendant who wishes to be tried does not have that right. Besides, the charges had achieved their objective, according to Wallace Connor, attorney for McGill and Gordon. The purpose behind them "was not so much as punish [Fitts as to serve as] a deterrent."[271] The desired effect had been achieved, though some thought it had made rural Williamsburg County "look medieval."[272]

Even though the South Carolina statute was subsequently declared unconstitutional,[273] the Fitts ordeal makes four important points about the American experience with criminal libel: First, either legislator could have filed a civil libel suit against Fitts had either believed he had been defamed.[274] Second, as it was a criminal case neither legislator risked any financial loss or costs.[275] Neither had to hire an attorney; neither had to pay any costs associated with the proceedings. The state acted to shield them,[276] without any determination that Fitts's accusations were true or false—clear evidence of the state's protecting its "best men."[277] Third, because not all criminal activity is prosecuted and because the state of South Carolina—through the actions of the prosecutor and the grand jury—moved to try Fitts for the crime of libel, there was a public presumption, based on Americans' faith in the objectivity and fairness of the law, that at least some evidence pointed to his guilt. Fourth, Fitts was penalized—through his weekend in jail

---

[271]Smith, *supra* note 33, at 17.

[272]Area resident John Crangle, *quoted in* Gatling, *supra* note 270, at 1A.

[273]Fitts v. Kolb, 779 F. Supp. 1502 (D.S.C. 1991).

[274]*See supra* text accompanying note 25.

[275]On the other hand,

> prosecution for criminal libel has significant social costs, including the high costs of investigating, arresting, and litigating criminal libel cases and the capricious manner in which such cases are prosecuted. As one court has noted, "one evil of a vague statute is that it creates the potential for arbitrary, uneven and selective enforcement. Nowhere is this more evident than in the area of criminal defamation."

Jeffrey Hunt & David Reymann, *Criminal Libel Law in the U.S.*, LIBEL DEFENSE RESOURCE CENTER BULL., March 27, 2002, 79, at 86 (quoting Gottschalk v. Alaska, 575 P.2d 289, 294 (Alaska 1978)). They also point out that a criminal prosecution may "provide an early and free litmus test for a potential civil plaintiff." *Id*. at 85.

[276]*See supra* text accompanying note 24. Criminal prosecution "is even more doubtful when it is used by prosecutors in behalf of famous and powerful persons [or persons warranting special community protection] who do not wish to bring a civil action themselves." CARTER ET AL., *supra* note 237, at 125.

[277]*See* NORMAN L. ROSENBERG, PROTECTING THE BEST MEN: AN INTERPRETATIVE HISTORY OF THE LAW OF LIBEL (1986). *See also* R.S.E. Pushkar, *Criminal Libel and Slander in the Military*, 9 A.F. J.A.G. L. REV. 40 (Nov.–Dec. 1967). It is also clear that the state will act to protect those of whom society expects (or, at least, historically expected) higher moral standards and behavior—women and teachers (the majority of whom, historically, were women). *See infra* text accompanying notes 280–347.

and through the bond requirements—before he was ever tried or convicted of anything whatsoever, all of which worked together as punishment, warning and prior restraint. Actions, such as "fining men or sending them to jail for criticizing public officials, not only jeopardizes the free, open public discussion which our Constitution guarantees, but can wholly stifle it."[278]

Even though concerns about potential breaches of the peace have disappeared and "a serious body of law on the subject of free speech" developed after the first world war,[279] Jim Fitts's experience is the American experience.[280] As the country matured, and especially well before the end of the Civil War, as a review of the case law of criminal libel demonstrates, the threat of violence became less and less "imminent," "clear" or even likely. In every instance, a civil libel claim would have been a fairer and less stigmatizing way to deal with the offending speech.

Theodore Lyman, to take an early example, was tried for the criminal libel of Daniel Webster in 1828, the gist of which

> was, that whereas [President John Quincy] Adams had ... charged that leading Federalists of Massachusetts had in 1808 had been guilty of treasonable designs to break up the Union, naming no one in particular, but libeling them all, Mr. Lyman had named Daniel Webster as a person to whom the libel of Mr. Adams applied, and thus made Adams's libel of all the leading Federalists of Massachusetts Mr. Lyman's own libel of Daniel Webster.[281]

Though the prosecution ended in a mistrial because the jury was "not convinced that the charge was ever really made,"[282] Webster just as easily "could have brought a civil action against [Lyman] for damages," had he chosen to do so.[283] In a case that was also more about a

---

[278]Garrison v. Louisiana, 379 U.S. 64, 80 (1964) (Black, J., concurring).

[279]FRIEDMAN, *supra* note 143, at 669.

[280]The cases cited by Leflar, and discussed in some detail, provide support. *See supra* note 104, at 986–1011.

[281]JOSIAH H. BENTON, JR., A NOTABLE LIBEL CASE 11 (repr. Fred B. Rothman & Co. 1985) (1904).

[282]*Id*. at 103.

[283]*Id*. at 34. The trial was all the more unusual, as

> Webster and Lyman were former political associates, and had been personal friends and neighbors from the time Mr. Webster came to Boston. They were on intimate social terms, met usually several times a week, and had for years belonged to a dinner club that met every Saturday. It would have been a very simple matter for Mr. Webster to have asked Mr. Lyman for an explanation as to whether he intended to charge him with having been engaged in a plot to break up the Union in 1808.

public issue than about defamation, in 1830, abolitionist William Lloyd Garrison found himself convicted of criminal libel after his public condemnation of Maryland slave trading in which he identified the owner and captain of a particular ship and called them "highway robbers and murderers."[284] Consequently, he served seven weeks in jail when he was unable to pay the $50 fine. In this situation, the civil action option did not help Garrison, as he was also subsequently sued for civil libel and lost, to no one's surprise, as the verdict was more of a commentary on Maryland residents' attitude toward slavery than it was an attempt to restore the ship owner's reputation. Similarly—though an incomplete list—accusations of pilferage made against a police constable,[285] for example, of bribery made against a Congressman,[286] of adultery made against a school teacher,[287] of the use of false weights made against livestock dealers,[288] of fiscal mismanagement made against a newspaper's managing editor,[289] of real estate fraud against a company and its president,[290] of prejudice and monopoly made against a news association executive,[291] of prostitution made against a married woman,[292] of false oath-taking made against a Catholic fraternal organization,[293] of Ku Klux Klan membership made against members of a Catholic fraternal organization,[294] of impropriety made against a state attorney general during a murder investigation and prosecution,[295] of forgery against a candidate for city office,[296] of thievery made against a former mayor,[297] of pimping and adultery made against a woman and her son,[298] of bootlegging made against a police chief,[299] of poor business practices made against the owner of a

---

Id. at 30.

Clearly, the case "was in reality and personal and political suit by Webster against Lyman, and was so treated by the public and the press." *Id*. at 58.

[284]Amy Reynolds, *William Lloyd Garrison, Benjamin Lundy and Criminal Libel: The Abolitionists' Plea for Press Freedom*, 6 COMM. L. & POL'Y 577, 592 (2001).

[285]*See* State v. Spear & Corbett, 13 R.I. 324 (1881).

[286]*See* State v. Conable, 46 N.W. 759 (Iowa 1890).

[287]*See* Vallery v. State, 60 N.W. 347 (Neb. 1894).

[288]*See* State v. Shippman, 86 N.W. 431 (Minn. 1901).

[289]*See* State v. Fosburgh, 143 N.W. 279 (S.D. 1913).

[290]*See* Kennerly v. Hennessy, 66 So. 729 (Fla. 1914).

[291]*See* People v. Eastman, 152 N.Y.S. 314 (Ct. Gen. Sess. 1915).

[292]*See* United States v. Davidson, 244 F. 523 (N.D. N.Y. 1917).

[293]*See* Crane v. State, 166 P. 1110 (Okla. Crim. App. 1917).

[294]*See* People v. Gordan, 63 Cal. App. 627 (1923).

[295]*See* State v. Dedge, 125 A. 316 (N.J. 1924).

[296]*See* Arnold ex rel. Florida v. Chase, 114 So. 856 (Fla. 1927).

[297]*See* Commonwealth v. Enwright, 156 N.E. 65 (Mass. 1927).

[298]*See* Wimberly v. State, 4 S.W. 2d 73 (Tex. Crim. App. 1927).

[299]*See* State v. Gardner, 151 A. 349 (Conn. 1930).

beauty shop,[300] and of laziness, inefficiency and dishonesty made by an outspoken district attorney against judges before whom he prosecuted cases,[301] all appear to be issues which could more properly and more fairly have been dealt with through civil libel actions.

It should not have been surprising that the Supreme Court in *Garrison v. Louisiana* would conclude that criminal libel, despite its differing history and purpose,[302] does not "serve interests distinct from those secured by civil libel laws,"[303] especially after the Court remarked on the unconstitutionality of a federal criminal statute—the Sedition Act of 1798[304]—in the civil libel case of *New York Times v. Sullivan*, even if it was *dicta*.[305] The crime of libel is thus substantively no different than the tort, especially "where criticism of public officials is concerned."[306] *Garrison*, despite arguments to the contrary, did not thus involve "purely private defamation,"[307] which at that time would not have implicated the *Sullivan* rule. The Court hinted that it might have accepted the kind of "narrowly drawn statute" proposed by a tentative draft of the Model Penal Code which would have criminalized so-called fighting words or group defamation, "especially likely to lead to public disorders,"[308] but concluded that the Louisiana statute was not of this type. Nor did it help that the Louisiana statute allowed a defense of truth to be negated "on a showing of malice in the sense of ill-will"[309]—in essence, a "good motives" and "justifiable ends" restriction of the defense[310]—as the Court noted that the public interest requires that freedom of speech be secured by restricting only "the knowing or reckless falsehood."[311]

---

[300]*See* State v. Johnson, 231 S.W. 2d 625 (Mo. Ct. App. 1950).

[301]*See* State v. Garrison, 154 So. 2d 400 (La. 1963).

[302]*See* Eberhard P. Deutsch, *From Zenger to Garrison: A Tale of Two Centuries*, 38 N.Y. St. B. J. 409 (Oct. 1966). *See also* Jane A. Finn, *Criminal Law—Criminal Libel—Constitutional Limitations on State Action—Garrison v. Louisiana*, 14 Am. U. L. Rev. 220 (1965); Ronald A. Naquin, *Constitutional Law—Freedom of Speech—Defamation*, 39 Tul. L. Rev. 355 (1965); *New York Times Rule Extended to Criminal Libel*, 40 Wash. L. Rev. 898 (1965); Martin L. Zimmerman, *Constitutional Law—State Power To Impose Criminal Sanctions for Criticism of Public Officials Limited by Federal Constitution to False Statements Made with Actual Malice*, 16 Syracuse L. Rev. 879 (1965).

[303]379 U.S. 54, 67 (1964).

[304]1 Stat. at Large 596 (1798).

[305]376 U.S. 254, 276 (1964).

[306]*Garrison*, 379 U.S. at 67.

[307]*Id.* at 76.

[308]Model Penal Code § 250.7, comment at 45 (Tentative Draft No. 13, 1961).

[309]379 U.S. at 71–72.

[310]*Id.* at 72–73.

[311]*Id.* at 73.

Despite the urging of two justices,[312] who recognized the broad prose-cutorial power still available to protect public officials,[313] the forego-ing leads to the conclusion that in 1964 the Court believed its 1952 *Beauharnais* ruling, upholding a state group defamation statute, to be good law still.

Of the accusations made against public officials and public figures since 1964,[314] this broad prosecutorial power has been widely used. As with the pre-1964 cases listed above, accusations of abuse of office made against a police chief,[315] of improper relationships made against a prominent businessman,[316] of professional misconduct made against a former Supreme Court justice,[317] of illegal drug deal-ing made against a county sheriff,[318] of unsuitability for elective of-fice made against a presidential candidate,[319] of an unspecified nature made against a movie actress which tended to expose her to contempt,[320] of theft made against a state trooper,[321] and of illegal ha-

---

[312]*Id.* at 82 (Douglas, J., concurring) (joined by Justice Black).

[313]"I believe that the Court is mistaken if it thinks that requiring proof that state-ments were 'malicious' or 'defamatory' will really create any substantial hurdle to block public officials from punishing those who criticize the way they conduct their office." *Id.* at 79–80 (Black, J., concurring) (joined by Justice Douglas).

[314]It must be noted that requiring actual malice to be proven for the conviction of those libeling public figures involved in issues of public interest is an assumption that could prove to be false. The requirement may be the rule in civil libel but is without a firm foundation in criminal libel. In civil libel, *Sullivan* has a significant progeny—Supreme Court decisions directly applying the rule. *See, e.g.*, Masson v. New Yorker Magazine, 501 U.S. 496 (1991); Milkovich v. Lorain Journal Co., 497 U.S. 1 (1990); Harte-Hanks Communications, Inc. v. Connaughton, 491 U.S. 657 (1989); Hustler Magazine v. Falwell, 485 U.S. 46 (1988); Anderson v. Liberty Lobby, 477 U.S. 242 (1986); Philadelphia Newspapers v. Hepps, 475 U.S. 767 (1986); Dun & Bradstreet v. Greenmoss Builders, 472 U.S. 749 (1985); Herbert v. Lando, 441 U.S. 153 (1979); Hutchinson v. Proxmire, 443 U.S. 111 (1979); Wolston v. Reader's Di-gest Ass'n, 443 U.S. 157 (1979); Time, Inc. v. Firestone, 424 U.S. 448 (1976); Gertz v. Robert Welch, Inc., 418 U.S. 323 (1974); Monitor-Patriot Co. v. Roy, 401 U.S. 265 (1971); Ocala Star-Banner v. Damron, 401 U.S. 295 (1971); Rosenbloom v. Metromedia, 403 U.S. 29 (1971); Greenbelt Co-op. Pub. Ass'n v. Bresler, 398 U.S. 6 (1970); St. Amant v. Thompson, 390 U.S. 727 (1968); Curtis Publ'g Co. v. Butts, 388 U.S. 130 (1966); Rosenblatt v. Baer, 383 U.S. 75 (1966). In criminal libel, *Garrison* has no progeny—no Supreme Court decisions directly applying the rule. 379 U.S. at 64. The Court has not addressed the applicability of civil libel's public figure rule in the area of criminal libel, even though lower courts have generally presumed its va-lidity. *See infra* text accompanying notes 315–49.

[315]*See* Commonwealth v. Ashton, 405 S.W. 2d 562 (Ky. 1965).

[316]*See* Commonwealth v. Armao, 286 A. 2d 626 (Pa. 1972).

[317]*See* United States v. Handler, 383 F. Supp. 1267 (D. Md. 1974).

[318]*See* Weston v. State, 528 S.W. 2d 412 (Ark. 1975).

[319]*See* State v. Anonymous (1976–8), 360 A. 2d 909 (Conn. Cir. no date).

[320]*See* Eberle v. Municipal Court, 127 Cal. Rptr. 3d 594 (Cal. App. 1976).

[321]*See* Gottschalk v. Alaska, 575 P.2d 289, 294 (Alaska 1978).

rassment made against a police chief,[322] also all appear to be issues more properly and more fairly—as well as, more easily—dealt with through civil libel actions (or through criminal charges of falsely reporting a crime, for example), if at all. Between 1990 and 2002, the most recent part of the post-*Garrison* period during which prosecutions for libel were supposed to have been have been rare,[323] Richard Hickey reported seventeen prosecutions[324]—not an insignificant number during a thirteen-year period—including charges of theft and unfitness for duty made against a police officer,[325] of fraud and child neglect made against an ex-girlfriend,[326] of misconduct made against a university vice president,[327] of criminal wrongdoing made against another,[328] of misbehavior made against police officers,[329] of brutality against an arresting officer,[330] of drunkenness and pedophilia made against a high school teacher,[331] of rape and battery made against a candidate for lieutenant governor,[332] of anti-Semitism made against county commissioners[333] and of misconduct made against police officers.[334]

The most egregious recent example of all that is wrong with the crime of libel involved 16-year-old Ian Lake, a "pink-and-green

---

[322]*See* Debra Gersh, *Newspaper Letter Writer Charged with Criminal Libel*, EDITOR & PUBLISHER, March 24, 1990, at 22.

[323]*See* Susan W. Brenner, *Complicit Publication: When Should the Dissemination of Ideas and Data Be Criminalized?* 13 ALB. L.J. SCI. & TECH. 273, 320 (2003).

[324]*Supra* note 258, at 105–106.

[325]*See Publishers Charged with Criminal Libel*, NEWS MEDIA & THE LAW, Spring 1990, at 22.

[326]*See* State v. Ryan, 806 P. 2d 935 (Colo. 1991).

[327]*See* State v. Powell, 839 P. 2d 139 (N.M. Ct. App. 1992).

[328]*See* State v. Helfrich, 922 P. 2d 1159 (Mont. 1996).

[329]*See* State v. Cardenas-Hernandez, 579 N.W. 2d 678 (Wis. 1998); *Deputy Is Accused on Defamation on the Internet*, NEW ORLEANS TIMES-PICAYUNE, Aug. 27, 1999, at A4.

[330]*See* Hamilton v. City of San Bernardino, 107 F. Supp. 2d 1239 (C.D. Calif. 2000).

[331]*See* Jennifer Farrell, *Parody Web Site: Offensive or Illegal?* ST. PETERSBURG TIMES, Dec. 18, 2000, at 1.

[332]*See* Ivey v. State, 821 So. 2d 937 (Ala. 2001). *See also Antiquated Libel Statute Declared Unconstitutional*, NEWS MEDIA & THE LAW, Summer 2001, at 14; *Top Court Overturns Lawyer's Conviction*, COLUMBUS LEDGER-ENQUIRER, July 7, 2001, at B4. The amicus brief submitted on behalf of the defendant by the Reporters Committee for Freedom of the Press is *available at*, http://www.rcfp.org/news/documents/iveyala.html (last visited Sept. 20, 2001).

[333]*See* State v. Shank, 795 So. 2d 1067 (Fla. Dist. Ct. App. 2001).

[334]Mangual v. Rotger-Sabat, 317 F. 3d 45 (1st Cir. 2003). *See also Puerto Rico: Libel Law Ruled Unconstitutional*, N.Y. TIMES, Jan. 23, 2003, at A19.

haired teen,"[335] described as weird by classmates,[336] who reacted to the taunts and harassment of Milford High School students by creating an Internet Web site and posting "an obscenity-laced home page,"[337] which "peppered forty-nine people with various profanities."[338] On it, he referred to school principal Walter Schofield as "the town drunk" and to female classmates as "sluts,"[339] and speculated that school teachers and staff "engaged in drug use or homosexuality."[340] School officials suspected Lake immediately, because of his "frequent run-ins with the principal ... and ... an altercation during a football game,"[341] and Schofield notified police on May 16, 2000. Two days later, police seized Lake's computer, sent it to the state crime laboratory for analysis, and arrested the teenager, who subsequently spent seven days in juvenile detention.[342] Upon his release, his family sent him to live with relatives in California.

A month later, Lake was charged with one count of violating Utah's criminal libel statute and another of violating its criminal defamation

---

[335]Katharine Biele, *When Students Get Hostile, Teachers Go to Court*, CHRISTIAN SCI. MONITOR, Aug. 22, 2000, at 1.

[336]Jon Katz, Criminal Libel, Free Speech and the Net (June 5, 2001), ¶ 9, Slashdot, *at* http://slashdot.org/features/00/06/01/1526235.shtml (last visited Sept. 5, 2002).

[337]Baird, *supra* note 16, at C1.

[338]Biele, *supra* note 335, at 1. Lake's father said "his son was fighting back against hostile peers. 'For him, it was just a tit-for-tat thing. Everything he has done up to this point was in retaliation for what other kids did, stuff that was just as vulgar and just as harmful.'" Katz, *supra* note 336, at ¶ 3.

[339]Baird, *supra* note 16, at C1. Jon Katz writes that "the anonymous Utah Web site was vulgar and offensive, but compared to many public flames, only tepid." Katz, *supra* note 336, at ¶ 6. "Flaming" is harsh, caustic, online criticism, which is usually anonymous.

[340]Jennifer K. Nii, *Libel Charges Will Stand Against Milford Student*, DESERET NEWS, Dec. 6, 2000, at B4. The site "did not contain threats of violence or references to weapons." National Organization Joins Fight Against Utah's Criminal Libel Law (Aug. 10, 2001), at ¶ 3, Hard News Café, Utah State University Department of Journalism & Communication, *at* http://www.hardnewscafe.usu.edu/archive/august2001/0810_criminallibel.html (last visited Oct. 1, 2002).

[341]Katz, *supra* note 336, at ¶ 9.

[342]Jon Katz argues this lengthy incarceration was the result of

post-Columbine hysteria, in which anger, alienation and offensive speech online is increasingly equated with danger.... If a teenager calls one of his classmates a slut outside of school (but not online), it's hard to imagine he'd be arrested, driven out-of-state, or charged with criminal libel.... Here, when troubled teenagers lash out at peers and teachers online, we don't sit down with teachers, counselors, parents and administrators. We don't call constitutional scholars, technologists and social scientists to ponder rational solutions to unprecedented techno-driven 21st century problems. ... We call 911 and turn a kid who has trouble fitting in into both a refugee and a criminal suspect.

Id. at ¶¶ 12, 22–23.

statute.[343] After the juvenile court refused to dismiss the libel charge on December 19, the state court of appeals "initially declin[ed] to take the case," but reversed itself and sent the appeal to the state supreme court on May 15, 2001.[344] Eighteen months later, the Utah Supreme Court unanimously declared the state's criminal libel statute unconstitutional,[345] after the Lakes spent more than $20,000 defending their son.[346] Thus was Ian Lake prosecuted and punished for his speech in much the same way as Jim Fitts was, without a conviction and at taxpayers' expense.[347] That several state court systems have declared the crime of libel antithetical to their state constitutions over the last forty years,[348] however, does not lessen the consequences and trauma associated with being arrested, charged, booked, jailed, indicted, tried, convicted and/or fined for speech which should never have been subject to criminal prosecution in the first place. Although Lake's prosecution was dropped after the state supreme court declared one of Utah's ten statutes dealing with criminal libel unconstitutional, online satire also resulted in a similar computer seizure and criminal libel charges in Colorado in January 2004,[349] proving once again the tenacity and resilience of the crime.

In 1999, two disaffected teenagers at Columbine High School, near Littleton, Colo., shot and killed twelve students and a teacher, before killing themselves. *See* Biele, *supra* note 335, at 1.

[343]Utah Code. Ann. § 76–9–501 (1999); Utah Code Ann. § 76–9–507 (1999). After the juvenile court dismissed the slander charge, the count remaining alleged the criminal libel of the high school principal. *See* Motion To Dismiss Petition, State of Utah v. Ian Michael Lake (July 31, 2000), The American Civil Liberties Union Protecting Constitutional Freedoms in Utah, *at* http://www.acluutah.org/lakemotion. htm (last visited Sept. 30, 2002).

[344]Joe Baird, *Libel Case Heading to High Court*, SALT LAKE TRIB., Aug. 4, 2001, at B1. *See also* Brief for Appellant, State of Utah v. Ian Michael Lake (Aug. 2, 2001), The American Civil Liberties Union Protecting Constitutional Freedoms in Utah, *at* http://www.acluutah.org/lakeappeal.htm (last visited Sept. 30, 2002); Joe Baird, *Libel Appeal Drawing National Attention*, SALT LAKE TRIB., Aug. 28, 2001, at B2.

[345]*In re* I.M.L. v. State, 61 P. 3d 1038 (Utah 2002). The state supreme court's opinion is also *available at*, http://courtlink.utcourts.gov/opinions/supopin/iml.htm (last visited Mar. 17, 2004). *See also* Alan Edwards, *Libel Case Out, Law 'Overbroad'*, DESERET NEWS, Nov. 16, 2002, at B1; Christopher Smart, *Utah Court Kills 1876 Libel Statute*, SALT LAKE TRIB., Nov. 16, 2002, at A1.

[346]A civil libel suit Schofield filed against the teenager in August 2000 was subsequently settled in the spring of 2001. *See* Angie Welling, *Web Defamation Case Ending*, DESERET NEWS, Jan. 8, 2003, at B4.

[347]Lake's father "believes his son has the basis for a federal civil rights lawsuit for violation of his due process rights." *Id.*

[348]*See supra* text accompanying notes 315–345.

[349]*See* Karen Abbott, *And This Little Piggy Isn't Libelous* ..., ROCKY MOUNTAIN NEWS, Jan. 21, 2004, at 20A; Karen Abbott, *Student Squeals Over Seizure*, ROCKY MOUNTAIN NEWS, Jan. 9, 2004, at 18A; Karen Abbott, *Salazar Drawn into Battle Over Libel Law: ACLU Challenges Its Constitutionality in Web Satire Case*, ROCKY

Criminal Libel Statutes Today

As a consequence of the "trend toward uniformity in the state criminal laws"[350] and the efforts of the American Law Institute to modernize and reorganize the law—which began in 1952 and which resulted in the Model Penal Code, the official draft of which was completed in 1962[351]—most criminal law today is statutory law rather than common law.[352] Most states have thus abolished common law crimes.[353] This trend, at least with regard to the crime of libel, reached its zenith in 1966, when the Supreme Court declared the common law of criminal libel unconstitutional.[354]

However, the drafters of the Model Penal Code went even further than the Supreme Court did in 1964, when the Court required proof of actual malice to justify a conviction for criminal libel.[355] The drafters did not even include a provision for a criminal libel section in their code, though they admitted that the question of the criminality of libel was "one of the hardest questions we confront in drafting a Model Penal Code."[356] The drafters finally concluded that libel should not be a crime, because

---

MOUNTAIN NEWS, Feb. 20, 2004, at 7A; Brittany Anas, *Poking Fun with 'The Howling Pig': Former UNC Student Runs Online Paper, Overcomes Professor's Libel Accusations*, DENVER POST, Feb. 8, 2004, at A29; *Bad Taste Is Not a Crime* (editorial), DENVER POST, Jan. 13, 2004, at B8; *Criminal Libel: Wipe It Off Books* (editorial), ROCKY MOUNTAIN NEWS, Jan. 10, 2004, at 14C; Jim Hughes, *Online Satire Wins Round in Court*, DENVER POST, Jan. 11, 2004, at A24; Howard Pankratz, *ACLU Targets State Libel Law After Student's Files Seized*, DENVER POST, Jan. 9, 2004, at A29;

[350]KLOTTER, *supra* note 13, at 6.

[351]The "Proposed Official Draft of the Model Penal Code [is] a carefully drafted code containing provisions relating to the general principles of criminal responsibility and definitions of specific offenses." JOSHUA DRESSLER, UNDERSTANDING CRIMINAL LAW 22 (2d ed. 1995). As a growing number of states have adopted the code or portions of it, the results have been "stunning." Sanford H. Kadish, *The Model Penal Code's Historical Antecedents*, 19 RUTGERS L. J. 521, 538 (1988). The code "has become a standard part of the furniture of the criminal law. *Id.* at 521. In addition, more and more courts are turning "to the Model Code and its supporting commentaries for guidance in interpreting non-Code criminal statutes." DRESSLER, *supra* note 351, at 23. *See also* MARKUS D. DUBBER, CRIMINAL LAW: MODEL PENAL CODE (2002).

[352]*See* KLOTTER, *supra* note 13, at iv.

[353]*See* DRESSLER, *supra* note 351, at 20.

[354]Ashton v. Kentucky, 384 U.S. 195 (1966).

[355]Garrison v. Louisiana, 379 U.S. 64, 67 (1964).

[356]Model Penal Code § 250.7, comment at 44 (Tentative Draft No. 13, 1961). The drafters "diffidently advanced"—in the place of criminal libel—a new § 250.7, "Fomenting Group Hatred," but did not finally include it in the tentative model code

penal sanctions cannot be justified merely by the fact that defamation is … damaging to a person in ways that entitle him to maintain a civil suit…. We reserve the criminal law for harmful behavior which exceptionally disturbs the community's sense of security…. It seems evident that personal calumny falls in neither of these classes in the U.S.A., that it is therefore inappropriate for penal control….[357]

In essence, prosecutions for the crime of libel are "inconsistent with the principles of imposing criminal liability in modern society."[358]

Yet twenty-three states, the District of Columbia,[359] and one territory still have statutes or constitutional provisions establishing, enabling or governing the prosecution of criminal libel:[360] Arkansas,[361] Colorado,[362] Florida,[363] Georgia,[364] Idaho,[365] Illinois,[366] Iowa,[367] Kan-

---

promulgated in 1962. *Id.*, at 41–42. Interestingly, *"Beauharnais v. Illinois* had almost no progeny…. Indeed, in revising its code of criminal law in 1961, Illinois did not re-enact the group libel statute despite its recent success." NELSON & TEETER, *supra* note 195, at 55 (referencing 343 U.S. 250 (1952)).

[357]Model Penal Code, *id.*

[358]Brenner, *supra* note 323, at 320–321.

[359]D.C. Code §§ 22–2301 through 22–2304 (1999).

[360]For a global perspective, *see* RUTH WALDEN, INSULT LAWS: AN INSULT TO PRESS FREEDOM (2000); Jeremy Feigelson & Erik Bierbauer, *Criminal Defamation: International Reforms Advance Against a Global Danger*, LIBEL RESOURCE DEFENSE CENTER BULL., March 27, 2002, at 107; Richard Winfield, *The Wasting Disease and a Cure: Freedom of the Press in Emerging Democracies*, COMMUNICATIONS LAWYER, Summer 2002, at 22; Elena Yanchukova, *Criminal Defamation and Insult Laws: An Infringement on the Freedom of Expression in European and Post-Communist Jurisdictions*, 41 COLUM. J. TRANSNAT'L L. 861 (2003).

[361]Ark. Code Ann. §§ 5–15–101 through 5–15–109 (2001).

[362]Colo. Rev. Stat. § 18–13–105 (2000). The constitutionality of Colorado's statute was partially upheld in *People v. Ryan*. 806 P. 2d 935 (Colo. 1991). The Colorado Supreme Court ruled that the statute was overbroad only to the extent that it criminalized libelous statements about public officials or public figures involving matters of public concern. Because truth is an absolute defense for criminal libel under Article II, § 10 of the Colorado Constitution, the statute is constitutional to the extent that it criminalizes libelous statements about private individuals.

[363]Fla. Stat. §§ 836.01 through 836.10 (2000). Fla. Stat. § 836.11 was declared unconstitutional in *State v. Shank*. 795 So. 2d 1067 (Fla. Dist. Ct. App. 2001).

[364]O.C.G.A. § 16–11–40 (2000). The statute's "breach of the peace" requirement was held to be unconstitutional by the state supreme court in *Williamson v. State*. 295 S.E. 2d 305 (Ga. 1982).

[365]Idaho Code §§ 18–4801 through 18–4809 (2000).

[366]720 Ill. Comp. Stat. 300/1 (2001). 720 Ill. Comp. Stat. 5/1–6 (l) (2001) specifies the venue for such prosecutions but does not authorize such prosecutions.

[367]While no state criminal libel statute exists, Article I, § 7 of the Iowa Constitution provides that truth may be used as a defense in criminal prosecutions for libel.

sas,[368] Louisiana,[369] Michigan,[370] Minnesota,[371] Nevada,[372] New Hampshire,[373] New Mexico,[374] North Carolina,[375] North Dakota,[376] Ohio,[377] Oklahoma,[378] South Dakota,[379] Utah,[380] Virgin Islands,[381] Virginia,[382] Washington,[383] and Wisconsin.[384] Of these, eighteen jurisdictions specifically criminalize defamation of living persons;[385] ten criminalize defamation of the dead;[386] six penalize accusations of

[368]Kan. Stat. Ann. §§ 21–4004 through 21–4006 (2000). Kan. Stat. Ann. § 21–4004 was upheld in *Phelps v. Hamilton*. 59 F. 3d 1058 (10th Cir. 1995).

[369]La. Rev. Stat. § 14:47 (2001). The statute has been held partially unconstitutional, insofar as it restricts expression about public officials. State v. Defley, 395 S. 2d 759 (La. 1981).

[370]Mich. Comp. Laws §§ 491.1108, 750.97, 750.370, 750.389, 750.409 (2001).

[371]Minn. Stat. §§ 609.27(1)(4), 609.77, 609.765, 628.22, 631.06 (2000).

[372]Nev. Rev. Stat. §§ 200.510 through 200.560 (2001). Though the statutes have not been held unconstitutional, the U.S. District Court endorsed "an agreement" between the Nevada Press Association and the state Attorney General that the state's criminal libel statutes are "unconstitutional." Nevada Press Association v. del Papa, CV–S–98–00991–JBR (1998). *See also* Hickey, *supra* note 258, at 101–102; LIBEL DEFENSE RESOURCE CENTER, 50-STATE SURVEY: MEDIA LIBEL LAW—1998–1999 670 (1999).

[373]N.H. Rev. Stat. Ann. § 644:11 (2001). The statute was cited with approval in *Keeton v. Hustler Magazine*. 465 U.S. 770, 776 (1984).

[374]N.M. Stat. Ann. § 30–11–1 (2001). The statute has been held to be partially unconstitutional, insofar as it applies to public statements involving matters of public concern. State v. Powell, 839 P. 2d 139 (N.M. Ct. App. 1992).

[375]N.C. Gen Stat § 14–47 (2000).

[376]N.D. Cent. Code § 12.1–15–01 (2001).

[377]Ohio Rev. Code Ann. §§ 2739.03, 2739.16, 2739.18, 2739.99 (Anderson 2001).

[378]21 Okla. Stat. §§ 771 through 781 (2000).

[379]While no state criminal libel statute exists, Article VI, § 5 of the South Dakota Constitution provides that truth may be used as a defense in criminal prosecutions for libel.

[380]Utah Code Ann. §§ 76–9–404, 76–9–501 through 76–9–509 (2001). Utah Code Ann. § 76–9–502 has been held to be unconstitutional. *In re* I.M.L., 61 P.3d at 1038.

[381]14 V.I. Code Ann. §§ 1177, 1183 (2001).

[382]Va. Code Ann. §§ 18.2–209, 18.2–416 through 18.2–418 (2001).

[383]Wash. Rev. Code Ann. §§ 9.58.010 through 9.58.020 (2001).

[384]Wis. Stat. § 942.01 (2000).

[385]Arkansas, Colorado, the District of Columbia, Georgia, Idaho, Kansas, Louisiana, Michigan, Minnesota, Nevada, New Hampshire, New Mexico, North Dakota, Oklahoma, Utah, Virginia, Washington, and Wisconsin. Ark. Code Ann. §§ 5–15–103 and 5–15–104 (2001); Colo. Rev. Stat. § 18–13–105 (2000); D.C. Code § 22–2302 (1999); O.C.G.A. § 16–11–40 (2000); Idaho Code § 18–4801 (2000); Kan. Stat. Ann. § 21–4004 (2000); La. Rev. Stat. § 14:47(1) (2001); Mich. Comp. Laws §§ 750.370 and 750.409 (2001); Minn. Stat. §§ 609.27(1)(4), 609.77, and 609.765 (2000); Nev. Rev. Stat. § 200.510 (2001); N.H. Rev. Stat. Ann. § 644:11 (2001); N.M. Stat. Ann. § 30–11–1 (2001); N.D. Cent. Code § 12.1–15–01 (2001); 21 Okla. Stat. § 771 (2000); Utah Code Ann. §§ 76–9–404 and 76–9–501 (2001); Va. Code Ann. §§ 18.2–209 and 18.2–417 (2001); Wash. Rev. Code Ann. § 9.58.010 (2001); Wis. Stat. § 942.01 (2001).

[386]Colorado, Georgia, Idaho, Kansas, Louisiana, Nevada, North Dakota, Oklahoma, Utah, and Washington. Colo. Rev. Stat. § 18–13–105 (2000); O.C.G.A. § 16–11–40 (2000); Idaho Code § 18–4801 (2000); Kan. Stat. Ann. § 21–4004 (2000);

fornication or lack of chastity;[387] six criminalize defamation of financial institutions, insurance companies, or corporations;[388] one criminalizes the defamation of agricultural products;[389] and eight criminalize threats, name-calling, or "fighting words."[390] In the area of libel, then, it is clear that state legislatures have not followed the Model Penal Code's lead as they have in most other areas of the criminal law. In fact, the *Garrison* ruling[391] appears to have both undermined and eviscerated the American Law Institute's modernization efforts with regard to the crime of libel.

CONCLUSIONS

The crime of libel should have no place in American law. First, its common law basis is a "false foundation laid by Coke ... beneath the equally false superstructure raised by Blackstone."[392] Second, it cannot ever be reconciled with the democratic, libertarian ideas on which America was founded, as criminal libel is the product of authoritarianism and is "the hallmark of all closed societies throughout the world."[393] Third, it is functionally identical to civil libel, because,

---

La. Rev. Stat. § 14:47(2) (2001); Nev. Rev. Stat. § 200.510 (2001); N.D. Cent. Code § 12.1–15–01 (2001); 21 Okla. Stat. § 771 (2000); Utah Code Ann. § 76–9–501 (2001); Wash. Rev. Code Ann. § 9.58.010 (2001).

[387]Arkansas, the District of Columbia, Florida, Michigan, Oklahoma, and Virginia. Ark. Code Ann. § 5–15–102 (2001); D.C. Code § 22–2304 (1999); Fla. Stat. § 836.04 (2000); Mich. Comp. Laws § 750.370 (2000); 21 Okla. § 779 (2000); Va. Code Ann. § 18.2–417 (2001).

[388]Florida, Illinois, Kansas, Michigan, Virginia, and Washington. Fla. Stat. § 836.06 (2000); 720 Ill. Comp. Stat. 300/1 (2001); Kan. Stat. Ann. § 21–4005 (2000); Mich. Comp. Laws §§ 49.1108, 750.97, 750.389 (2001); Va. Code Ann. § 18.2–209 (2001); Wash. Rev. Code Ann. § 9.58.010 (2001).

[389]Colo. Rev. Stat. § 12–16–115 (2000).

[390]Florida, Georgia, Idaho, Kansas, Nevada, Ohio, Oklahoma, and Virginia. Fla. Stat. § 836.05 (2000); O.C.G.A. § 16–11–39 (2000); Idaho Code § 18–4809 (2000); Kan. Stat. Ann. § 21–4006 (2000); Nev. Rev. Stat. § 200.560 (2001); Ohio Rev. Code Ann. § 2739.18 (Anderson 2001); 21 Okla. Stat. § 778 (2000); Va. Code Ann. § 18.2–416 (2001).

[391]379 U.S. 64 (1964).

[392]Brant, *supra* note 114, at 19.

[393]HARRY KALVEN, JR., THE NEGRO AND THE FIRST AMENDMENT 15 (1965). The absence of libel as a crime

> is the true pragmatic test of freedom of speech. This I would argue is what freedom of speech is about. Any society in which seditious libel is a crime is, no matter what its other features, not a free society. A society can, for example, either treat obscenity as a crime or not treat it as a crime without thereby altering its basic nature as a society. It seems to me it cannot do so with seditious libel. Here the response to this crime defines the society.

Id. at 16.

"courts have never adequately worked out a distinction between the tort and the crime,"[394] now that truth may be used as a defense. Fourth, its purpose—the "protection of individual reputation is probably the only real justification of the modern law of criminal libel"[395]—is identical to that of civil libel, now that prevention of violence is no longer a legal justification for its existence.[396] Civil libel, with its possibility of monetary damages, both compensatory and punitive, is "the most satisfactory and popular method of dealing with defamations between individuals."[397] Finally, civil libel is also the fairest way of dealing with defamation. The impact of criminal law is "felt not only by those convicted," but also by those who are "merely prosecuted" or "threatened with prosecution," and by "countless others" who cannot "accurately judge the boundaries imposed on freedom or who [are] fearful to take the risk."[398] The crime of libel "is often available as a device for punishing criticism of the men who direct the conduct of government. Indeed, examination of the cases reveals that in recent years there has been a tendency to use criminal libel to attain ends theoretically foreclosed by the absence of seditious libel."[399] Plus, the prospect of "its enforcement is always pres-

---

In fact, the crime of libel is now "widely regarded as a threat to human rights." U.S. Ready, *supra* note 63, at ¶ 3. To date, the United Nations, the Organization of American States, the Organization for Security and Cooperation in Europe, and Reporters Without Borders have all called for the decriminalization of defamation worldwide. Free Expression Chiefs Call for Action on Criminal Defamation (Nov. 29, 1999), *available at* http://www.article19.org/docimages/535 .htm (last accessed Sept. 5, 2002). *See also* Maria Trombly, *European Journalists Discuss Libel Law*, QUILL, Jan./Feb. 2004, at 36.

[394]Kelly, *supra* note 84, at 318.

[395]Bahn, *supra* note 32, at 528.

[396]The only purposes remaining are improper ones:

(1) to circumvent the [constitutional] restrictions placed on civil libel litigation ... or (2) to punish an indigent who could not be reached by a civil judgment for damages. The first is clearly an impermissible attempt to circumvent the First Amendment; the second, while not as obviously invalid as the first, raises quite serious problems of equal protection as well as the First Amendment ones.

United States v. Handler, 383 F. Supp. 1267, 1278 (D. Md. 1974).

[397]Kelly, *supra* note 84, at 299.

[398]Emerson, *supra* note 38, at 892. In civil libel, this is known as the "chilling effect." *See* ERIC BARENDT ET AL., LIBEL AND THE MEDIA: THE CHILLING EFFECT (1997); FORER, *supra* note 12; Michael Massing, *The Libel Chill: How Cold Is It Out There?* COLUM. JOURNALISM REV., May/June 1985, at 31.

[399]Bahn, *supra* note 32, at 530. This was what happened to Jim Fitts. He was set up. The issue was not one of reputation but of power and control. His accusers understood how the criminal justice system worked and used it to their advantage, without regard to whether they had actually been defamed or not. The magistrate judge owed his position, to which he had been elected in the state legislature, to the support of the two legislators who now claimed to have been defamed. Fitts's indictment by the grand jury was based upon evidence developed and presented by the so-

ent,"[400] even though laws proscribing the subversive criticism of government or its officials have disappeared.

Some who believe *Beauharnais v. Illinois*[401] was decided correctly might argue that without the crime of libel, "there is no satisfactory civil remedy for group libel"[402] or for libel of the dead. The verdict of history in both of these instances supports the conclusion that breach of the peace, disorderly conduct or incitement to riot statutes—all based on the requirement that real, actual violence result—would be a more appropriate method of dealing with such situations. Others might argue that without the crime of libel, "the bankrupt libeler" and the "opulent defamer,"[403] as well as the person "mentally deranged and in need of restraint,"[404] would be able to harm reputations with impunity. But even if civil libel were not able to offer a practical remedy in these unlikely situations, the First Amendment—especially when the "vindictive ... sordid private vendettas" that typify criminal libel today are considered[405]—would still

---

licitor and his two assistants, one a cousin and the other a nephew of the two legislators. The charges were dropped just as it appeared public opinion was shifting in Fitts's favor, but after the legislators won their political party's re-nomination for office, which was tantamount to reelection because of the disparate strength of the Democratic and Republican parties in Williamsburg County at that time. *See* Joe Drape, *Editor Uses Paper To Shake Up S.C. County*, ATLANTA J.-CONST., June 26, 1988, at 6A; Joe Drape, *South Carolina Editor Indicted in Libel Case*, ATLANTA J., June 28, 1988, at 4A. *See supra* text accompanying notes 260–272. In discussing the 2001 Ian Lake case, Jon Katz notes the use of criminal libel

> makes offensive speech a crime. The whole point of the First Amendment is to protect offensive speech, even when it's obnoxious. When it becomes harmful, erroneous or defamatory, [civil] libel has always been the appropriate legal recourse.... But ... the police aren't supposed to get involved.... The outcome of this case and others like it is critical. Free speech isn't the right to speak for free. The right to free speech in the United States means the right to be free from punishment by the government in retaliation for most speech.

Katz, *supra* note 336, at ¶¶ 14–15.

[400]Kelly, *supra* note 84, at 318. In holding a Georgia statute prohibiting "opprobrious words or abusive language" to be unconstitutionally overbroad, the Supreme Court acknowledged that "persons whose expression is constitutionally protected may well refrain from exercising their rights for fear of criminal sanctions provided by a statute susceptible of application to protected expression." Gooding v. Wilson, 405 U.S. 518, 521 (1972).

[401]343 U.S. 250 (1952).

[402]Kelly, *supra* note 84, at 330. *See also A Communitarian Defense of Group Libel Laws*, 101 HARV. L. REV. 682 (Jan. 1988); K. Lasson, *In Defense of Group Libel Laws, Or Why the First Amendment Should Not Protect Nazis*, 2 HUM. RTS. ANN. 289 (1985). *But see* Evan P. Schultz, *Group Rights, American Jews and the Failure of Group Libel Laws, 1913–1952*, 66 BROOK. L. REV. 71 (2000).

[403]Veeder, *supra* note 87, at 46.

[404]Spencer, *supra* note 52, at 390.

[405]*Id.* at 390–91.

stand for the proposition that speech is best corrected by speech and that more speech is better for society than less.[406]

It cannot be doubted that "the problem of maintaining a system of freedom of expression in a society is one of the most complex any society has to face."[407] Criminal libel is "a direct restriction on speech."[408] "Arbitrary and discriminatory prosecutions are encouraged" by such an unclear rule.[409] As is now happening in high-profile civil libel cases with little chance of ultimate success, many file criminal complaints, not because they believe they will eventually win or that the alleged libeler will ever be convicted, but for the publicity value of showing themselves as having been wronged.[410] They thus win by complaining. Yet, because it is "more important that truth be heard than [a] society take no risk of violence,"[411] government must not have "untrammeled power" to sanction criminally that which is "part and parcel of the political process."[412] Experience teaches "that limitations imposed on discussion, as they operate in practice, tend readily and quickly to destroy the whole structure of free expression."[413]

As noted, it is true that "scant, if any, evidence exists that the First Amendment was intended to abolish" criminal libel.[414] But that is an argument for the vitality of criminal libel based upon silence, not one based upon evidence. Jurist Roscoe Pound, arguably "America's greatest legal scholar,"[415] believed "that the law consists, not in the actual rules enforced by decisions of the courts at any one time, but the principles from which those rules flow; that old principles are modified from time to time as changed conditions and new states of fact require."[416] Thus, while "conditions in 1791 must be considered ... they do not arbitrarily fix the division between lawful and unlawful speech for all time."[417] In addition, the nation's "most eminent judges" of the twentieth century believed that "the First Amend-

---

[406]Whitney v. California, 274 U.S. 357, 375 (1927).

[407]Emerson, *supra* note 38, at 889.

[408]Kelly, *supra* note 84, at 318.

[409]*Id.* at 320.

[410]*See* RANDALL P. BEZANSON ET AL., LIBEL AND THE PRESS 78 (1987).

[411]Kelly, *supra* note 84, at 326.

[412]Bahn, *supra* note 32, at 533.

[413]Emerson, *supra* note 38, at 893.

[414]Gertz v. Robert Welch, Inc., 418 U.S. 323, 381 (1974).

[415]SCHWARTZ, *supra* note 144, at 467.

[416]Williams v. Miles, 94 N.W. 705, 708 (Neb. 1903).

[417]CHAFEE, *supra* note 40, at 14.

ment was intended to bar criminal defamation,"[418] despite more recent *dicta* to the contrary.[419]

Libertarian governments "recognize the duty of the state to protect the reputations of individuals."[420] Yet this duty may be wholly and completely fulfilled through the availability of the tort of libel to those harmed. While the facts surrounding the Fitts and Lake cases may be egregious, they are neither atypical nor uncommon.[421] Their outcome was predictable, for in the words of Thomas Emerson, the use of criminal libel statutes "can only result in suppressing unpopular expression."[422]

Thus, it must be concluded that the Supreme Court did not go far enough with its *Garrison* ruling. The Court must erase the crime of libel from the American legal lexicon completely, for the American "legal system [is] an extremely complicated beast—a beast with fifty separate heads, bodies, and tails."[423] More than a half-century ago, "the possibility of abuse" was not deemed a good enough reason to deny Illinois the power to criminalize libel.[424] Forty years ago, the Court felt that "the fear of damage awards under a rule such as that invoked by the Alabama courts here may be markedly more inhibiting than the fear of prosecution under a criminal statute,"[425] concluding that "presumably a person charged with violation of [the Alabama criminal libel] statute enjoys ordinary criminal-law safeguards such as the requirements of an indictment and of proof beyond a reasonable doubt."[426] The Court was wrong; the fear of prosecution is more inhibiting and subject to far greater abuse. The

---

[418]Gottschalk v. Alaska, 575 P.2d 289, 291 (Alaska 1978). *See, e.g.,* Garrison v. Louisiana, 379 U.S. 64, 80 (1964) (Black, J., concurring) (joined by Justice Douglas); Beauharnais v. Illinois, 343 U.S. 250, 287 (1952) (Jackson, J., dissenting); Abrams v. United States, 250 U.S. 616, 624 (1919) (Holmes, J., dissenting) (joined by Justice Brandeis).

[419]Keeton v. Hustler Magazine. 465 U.S. 770, 776 (1984).

[420]Siebert, *Libertarian Theory,* in SIEBERT ET AL., *supra* note 41, at 54.

[421]*See, e.g.,* the case of "Happy" Howard Williamson. James Dodson, *The Trouble with Being Happy,* ATLANTA WEEKLY, April 18, 1982, at 10; Williamson v. State, 8 Media L. Rep. 2044 (Ga. 1982); Williamson v. State. 295 S.E. 2d 305 (Ga. 1982).

[422]Emerson, *supra* note 38, at 924.

[423]LAWRENCE W. FRIEDMAN, LAW IN AMERICA 12 (2002). Actually,

> there are more than fifty systems within the territory controlled by the United States. The federal system can be counted as number fifty-one; and in addition, there is Puerto Rico...; there is Guam, and the Virgin Islands; and there are also the legal systems of many of the native peoples who live inside American borders.

Id.

[424]Beauharnais v. Illinois, 343 U.S. 250, 263 (1952).

[425]New York Times Co. v. Sullivan, 376 U.S. 254, 277 (1964).

[426]*Id.*

Court's concomitant ruling in *Garrison* did place some limits on "an antiquated legal concept."[427] But the ruling was based on the assumption that law enforcement officials, knowing how difficult it would be to prove actual malice, would choose not to manipulate the judicial system in favor of any "best man" or woman.[428] Based on this faulty assumption, applying the *Sullivan* rule to the crime of libel provides inadequate protection for speech. Forty years have proven that the *Garrison* limits are not enough, at least not in this area of the law. Though the crime of libel today may indeed be "a largely unenforceable offense,"[429] that has not stopped those who would use its sledgehammer effect—or the threat of its use—to try to control speech, even in the face of eventual failure. Though not referring to the exact threat criminal libel poses today, Zechariah Chafee's words still ring true: "Surely, language which is immune from civil defamation suits ... ought to be equally immune from the sterner rigors of the penitentiary."[430] The jurists who drafted the Model Penal Code—including chief reporter Herbert Weschler of the Columbia University School of Law, who also served as lead appellate counsel in *Sullivan*[431]—had it correct: Libel as a crime, in any of its many forms, has no place in American law.[432]

---

[427]379 U.S. 64, 67 (1964). *See also* Jane Kirtley, *Overkill in Kansas*, AM. JOURNALISM REV., Sept. 2002, at 74.

[428]More than sixty years ago and just prior to his appointment to the Supreme Court, Robert Jackson—at the time U.S. attorney general—understood the dilemma:

> What every prosecutor is practically required to do is to select the cases for prosecution and to select those in which the offense is the most flagrant, the public harm the greatest, and the proof the most certain ... . If the prosecutor is obliged to choose his case, it follows that he can choose his defendants. Therein is the most dangerous power of the prosecutor: that he will pick people that he thinks he should get, rather than cases that need to be prosecuted. With the law books filled with a great assortment of crimes, a prosecutor stands a fair chance of finding at least a technical violation of some act on the part of almost anyone ... . It is in this realm—in which the prosecutor picks some person whom he dislikes or desires to embarrass, or selects some group of unpopular persons and then looks for an offense—that the greatest danger of abuse of prosecuting power lies. It is here that law enforcement becomes personal, and the real crime becomes that of being unpopular with the predominant or governing group, or being attached to the wrong political views.

The Federal Prosecutor, an address delivered at the second annual Conference of United States Attorneys, Apr. 1, 1940, *quoted* in Morrison v. Olson, 487 U.S. 654, 728 (1988) (Scalia, J., dissenting).

[429]Stevens, *supra* note 66, at 526.

[430]CHAFEE, *supra* note 40, at 95.

[431]376 U.S. at 255.

[432]Neither criminal libel nor the more narrow crime of group libel was included in the American Law Institute's final version of the Model Penal Code (1985). Section 250.7 of the final version is: "Obstructing Highways and Other Public Passages." *See supra* note 356.

Three factors are generally used to determine when conduct should be criminalized: (1) "the enforceability of the law;" (2) "the effects of the law;" and (3) "the existence of other means to protect society against the undesirable behavior."[433] Even though the crime of libel is obviously an enforceable offense, the other two factors argue overwhelmingly for its abolition as a crime: the effects of its enforcement on freedom of speech and the existence of the tort of civil libel to protect society against any abuse of that freedom. The Supreme Court must act. Until it does, criminal libel will continue to hang on the face of the First Amendment as spittle does from the mouth of a baby, who is not mature enough intellectually to know any better or mature enough physically to wipe it off. America's ideal of free expression in the twenty-first century merits the Court's total commitment.

---

[433]KLOTTER, *supra* note 13, at 5 ("Too often, laws are enacted ... without giving adequate consideration to the possible negative consequences. Nevertheless, criminal justice personnel are charged with enforcing these laws ... until they are repealed or declared to be unconstitutional.").

THE AD THAT CHANGED LIBEL LAW: JUDICIAL REALISM AND SOCIAL ACTIVISM IN *NEW YORK TIMES CO. V. SULLIVAN*

SUSAN DENTE ROSS*
R. KENTON BIRD**

The 1964 decision by the Supreme Court of the United States in New York Times Co. v. Sullivan *transformed libel law by extending constitutional protection to the publication of false and defamatory statements about public officials made without actual malice, that is, without knowledge of falsity or reckless disregard for the truth. Less well recognized is the decision's advancement of advocacy advertising and unhindered news coverage as a means to counter racism in the United States. Civil rights history, increasing visibility of advocacy advertisements and the Court's reliance on thin legal precedent suggest the decision embodies judicial realism and social activism.*

Justice William J. Brennan, writing for the majority in *New York Times Co. v. Sullivan*,[1] noted that government policies that "discourage newspapers from carrying 'editorial advertisements' ... might shut off an important outlet for the promulgation of information and ideas by persons who do not themselves have access to publishing facilities."[2] In his concurrence, Justice Hugo L. Black also noted that "if newspapers, publishing advertisements dealing with public issues, thereby risk liability, there can also be little doubt that the ability of

---

*Associate Professor and Director, AccessNorthwest, E.R. Murrow School of Communication, Washington State University.

**Assistant Professor and Interim Director, School of Journalism and Mass Media, University of Idaho.

[1] New York Times v. Sullivan, 376 U.S. 254 (1964).
[2] *Id.* at 266.

minority groups to secure publication of their views on public affairs and to seek support for their causes will be greatly diminished."[3]

The role of advocacy advertising as a tool to offer an effective voice to minorities in this country was not pivotal to Justice Black's concurrence, nor was it a central concern of the majority opinion. Indeed, the Court's recognition that advocacy advertising plays a critical role in empowering minority groups seeking social change seems to have passed with little notice into the annals of Supreme Court *dicta*.[4]

The Court's assertion that advocacy advertising plays an important social, democratic and political role has been given little attention by courts and legal scholars for four decades.[5] It warrants greater notice. As Justice Brennan noted nine years after the *Sullivan* decision, "We have explicitly recognized that editorial advertisements constitute 'an important outlet for the promulgation of information and ideas by persons who do not themselves have access to [media] facilities,' and the unavailability of such editorial advertising can serve only 'to shackle the First Amendment in its attempt to secure the widest possible dissemination of information from diverse and antagonistic sources.'"[6]

On the fortieth anniversary of the Supreme Court ruling widely acknowledged as having revolutionized libel law in America, it seems prudent to explore the context in which the Court decided to extend constitutional protection from libel damages to such advertisements. This article opens with a brief discussion of the state of advocacy ad-

---

[3]*Id.* at 300 (Black, J., concurring).

[4]A Lexis–Nexis search on March 15, 2004, found two references in Supreme Court cases, two references in circuit court of appeals rulings, and two law journal references to the majority opinion's comment and none to Black's concurrence. The majority passage is cited in McConnell v. FEC, 124 S.Ct. 619, 723 (2003) (Scalia, J., dissenting); CBS v. Democratic Nat'l. Comm., 412 U.S. 94, 192 (1973) (Brennan, J., dissenting); U.S. Southwest Africa/Namibia Trade & Cultural Council v. United States, 708 F.2d 760, 769 (D.C. Cir. 1983); and Business Executives' Move for Vietnam Peace v. FCC, 450 F.2d 642, 658 (D.C. Cir. 1971). The two law review references are in Note, *Philadelphia Newspapers v. Hepps Revisited : A Critical Approach to Different Standards of Protection for Media and Nonmedia Defendants in Private Plaintiff Defamation Cases*, 58 GEO. WASH. L. REV. 1268 (1990); and Kurt D. Dykstra, Comment, *Sending the Parties "PAC-ing"? The Constitution, Congressional Control, and Campaign Spending After Colorado Republican Federal Campaign Committee v. Federal Elections Commission*, 81 MARQ. L. REV. 1201 (1998). *But see* JEROME BARRON, FREEDOM OF THE PRESS FOR WHOM? 10 (1973) (calling Brennan's comments "intriguing").

[5]The authors' Lexis–Nexis search on Feb. 7, 2004, of all Supreme Court decisions, all federal court of appeals decisions, and all law review articles in the database did not find a single reference to the cited text.

[6]*CBS*, 412 U.S. at 192.

vertising and the importance of such ads to newspapers during the years leading up the to the Court's 1964 ruling in *Times v. Sullivan*. An exploration of news coverage of the civil rights movement in the mainstream media during that era precedes a description of the advertisement itself. An overview of libel law prior to 1964 sets up a summary of the Court's decision and an analysis of the precedents relied upon by the Court in *Sullivan*. After discussing the historical and social context of the Court's decision and its influence on subsequent reporting of the civil rights movement, the authors argue that the decision, like most major court rulings, is, in large part, a product of its time. The decision's greatest contribution may have been outside the law, where it came to symbolize national commitment to racial equality.

ADVOCACY ADVERTISING CIRCA 1964

American Telephone & Telegraph, with the assistance of N.W. Ayer & Son advertising agency, launched one of the first documented advocacy advertising campaigns in 1908. The series of five ads, placed in national magazines, was intended to overcome public animosity toward the company's monopoly position in the industry.[7] Six years later, famed public relations agent Ivy Lee wrote the copy for four newspaper ads for Colorado Fuel & Iron Co. during a prolonged labor dispute. The ads, which ran in Colorado newspapers, articulated the company's opposition to unions and defended the wages it paid to miners.[8] Advocacy ads became a means of associating corporations with popular causes, a direct response to attacks from muckraking journalists during the Progressive Era and a mechanism for organizing labor during the 1930s.[9] However, advocacy advertising bloomed as the modern advertising industry exploded and fueled the post-World War II boom of consumerism in the United States. During this fertile period of growth in what would become a multi-billion dollar industry, the idea

---

[7]*See* Noel L. Griese, *AT&T: 1908 Origins of the Nation's Oldest Continuous Institutional Advertising Campaign*, 6 J. ADVERTISING 18 (Summer 1977). *See also* S. PRAKASH SETHI, ADVOCACY ADVERTISING AND LARGE CORPORATIONS (1977); Quentin.J. Schulze, *Advertising and Public Utilities 1900–1917*, 10 J. ADVERTISING 41 (1981).

[8]*See* Kirk Hallahan, *Ivy Lee and the Rockefellers' Response to the 1913–1914 Colorado Coal Strike*, 14 J. PUB. REL. RES. 264, 277–78 (2002).

[9]*See* Roland Marchand, *The Fitful Career of Advocacy Advertising: Political Protection, Client Cultivation, and Corporate Morale*, 29 CALIF. MGMT. REV. 128 (1987); Richard Tansey & Michael R. Hyman, *Ethical Codes and the Advocacy Advertisements of World War II*, 12 INT'L J. ADVERTISING 351 (1993).

that strategic advertising messages could do far more than sell washing machines and vacuum cleaners took hold.[10]

By the 1950s, an array of organizations began to place ads advocating social change in leading newspapers. For example, a pair of full-page ads urging elimination of bigotry and prejudice appeared in the *New York Times* in 1949 and 1951 sponsored by *Woman's Home Companion* magazine.[11] On July 19, 1959, the *Times* published an ad paid for by Moral Re-Armament dominated by a photograph of singer/actress Muriel Smith standing before an American flag. The ad, which bore the title "A Magna Carta for this Modern Generation," urged for the end of racism as the only means to halt advancing communism. Six months later, on January 17, 1960, the National Urban League ran a half-page ad in the *Times*. A black and white photograph showed a bespectacled black man in a white lab coat extending a pill in his left hand. The ad headline asked, "Would you take the pill?" and the copy encouraged the elimination of racism in America.[12]

Between 1945 and 1964, a variety of civil rights groups sponsored at least fourteen advertisements in the *Times* promoting racial equality.[13] Prominent among them was an advertisement titled "Heed Their Rising Voices," which spawned the lawsuit in *New York Times v. Sullivan*. The ad appeared early in 1960, almost two years before the *Times* became a leader among newspapers by publicly declaring a policy to accept all ads without censorship even when they presented positions contrary to the newspaper's own editorials.[14] A *New York Times* editorial at the end of 1961 reported, "[W]e think the principle of freedom of the press not only requires us to report events and occurrences of which we disapprove ... but also imposes on us the obligation to accept advertising of books whose contents we reject and of political parties and movements whose goals we despise."[15]

---

[10]*See* SETHI, *supra* note 7, at 14–15.

[11]*See How to Beat the Bigots*, N.Y. TIMES, Sept. 24, 1951, at 17; *Is Prejudice Poisoning Our Kids?*, N.Y. TIMES, Oct. 24, 1949, at 14.

[12]*See* Susan D. Ross, Raising Another Voice (unpublished manuscript on file with author).

[13]*See* Susan D. Ross, *"Heed Their Voices": Civil Rights, Social Movements, and Advertising in The New York Times*, 75 JOURNALISM &MASS COMM. Q. 518 (1998). The first civil rights ad uncovered by this researcher is dated February 1954, two years prior to the Montgomery bus boycotts. Unfortunately, the photograph, the headline and the name of the publication are missing from the clip filed in the Schomburg Collection in the Library of Congress, making it impossible to determine where the ad ran. However, the ad, subtitled "We're in the FIGHT for Freedom!" closely resembles the ads published in the *New York Times*.

[14]Editorial, *The Freedom of Advertising*, N.Y. TIMES, Dec. 28, 1961, at 26.

[15]*Id.*

In 1961, V.O. Key noted and denigrated the growing phenomenon of issue-oriented advertisements in his influential work, *Public Opinion and American Democracy*.[16] He viewed these ad campaigns as "propagandizing" efforts whose effects were "on the order of the dance of the rainmakers. ... Sometimes these campaigns have their effects—just as rain sometimes follows the rainmaker's dance."[17] Others suggested such ads provided a vital counterbalance to the reality that "use [of] mass media as a forum for the expression of opinion by the dissenters of society is at best uncertain."[18]

Yet the ads did not stop. To the contrary, they became a critical part of national debate of important public issues. For example, oil companies—among the largest corporations in America during the 1970s—came under public and political attack following the oil crisis in 1973. In response, Mobil Oil employed "social responsibility campaigns in the media" to create a more positive image and to defuse political and public concerns that oil company price-gauging and enormous profits warranted regulatory action.[19] The power of such ads, according to one scholar and the company's own CEO, was to make Mobil Oil's self-interested messages appear more objective, particularly because the ads appeared in credible media outlets, often on op-ed pages. Control over the content and presentation of these ads allowed Mobil Oil to soften its image, distract attention from its profits and counterbalance negative news stories.[20]

Since the 1960s, a diverse but non-systematic body of research has examined the phenomenon alternately called issue advertising, advertorials, advocacy advertising, outside lobbying, editorial advertising, social marketing and strategic use of media. Sociologists have highlighted the essential role of media messages, including but not limited to advertisements, in organizing movements and effecting social change.[21] In contrast, political scientists generally have found little direct effect between mediated lobbying through ads and policy

---

[16]V.O. KEY, PUBLIC OPINION AND AMERICAN DEMOCRACY (1961).

[17]*Id.* at 528.

[18]Robert J. Gwyn, *Opinion Advertising and the Free Market of Ideas*, 34 PUB. OPINION Q. 246, 255 (1970).

[19]*See* Ross L. Watts & Jerod L. Zimmerman, *Towards a Positive Theory of the Determination of Accounting Standards*, 53 ACCOUNTING REV. 112, 115 (1978).

[20]*See* S. Prakash Sethi, *Advocacy Advertising—The American Experience*, 21 CAL. MGMT. REV. 55 (1978); S. Prakash Sethi, *Business and the News Media, The Paradox of Informed Misunderstanding*, 19 CAL. MGMT. REV. 52 (1977); S. Prakash Sethi, *Issue-Oriented Corporate Advertising, Tax Treatment of Expenditures*, 19 CAL. MGMT. REV. 5 (1976).

[21]*See, e.g.,* DOUG MCADAM & DAVID A. SNOW (eds.), SOCIAL MOVEMENTS: READINGS ON THEIR EMERGENCE, MOBILIZATION, AND DYNAMICS (1997).

change.[22] Communication scholars and others have provided applied studies offering insight into how to design, improve and use advertorial campaigns to respond to organizational criticism or advance corporate goals.[23] Descriptive case studies have clarified the nature and functions of advocacy advertising to alert policymakers of the views and interests of the ads' sponsors and to influence opinions and attitudes toward their central issues.[24] Yet, although a single advocacy ad revolutionized American libel law, courts and legal scholars generally have failed to examine or articulate fully the role of such ads in advancing the fundamental First Amendment "principle that debate on public issues should be uninhibited, robust and wide-open."[25]

Today much research accepts the notion that strategic use of media is vital to effective social movements, social change, and political and social participation by minority groups.[26] The ads generally are said to achieve their objectives through rhetorical and narrative strategies that evoke and resonate with the embedded attitudes and beliefs of mainstream readers and the dominant culture.[27] A group of

---

[22]See, e.g., KEN KOLLMAN, OUTSIDE LOBBYING: PUBLIC OPINION AND INTEREST GROUP STRATEGIES 4 (1998); STEPHEN MILLER, SPECIAL INTEREST GROUPS IN AMERICAN POLITICS (1983).

[23]See, e.g., R.M. Detwiler, The Myths of Persuasion, 38 PUB. REL. J. 52 (1982); A.H. Edelson, Advocacy Advertising, 52 ADVERTISING AGE 47 (1981); R.G. Meadow, The Political Dimensions of Non-product Advertising, 31 J. OF COMM. 69 (1981); H. Waltzer, Corporate Advocacy Advertising and Political Influence, 14 PUB. REL. REV. 41 (1988).

[24]See KOLLMAN , supra note 22, at 8.

[25]Times v. Sullivan, 376 U.S. 254, 270 (1964).

[26]See, e.g., SEYMOUR H. FINE, THE MARKETING OF IDEAS AND SOCIAL ISSUES 195–214 (1981); SEYMOUR H. FINE, SOCIAL MARKETING: PROMOTING THE CAUSES OF PUBLIC AND NONPROFIT AGENCIES (1990); P. SZTOMPKA, THE SOCIOLOGY OF SOCIAL CHANGE (1999); LAWRENCE WALLACK ET AL., NEWS FOR A CHANGE 152 (1999); Roland J. Adams et al., Media Advocacy: A Case Study of Philip Sokolof's Cholesterol Awareness Campaigns, 27 J. OF CONSUMER AFFAIRS 145 (1993); Christina D. Economos et al., What Lessons Have Been Learned From Other Attempts to Guide Social Change? 59 NUTRITION REV. S40 (2001); K.F.A. Fox & P. Kotler, The Marketing of Social Causes: The First Ten Years, 44 J. OF MARKETING 24 (1980); Doug McAdam, Tactical Innovation and the Pace of Insurgency, in SOCIAL MOVEMENTS, supra note 21, at 340–41 (noting the vital role an "established communication network" plays in the diffusion of social movements but failing to specifically acknowledge the role of mass media); David A. Snow et al., Frame Alignment Processes, Micromobilization, and Movement Participation, in SOCIAL MOVEMENTS, supra note 21, at 235, 238, (identifying the mass media as a mechanism of "frame bridging" between movements and individuals); Lawrence Wallack, Media Advocacy: Promoting Health Through Mass Communication, in HEALTH BEHAVIOR AND HEALTH EDUCATION 370 (K. GLANZ et al., eds. 1990).

[27]For an introduction to the role of rhetoric and narrative in opinion formation, see, e.g., EYTAN GILBOA, MEDIA AND CONFLICT, FRAMING ISSUES, MAKING POLICY,

scholars has linked the effectiveness of advocacy messages to their ability to: (1) convey a sense of crisis to the public, (2) support the crisis claim credibly, (3) align goals with dominant values, (4) provide a sense of urgency to catalyze both internal and external audiences and (5) enlist the support of government and other important elite groups.[28]

Advocacy ads both define and draw attention to a central issue or conflict; they reinforce the identity of a group or movement and align members; they solicit moral and financial support. Advocacy advertisements may be used to develop a public climate favorable to group goals or to promote active public support for group views on controversial issues. Alternately, advocacy ads and other strategic media messages may "expand ... conflict by bringing new and favorably disposed and influential participants into play" on an issue.[29] The functions of advocacy advertising parallel the vital role media more generally play in social change and expand the ability of newspapers to serve as an effective conduit for alternate voices.[30] The Court itself acknowledged this function in *Sullivan* and in subsequent cases.[31]

Scholars from many fields have noted an increase in advocacy advertisements since the 1970s or even earlier.[32] For example, one recent study of advocacy ads in the *New York Times* between 1985 and 1998 found growth in the number of ads, the diversity of topics covered and the range of sponsoring organizations.[33] The study also noted that the frequency and content of the ads tended to shift in correlation with important political and social issues, reinforcing the notion that such ads advance an important public policy objective of enhancing open debate in a democratic society.

SHAPING OPINION (2002); TEUN VAN DIJK, ELITE DISCOURSE AND RACISM (1993). *See also* Mark P. Orbe, *From the Standpoint(s) of Traditionally Muted Groups: Explicating a Co-cultural Communication Theoretical Model*, 8 COMM. THEORY 1, 8–9 (1998) (offering a summary of communicative practices used by "muted" groups).

[28]*See* Economos et al., *supra* note 26 at S44–46.

[29]C. Brown, *Daring to be Heard: Advertorials by Organized Interests on the Op-Ed Page of the New York Times, 1985–1998*, 18 POL. COMM. 23 (2001).

[30]*See* SETHI, *supra* note 7 at 9.

[31]*See, e.g.*, First Nat'l Bank v. Bellotti, 435 U.S. 765, 777 (1978); Buckley v. Valeo, 424 U.S. 1, 48–49 (1976).

[32]*See* Brown, *supra* note 29, at 23. *See also* R. Shaiko, *More Bang for the Buck: The New Era of Full-Service Public Interest Organizations*, *in* INTEREST GROUP POLITICS 109 (A. CIGLER & B. LOOMIS eds., 3d ed. 1991); J.R. Nowling, *Op-ed: New Opportunity for PR*, 31 PUB. REL. J. 20 (1975).

[33]*See* Brown, *supra* note 29, at 23.

THE BUSINESS OF NEWS AND THE CIVIL RIGHTS MOVEMENT CIRCA 1964

In 1950, before television became a serious competitor for news coverage and advertising dollars, American newspapers enjoyed substantial power and influence. Over the next two decades, the original newspaper chains stepped up their acquisitions, and many papers merged with competitors or ceased publication. Newhouse, Knight, the Tribune Co. and other companies laid the groundwork for nationwide chains that came to dominate the industry by the 1970s.[34] The growth of the chains, coupled with the decline of family ownership, signaled a more bottom-line, less personalized approach to newspapers. By 1960, these trends "transformed the news industry in the United States from a brawling, competitive, localized business into an order dominated by a double handful of fiefs of imperial power and wealth," British journalist Godfrey Hodgson wrote in his sweeping political and cultural history of the United States in the 1960s and early 1970s.[35]

The circulation of U.S. newspapers rose from fifty-two million copies a day in the late 1940s to sixty-two million in the late 1960s. Advertising revenues rose, too. Even as the television networks became major competitors for national advertising (promoting brand-name products), newspapers posted gains in this area, recording more than $1 billion a year in revenues in the late 1960s, nearly four times the figure for the mid-1940s.[36] In 1960, roughly three quarters of the revenue of the *Times* came from advertisements, and ads sales in Alabama averaged $3,600 a month.[37] Yet the financial success of the news industry was not shared equally. Rising production costs, union resistance to automation of parts of the production process, and a series of strikes, especially at metropolitan newspapers, pushed some papers' balance sheets into the red. For example, the *New York Herald Tribune*, the *New York Times*'s principal competitor for up-scale morning readers in the first half of the twentieth century, lost an estimated $15 million to $20 million between 1955 and 1965.[38]

---

[34]*See* JEAN FOLKERTS & DWIGHT L. TEETER JR., VOICES OF A NATION: A HISTORY OF MASS MEDIA IN THE UNITED STATES 494 (2003).

[35]GODFREY HODGSON, AMERICA IN OUR TIME 138 (1976).

[36]ERNEST C. HYNDS, AMERICAN NEWSPAPERS IN THE 1970S 81 (1975).

[37]New York Times v. Sullivan, 144 So.2d 25, 30 (Ala. 1962).

[38]*See* JOHN HOHENBERG, THE NEWS MEDIA: A JOURNALIST LOOKS AT HIS PROFESSION 51 (1968). The *Herald Tribune* merged with two competing dailies in 1966, but the merged *World Journal Tribune* died the following year. *See* HYNDS, *supra* note 36, at 85.

In New York, nine major dailies competed for readers after World War II, selling more than six million copies a day during the week and more than ten million copies on Sundays.[39] The *Times*'s circulation grew by more than 40% during the 1950s, from 523,446 in 1950 to 751,228 in 1960.[40] Although not the largest circulation U.S. newspaper (that honor belonged to the *Daily News*), the *Times* steadily increased its lead over the *Herald Tribune,* and advertisers followed the readers.[41] By 1950, the *Times*'s stature was such that David Halberstam, writing almost thirty years later, described it as "the most influential paper not just in the country but in the world. More, it had significantly changed the nature and tone of journalism, moving away from the intense partisanship and parochialism of a previous era, when papers existed only as an extension of a publisher's political or commercial will." At the *Times*, Halberstam observed: "[P]ower was invested, not in the publisher, not in the editorial page, but finally in the reporter. The publisher deliberately diminished his own role. It was journalism that left it to the reader to make judgments. The *Times*'s role was only in selecting where the reporters should go and what they should cover ... "[42] The *Times*'s unique national position, organizational policies and particular history all contributed to its leadership in coverage of the civil rights movement.

The *Times*'s decision to devote considerable resources to covering the civil rights movement in the South clearly elevated the struggle for equality for African Americans to a national story. "The South had always held special significance for the *New York Times* because it was from the South, the Reconstruction South, that [Adolph] Ochs [publisher from 1896 to 1935] emerged," Harrison Salisbury wrote.[43] Former *Los Angeles Times* reporter Jack Nelson noted that "most newspapers left the coverage of civil rights to the wire services, which mostly offered bland reports." The exception, Nelson wrote, was the *New York Times*, "which was so far out front in covering the story, not only focusing on it long before other news organizations, but also devoting more resources and top news space to it and thereby helping make it part of the government's agenda."[44]

---

[39]*See* MICHAEL EMERY, EDWIN L. EMERY & NANCY L. ROBERTS, THE PRESS AND AMERICA: AN INTERPRETIVE HISTORY OF THE MASS MEDIA 352 (2000).

[40]*Chronology*, N.Y. TIMES, Nov. 14, 2001, F30, F33.

[41]*See* EMERY ET AL., *supra* note 39, at 352; DAVID HALBERSTAM, THE POWERS THAT BE 218 (1979).

[42]HALBERSTAM, *supra* note 41, at 219.

[43]HARRISON E. SALISBURY, WITHOUT FEAR OR FAVOR 352 (1980).

[44]Jack Nelson, *Reporting on the Civil Rights Movement*, 57 NIEMAN REPORTS 6 (Fall 2003).

Salisbury points to the paper's decision to assign John Popham, a former Marine Corps officer from the Tidewater region of Virginia, to cover the South in the early 1950s as the first step on the road to *New York Times v. Sullivan*. "The South was not yet a story [before 1954], but Popham was covering it, and, as he was later to say, 'accumulating.' Not for the day but for next year and the year after," Salisbury wrote.[45] By the mid-'50s, the *Times* assigned Claude Sitton to cover eleven southern states, including Alabama. Based in Atlanta, Sitton and other *Times* staffers spent roughly thirty days each year covering news in Alabama.[46]

Indeed, the *Times* covered civil rights issues extensively at least a year before the *Brown v. Board of Education*[47] decision to which many point as the official starting point of the modern civil rights movement.[48] An unpublished content analysis of every other issue of the *Times* in 1953 found an average of more than two articles per week dealing with civil or equal rights coverage.[49] "The Times was engaging in regular coverage of many types of stories—everything from listing a United Negro College Fund Drive to stories about civil rights violations," researcher Debra Smith wrote.[50] Among the most frequently covered stories were those dealing with legislation, court rulings and civil rights violations, and these often appeared on the front page, she observed. Smith concluded that because of its agenda-setting role, the *"Times'* coverage was laying the groundwork for people to view civil rights as an important issue."[51]

The civil rights movement did not simply burst onto the national news agenda. Instead, individual stories and isolated events attracted coverage, and gradually, over time, reporters and editors began to perceive the civil rights movement *as* a movement, as a news story on its own merits. As *Times* columnist Anthony Lewis observed in 1964, "There were many factors working before 1954 for change in American race relations ... But revolutions require a spark, a catalyst. ... Change does not just begin at a point in time; it builds on history."[52]

---

[45]SALISBURY, *supra* note 43, at 355.

[46]*See* New York Times v. Sullivan, 144 So.2d 25, 29 (Ala. 1962).

[47]347 U.S. 483 (1954).

[48]*See infra* notes 52–55 and accompanying text.

[49]*See* Debra A. Smith, The Shaping of the American Civil Rights Movement: The Role of the New York Times in 1953 (2001) (unpublished master's thesis, Washington State University).

[50]*Id.* at 40.

[51]*Id.* at 43.

[52]ANTHONY LEWIS, PORTRAIT OF A DECADE: THE SECOND AMERICAN REVOLUTION 5 (1964).

Lewis identified the spark that ignited the civil rights movement, and media attention to it, as the Supreme Court's 1954 decision in the school desegregation cases known collectively as *Brown v. Board of Education*.[53] But there is no consensus. Smith argued that the modern civil rights movement began with a bus boycott in Baton Rouge, Louisiana, in June 1953.[54] Others set the inception of the movement as the arrest of Rosa Parks on December 1, 1955, which triggered the Montgomery bus boycott, or perhaps the crisis in Little Rock, Arkansas, in the fall of 1957, in which President Dwight Eisenhower sent 1,000 soldiers to assure peaceful integration of Central High School.[55] Another 1955 event, the trial of two Mississippi men accused of the kidnapping and murder of Chicago teenager Emmett Till, attracted significant media attention to the region. "The Till trial was the first of the major civil rights stories that took TV reporters all across the South," two journalism historians state.[56]

Television news became national in scope in the late 1950s. Hodgson attributes this to the networks' desire for bigger audiences (and accompanying advertising revenues) and their strategy to counter negative publicity resulting from recent scandals about rigged television quiz shows.[57] He notes that 1961 was the first year in which a majority of Americans identified television as their primary source of world, and by implication, national news.[58] As a result, the increasingly violent clashes over civil rights in the South acquired an unprecedented visual dimension. William Small described the images: "On television, with its rapidly growing audience and rapidly increased news coverage, there was a college [sic] of vivid scenes: young Negroes dragged out of buildings, grim-jawed sit-ins surrounded by angry whites, hoodlums pouring mustard on the heads of blacks at a lunch counter, police moving in with brutal swiftness."[59] Many observers believe televised images of police across the South turning attack dogs and fire hoses on black children and bludgeoning civil rights marchers catalyzed support across the nation for the movement.[60]

---

[53]*Id.*

[54]*See* Smith, *supra* note 49, at 5.

[55]*See* PETER B. LEVY, THE CIVIL RIGHTS MOVEMENT 7–11 (1998).

[56]Henry D. Marsh & David R. Davies, *The Media in Transition, 1945–1974, in* THE MEDIA IN AMERICA 450 (W. David Sloan ed., 2002).

[57]HODGSON, *supra* note 35, at 143.

[58]*Id.* at 140.

[59]WILLIAM SMALL, TO KILL A MESSENGER: TELEVISION NEWS AND THE REAL WORLD 41–57 (1970).

[60]*See, e.g.,* NORMAN ROSENBERG, PROTECTING THE BEST MEN 246 (1985).

In the mid-1950s, though, the story belonged to the print media. Critics give American newspapers mixed reviews for their coverage of the movement in its early years. John Hohenberg, long-time administrator of the Pulitzer prizes, observed that newspapers, especially in the South, too often supported the status quo of segregation. "While there have been instances of superb work by all sections of the media on this story in every part of the nation, the record on the whole is not one that satisfies most thoughtful journalists," he wrote.[61] Nonetheless, many editors in the South spoke out for racial equality, often at considerable financial and personal risk, he wrote.[62]

Jack Nelson, who became the first Atlanta correspondent for the *Los Angeles Times* in 1965, assessed the challenges that reporters covering the South faced in the 1950s and 1960s. Writing in 2003, he recalled, "In those years, the white establishment dug in its heels, and the Ku Klux Klan, the white citizens councils and other racists lashed out at the media, as well as the civil rights movement, in a last-ditch effort to preserve segregation."[63] It was against this background that Alabama officials sought to use their state's libel laws to limit, and if possible, stop coverage of African-Americans' struggle for equality.

THE ADVERTISEMENT

The full-page ad that triggered Luther B. Sullivan's libel suit has been called a "paid political ... plea for funds to finance new campaigns of nonviolent civil disobedience."[64] In contrast, the Court called it "an expression of grievance and protest on one of the major public issues of our time."[65] Either way, the ad titled "Heed Their Rising Voices" was purchased for $4,800[66] and appeared on March 29, 1960, on page 25 of the *New York Times*.[67] Signed by sixty-four prominent individuals, including celebrities and luminaries Harry Belafonte, Marlon Brando, Sidney Poitier and Eleanor Roosevelt, the ad encouraged readers to join blacks in the use of nonviolent protest to fight southern segregation and oppression.

---

[61]HOHENBERG, *supra* note 38, at 101.
[62]*Id.*
[63]Nelson, *supra* note 44, at 6.
[64]ROSENBERG, *supra* note 60, at 235.
[65]*Times v. Sullivan,* 376 U.S. 254, 271 (1964).
[66]BARRON, *supra* note 4 at 8.
[67]*Heed Their Rising Voices,* N.Y. TIMES, Mar. 29, 1960, at 25.

The ad began by identifying the voice of the civil rights movement with the authority and credibility of the *New York Times* both by mimicking the design of a *Times* news page and by leading off with a quote from a *New York Times* editorial of ten days earlier. That editorial, in support of a civil rights bill then pending in Congress, described the "growing movement of peaceful mass demonstrations by Negroes" as "something understandable and also something ominous." It concluded by calling on Congress to "heed their rising voices," a line from which the advertisement drew its title.[68]

The ad's stated purpose was to raise funds for "the defense of Martin Luther King, the support of the embattled students and the struggle for the right-to-vote" [sic]. However, most of the ad copy presented information on the civil rights movement's perspective of the desegregation struggle and the fight to register black voters in the South. Justice was the issue, not race, the ad suggested. Civil rights was not a fight for Negro equality but the fight to advance American values and the American dream. The students in the movement were "freedom fighters," (a term which, at that time, had not gained its negative connotation), restrained, dignified, inspirational, non-violent and courageous "protagonists of democracy." Dr. Martin Luther King was "the one man who, more than any other, symbolizes the new spirit now sweeping the South." This spirit was "quiet, heroic," inspired, non-violent and "world famous." The movement embodied the essence of "*our* America"—the essence of participatory democracy and equality.

A call to the righteous, the ad pushed beyond the *Times* editorial from which it drew its original strength. "*We* must heed their rising voices—yes—but we must add our own" to oppose the "intimidation and violence," the "tear gas, ... fire hoses, and... open barbed-wire stockade[s]" of "the Southern violators." The ad systematically and graphically alienated readers from the *apparatchik* of southern states opposing equal rights. The "official state apparatus and police power" that embodied the South was both ruthless and violent. They "attempt[ed] to starve [students] into submission; ... They have bombed; ... They have assaulted" and attempted to "*behead* this affirmative movement" (emphasis in original). To join the movement was to join all "men and women of goodwill [to] do more than applaud the rising-to-glory of others" and to "join hands with" the "upholders of the Constitution."

---

[68] Editorial, *Amendment XV*, N.Y. TIMES, Mar. 19, 1960, at 20.

Justice Black would echo this theme and make it a central tenet of his concurrence in *Sullivan*:

> One of the acute and highly emotional issues in this country arises out of efforts of many people, even including some public officials, to continue state-commanded segregation of races in the public schools and other public places, despite our several holdings that such a state practice is forbidden by the Fourteenth Amendment.[69]

According to policy, the *Times* advertising department accepted the ad without verifying its accuracy.[70] The ad contained errors. For example, one paragraph of the ad said that after protesting college students sang "My Country, 'tis of Thee" at the Alabama State Capitol in Montgomery, "truckloads of police armed with shotguns and tear-gas ringed the Alabama State College campus," padlocked the dining hall in an attempt to starve students into submission, and student leaders were expelled. In fact, the students had sung "The Star-Spangled Banner," and although large numbers of armed police were sent to the campus, they did not "ring" it. Students without meal tickets were barred from the dining hall, which was not padlocked. And the nine student leaders were expelled for seeking service at the segregated Montgomery courthouse lunch counter on a different day, not for singing during the protest at the Capitol.[71]

A second paragraph of the ad said "Southern violators" subjected Dr. Martin Luther King, Jr., to "intimidation and violence … . They have bombed his home almost killing his wife and child. They have assaulted his person. They have arrested him seven times—for 'speeding,' 'loitering' and similar 'offenses.' And now they have charged him with perjury, a *felony* under which they could imprison him for *ten years*" (emphasis in original). In fact, King had been arrested twice; the assault charge was contested; and the bombing occurred during the tenure of a previous commissioner of police.[72]

---

[69]376 U.S. at 294 (Black, J., concurring).

[70]*Id.* at 260–61 n.27. *See also* W. WAT HOPKINS, ACTUAL MALICE: TWENTY-FIVE YEARS AFTER TIMES V. SULLIVAN 17 (1989) (reporting that the trial record showed a staff member in the newspaper's advertising acceptability department testified that he saw no reason to question the advertisement's content because the persons whose names were listed in the ad as sponsors were well known); ANTHONY LEWIS, MAKE NO LAW 5–7 (1991) (noting the newspaper's routine practice of checking ads for fraud, deception, smut and "attacks on personal character").

[71]*Sullivan*, 144 So.2d 25, 47–48 (Ala. 1962).

[72]376 U.S. at 257–60.

THE *SULLIVAN* LAWSUIT

Sullivan, one of three elected Montgomery city commissioners and the commissioner in charge of police, wrote to the *Times*, claiming that the ad falsely accused him of repression, and he demanded a retraction and apology.[73] The newspaper refused and asked for clarification of how the ad, which did not name Sullivan, had libeled him. Rather than respond, Sullivan sued the newspaper for half a million dollars. Soon thereafter, the Alabama governor, the mayor of Montgomery and two other city officials also filed suits totaling $2.5 million.[74] During the trial in Alabama, Sullivan said he was clearly identifiable because he was recognized as the supervisor of the Montgomery police. He claimed the ad's negative characterization of Montgomery police reflected adversely on him and damaged his reputation.[75]

The judge, Walter B. Jones, instructed the all-white, all-male jury that Alabama law imposed strict liability for libel, which meant that damage to Sullivan's reputation was presumed because the content was *per se* libelous.[76] Judge Jones, "a great admirer of the Confederacy" who celebrated its founding annually by seating the "jurors in his courtroom in Confederate military uniforms,"[77] told the jury that general and punitive damages could be awarded without any showing of financial loss, and their job consisted only of determining whether the statements were published and were "of and concerning" Sullivan.[78] After less than two hours of deliberation, the jury awarded Sullivan $500,000. The state supreme court affirmed the judgment.[79] In concluding that the unprecedented award was appropriate, the Alabama Supreme Court wrote:

> The *Times* adamantly refused to right the wrong it knew it had done the plaintiff. In the trial below none of the defendants questioned the falsity of the allegations in the advertisement. On the other hand, during his testimony it was the contention of the Secretary of the *Times* that the advertisement was "substantially correct." In the face of this cavalier ignoring of the falsity of the advertisement, the jury could not

---

[73]*Id.* at 261.
[74]*Id.* at 278 n.18.
[75]*Id.* at 258.
[76]144 So. 2d at 37, 41.
[77]Anthony Lewis, *Thoughts That We Hate*, 1994 Knight Lecture at Stanford University, *available at* http://knightfellows.stanford.edu/lectures/knight/1994/.
[78]144 So. 2d at 39.
[79]*Id.* at 52.

have but been impressed with the bad faith of the *Times*, and its maliciousness inferable therefrom.[80]

Even though Sullivan's lawsuit stemmed from an advertisement, it was part of a larger southern campaign intended to deter aggressive and thorough coverage of white southern resistance to civil rights for African Americans. According to Justice Black:

> The half-million-dollar verdict does give dramatic proof ... that state libel laws threaten the very existence of an American press virile enough to publish unpopular views on public affairs and bold enough to criticize the conduct of public officials. The factual background of this case emphasizes the imminence and enormity of that threat. ... Moreover, this technique for harassing and punishing a free press—now that it has been shown to be possible—is by no means limited to cases with racial overtones; it can be used in other fields where public feelings may make local as well as out-of-state newspapers easy prey for libel verdict seekers.[81]

In reflecting on the decision a quarter century later, Rodney Smolla wrote: "The last desperate reaction of a clinging Jim Crow regime was to try to suppress the message itself, using whatever pretextual legal devices were at hand, including the law of libel. If one could not stop the marches, one might at least keep the marches off television and out of the newspapers."[82]

LIBEL LAW CIRCA 1963

As one historian has noted, "[U]ntil the early 1960s, defamation law was not a prominent free-expression issue."[83] For centuries prior to the Supreme Court's 1964 ruling in *New York Times v. Sullivan*, courts considered legal punishment for libel to be the logical and necessary remedy for the harms it causes. Common law long had held that defamation of private persons was a serious crime because it both harmed individual reputation and incited public quarrels and vengeance.[84] English statutory law made it an even greater crime to

---

[80]376 U.S. at 286.

[81]*Id.* at 294–95 (Black, J., concurring).

[82]RODNEY A. SMOLLA, SUING THE PRESS 43 (1986). *See also* Lynne Flocke, *Times v. Sullivan and the Civil Rights Movement, available at* http://civilrightsandthe press.syr.edu/reflectionhtml.

[83]ROSENBERG, *supra* note 60, at 208.

[84]*See* Beauharnais v. Illinois, 343 U.S. 250, 253–54 (1952).

defame public officials because libel of government impugned and undermined the very authority of the state.[85]

As early as 1275, English law made it criminal to distribute false news "from which discord might result between the king and his people."[86] The law later expanded to criminalize any speech that bred scandal about virtually any government official that might prompt unrest or civil discontent. Truth was not a defense, and malicious intent was not required to make seditious defamation a crime. British licensing of printing and publishing in the 1500s and 1600s was a logical extension of these libel laws and the crown's desire to suppress speech that might incite the people to challenge the supremacy of the rulers.[87]

The English licensing system ended in 1694, but judicial attitudes favoring punishment for licentious and libelous expression retained sway. Freedom of the press was understood to mean only freedom from prior restraint.[88] Even after the drafting of the American Constitution, it was generally accepted that punishment for defamation did not infringe on protected freedoms of speech and press.[89] As First Amendment historian Leonard Levy wrote, "In colonial America, as in England, the common law of criminal libel was strung out like a chicken wire of constraint against the captious and the chancy, making the open discussion of public issues hazardous, if not impossible, except when public opinion opposed administration policy."[90]

Early political leaders generally accepted that libel law should punish licentious criticism of government.[91] "Those who made the republican Revolution and established the nation's legal-constitutional framework ... placed great importance on the use of libel law to protect the reputations of the best men," Norman Rosenberg wrote in his insightful history of libel. "The law of libel not only safeguarded the reputations of individual political leaders but served ... to ensure that virtuous men would seek governmental position, that voters would not be fooled into selecting knaves and fools, and that public opinion itself would not become corrupted."[92]

---

[85]See FREDERICK S. SIEBERT, FREEDOM OF THE PRESS IN ENGLAND 1476–1776 117–20 (1952).

[86]EDWARD G. HUDON, FREEDOM OF SPEECH AND PRESS IN AMERICA 8 (1963).

[87]See SIEBERT, supra note 85, at 117–20.

[88]See 4 WILLIAM BLACKSTONE, COMMENTARIES ON THE LAWS OF ENGLAND 151–52 (1765).

[89]See LEONARD W. LEVY, EMERGENCE OF A FREE PRESS 3–15 (1985).

[90]LEONARD W. LEVY, LEGACY OF SUPPRESSION 21 (1960).

[91]See ROSENBERG, supra note 60, at 56.

[92]Id. at 151–52.

Even if one accepts the alternate view presented by Harvard University professor Zechariah Chafee that speech freedom in Colonial America meant "the right of unrestricted discussion of public affairs,"[93] libel law was nonetheless considered to be a legitimate means to punish abuse of the freedoms of speech and press. In the colonies and for nearly two centuries after, the common law of defamation punished individuals whose intolerable and unreasonably pernicious speech caused harm to others. Thus, in 1941, Chafee reasoned that "the law ... punishes a few classes of words ... because the very utterance of such words is considered to inflict a present injury upon listeners, readers, or those defamed."[94] Yet as early as the antebellum period in the nineteenth century, some liberal jurists focused less on the need to protect or recompense citizens for licentious speech than on the need to promote open debate in the service of a self-righting democracy.[95] Beginning in the mid-1800s, some lawyers and scholars argued that a qualified privilege for false and libelous statements would increase and enhance political debate without undue harm.[96]

Nonetheless, until 1964 the Supreme Court held broadly "that punishment for the abuse of the liberty accorded to the press is essential to the protection of the public."[97] The Court reasoned that because personal abuse, epithets and libel were "not in any proper sense communication of information or opinion safeguarded by the Constitution, ... [their] punishment as a criminal act would raise no question under that instrument."[98] Until its ruling in *Sullivan*, the Court maintained that libel played "no essential part in the exposition of ideas"[99] and so did not fall "within the area of constitutionally protected speech."[100] Yet, in its 1964 decision in *Sullivan*, the Court found the Constitution did protect the publication of certain libels of public officials.

THE *SULLIVAN* DECISION

Justice Brennan wrote the majority opinion in the Supreme Court's unanimous decision in *New York Times v. Sullivan* reversing the lower courts. The opinion cast aside Sullivan's argument that the case did not raise First Amendment concerns because it involved

---

[93]ZECHARIAH CHAFEE, FREE SPEECH IN THE UNITED STATES 18 (1941).
[94]*Id.* at 149.
[95]*See* ROSENBERG *supra* note 60, at 152.
[96]*See id.* at 177.
[97]Near v. Minnesota, 283 U.S. 697, 715 (1931).
[98]Cantwell v. Connecticut, 310 U.S. 296, 309–10 (1940).
[99]Chaplinsky v. New Hampshire, 310 U.S. 296, 571 (1942).
[100]Beauharnais v. Illinois, 343 U.S. 250, 266 (1952).

paid commercial speech that did not warrant constitutional safeguards and flatly rejected the common law standard of strict liability for political libel.[101] Instead, the Court concluded, public officials can prevail in a libel suit only if they establish, with "convincing clarity," that the libel was published with knowledge of its falsity or with reckless disregard for the truth.[102]

Writing in concurrence, Justices Black and Arthur Goldberg argued that the First Amendment required more—that it posed an absolute ban to the award of libel damages for citizens' criticism of the official conduct of public officials.[103] But the majority did not embrace this sweeping principle. Instead, it extended the "actual malice" standard to media defendants.[104] In so doing, at least one observer says, the Court "not only ignored the clear-and-present-danger rationale followed in *Beauharnais v. Illinois*,[105] but all other traditional First-Amendment tests."[106]

The Court's decision in *Sullivan* rested less on established tests and precedents than on broad First Amendment principles and goals. Drawing on the lessons of history, Justice Brennan wrote that the central meaning and purpose of the First Amendment clearly was to advance "debate on public issues [that] should be uninhibited, robust and wide open, and that it may well include vehement, caustic and sometimes unpleasantly sharp attacks on government and public officials."[107] Libel laws that chilled political criticism, curbed "the vigor ... [and] the variety of public debate," encouraged media self-censorship and violated the "profound national commitment" to unfettered, energetic exchange of ideas embodied in the First Amendment, Brennan wrote.[108] Such libel laws violate the Constitution because they fail to protect the "breathing space" free expression needs to survive.[109] "Any other conclusion," Brennan wrote, "would discourage newspapers from carrying 'editorial advertise-

---

[101]376 U.S. 254, 266 (1964).

[102]*Id.* at 285–86. *See also* White v. Nichols, 44 U.S. 266 (1845) (in which the Court first required a defendant to prove "actual malice" to overcome the immunity of a privileged libelous communication).

[103]*Id.* at 293 (Black, J., concurring); *id.* at 298 (Goldberg, J., concurring).

[104]The Court previously had required a showing of actual malice to overcome qualified privilege of official government communications or to sustain payment of exemplary damages against state officials. *See* Scott v. Donald, 165 U.S. 58, 86 (1897); White v. Nichols, 44 U.S. 266 (1845).

[105]343 U.S. at 253, 266 (1952).

[106]ROSENBERG, *supra* note 60, at 245.

[107]376 U.S. at 270.

[108]*Id.* at 278–79.

[109]*Id.* at 271–72.

ments' of this type, and so might shut off an important outlet for the promulgation of information and ideas."[110]

THIN PRECEDENT IN THE COURT'S *SULLIVAN* DECISION

In *New York Times v. Sullivan*, the Court faced the question of whether the Constitution imposed any "limitations upon the power to award damages for libel of a public official."[111] Despite "175 years of settled legal practice" in the area,[112] the Court said its decision was "compelled by neither precedent nor policy."[113] Thus, writing on a clean slate, the Court had virtually unfettered discretion to select the legal foundations of its decision. Far from being arbitrary or capricious, a court's selection of legal context reflects the meaning the case holds for the members of the court.[114] The choice of legal foundations also often is determinative of outcome and is, thus, fertile ground for judicial realism and judicial activism.

A plain reading of the facts in *Sullivan* would characterize the case as a libel suit brought by a public official whose official actions were caustically but, at best, indirectly criticized in a paid newspaper advertisement about desegregation in the South that contained some errors. It is noteworthy, therefore, that in deciding the case the Supreme Court called centuries of libel jurisprudence "'mere labels' of state law"[115] and relied at least as heavily on its prior restraint, contempt and offensive speech precedents as it did upon its prior libel decisions.

Such choices make sense when the First Amendment is conceived as a tool to advance more fundamental social objectives. Justice Brennan believed in the functional value of the First Amendment. To him, free speech was worthy of protection because it improved society by enhancing the search for truth, the interplay of ideas and the processes of democracy.[116] The Court's choices also make sense when the case is viewed through the constitutional prism of equal opportunity and treatment for all members of society.

---

[110]*Id.* at 266.

[111]*Id.* at 268.

[112]ARCHIBALD COX, THE ROLE OF THE SUPREME COURT IN AMERICAN GOVERNMENT 38 (1976).

[113]376 U.S. at 269.

[114]*See* ALAN GARFINKEL, FORMS OF EXPLANATION (1981); Matthew D. Bunker & Emily Erickson, *The Jurisprudence of Precision: Contrast Space and Narrow Tailoring*, 6 COMM. L. & POL'Y 259 (2001).

[115]376 U.S. at 269 (citing NAACP v. Button, 371 U.S. 415, 429 (1963)).

[116]*See* W. WAT HOPKINS, MR. JUSTICE BRENNAN AND FREEDOM OF EXPRESSION 84 (1991).

Libel

In *Sullivan*, the Court referred only in passing to its own defamation precedents in *Schenectady Union Publishing v. Sweeney*,[117] *Beauharnais v. Illinois*,[118] *Barr v. Mateo*[119] and *Farmers Educational and Cooperative Union v. WDAY*.[120] These cases rely on legal tradition and generally support damages for libel. Their central holdings generally contradict the logic of *Sullivan* and are roundly ignored. Thus, in referencing *Schenectady Union Publishing*, the *Sullivan* decision neglected to mention that the Court's *per curiam* ruling had let stand an appeals court finding that "freedom of speech is, as it always has been, freedom to tell the truth and comment fairly upon facts and not a license to spread damaging falsehoods in the guise of news gathering and its dissemination."[121] The case involved a libel suit brought against a Schenectady, N.Y., newspaper by an Ohio representative to Congress after the newspaper printed a press release that claimed the congressman opposed the appointment of a judge because he was a naturalized citizen and a Jew.[122]

And the *Sullivan* opinion attended more to *dicta* in *Beauharnais v. Illinois* than to the Court's central holding affirming a criminal conviction for group libel of the Negro race.[123] The Court upheld an Illinois law prohibiting depraved portrayals based on class, race, color, creed or religion that exposes the group to contempt or produces riots. Justice Felix Frankfurter, writing for the majority, tied his opinion to the Court's holding in *Chaplinsky v. New Hampshire*[124] and reasoned that libelous "utterances are not ... within the area of constitutionally protected speech."[125] The decision also rested upon the theory that racist speech presented a danger to society because it would engender inter-racial violence.

Rather than rely on this central holding, the *Sullivan* majority highlighted *Beauharnais dicta* noting that punishment for libel may not "encroach[] on freedom of utterance."[126] In a sleight of hand, the *Sullivan* decision tortured the syntax and logic of a *Beauharnais* foot-

---

[117] 316 U.S. 642 (1942).
[118] 343 U.S. 250 (1952).
[119] 360 U.S. 564 (1959).
[120] 360 U.S. 525 (1959).
[121] 122 F.2d 288, 291 (2d Cir. 1941).
[122] *Id.*
[123] 343 U.S. at 261.
[124] 315 U.S. 568 (1942).
[125] *Id.* at 572.
[126] 376 U.S. at 268.

note to conclude that the case established precedent that "the right, as
well as the duty, of criticism must not be stifled."[127] Criticism of public
officials is critical, according to *Sullivan*'s interpretation of
Beauharnais, because "public men, are, as it were, public property. ...
[T]he whole doctrine of fair comment as indispensable to the democratic political process would come into play."[128] In the earlier case,
however, the statement arose not as an assertion of a right to criticize
but as a consideration that would be necessary if a hypothetical "statute sought to outlaw libels of political parties."[129]

The Court in *Sullivan* drew on an analogy between *Barr v. Mateo*,
which held that absolute privilege protects public officials' official
comments from libel, and the facts in *Sullivan* to support its constitutional analysis.[130] *Barr* reasoned that a federal official's comments
within even the outermost limits of his duties must be privileged unless actual malice is proven or else the threat of damages would "inhibit the fearless, vigorous and effective administration of policies of
government" and "dampen the ardor of all but the most resolute."[131]
Yet Justice Brennan pointed to no evidence in *Barr* that, as he said in
Sullivan, the "privilege for criticism of official conduct is appropriately analogous to the protection accorded a public official when *he* is
sued for libel by a private citizen" and should be absolute in order not
to inhibit expression or dampen the ardor of citizen-critics.[132] Similarly, in his concurrence Justice Black relies on *Barr* to conclude,
without supporting evidence, that an informed citizenry requires
"the freedom ... to applaud or to criticize the way public employees
do their jobs."[133]

The only mention of *Farmers Educational and Cooperative Union*
appeared in the concurrence by Justice Goldberg.[134] The case involved libelous statements made by a political candidate in an advertisement responding to another candidate's broadcast speech. The
Court's decision removed liability from broadcasters for libelous material contained in political advertisements on the basis that liability
would trigger an "excess of caution" in broadcasters and chill public
discussion of important public issues.[135] This potentially substantial

[127]*Id.*
[128]*Id.*
[129]*Beauharnais,* 343 U.S. 250, 264 (1952).
[130]376 U.S. at 282.
[131]360 U.S. 564, 571 (1959).
[132]376 U.S. at 282 (emphasis in original).
[133]*Id.* at 304 (Black, J., concurring).
[134]*Id.* at 300 (Goldberg, J., concurring).
[135]360 U.S. 525, 530 (1959).

precedent warranted only a fleeting comment in the opinion noting that protection from libel damages is vital to reduce the chilling effect of lawsuits and protect expression of non-media owners.[136]

Prior Restraint

Several of the Court's previous rulings limiting the power of government to impose various forms of prior restraint play a prominent role in the *Sullivan* decision. With the exception of the majority's reference to the commercial speech case, *Valentine v. Christensen*,[137] the Court used these cases to establish that prior restraints are unconstitutional. In relying on the cases to establish a First Amendment objection to curtailments of political speech, the Court failed to address the crucial distinction it long had established between prior restraints and *post hoc* punishment for abusive speech.[138] In addition, the Court again relied heavily on *dicta* and isolated phrases rather than on the central holdings of precedential decisions.

In an example of this tendency, the Court mentioned its 1942 decision in *Valentine* primarily to distinguish the commercial speech at issue in that case from the advocacy advertisement central to *Sullivan*.[139] Yet the distinction between the two is far from clear. In *Valentine*, the Court affirmed punishment under an anti-littering ban for the distribution of commercial advertising leaflets. Initially, a commercial exhibitor had used handbills to invite paying visitors to his submarine. When told the hand-outs violated city law, he printed a protest against city policy on the reverse side to evade the law. In *Valentine*, Justice William O. Douglas refused to "indulge nice appraisal based upon subtle distinctions" about whether the added commentary should remove the handbill from the realm of purely commercial speech.[140] Instead, writing for the Court, he affirmed the law and said that while government may not place undue burdens on free speech in a public forum, "the Constitution imposes no such restraint on government as respects purely commercial advertising."[141]

The Court in *Sullivan* called any reliance on *Valentine* "wholly misplaced."[142] The Court said *Valentine's* "holding was based upon the factual conclusions that the handbill was 'purely commercial ad-

---

[136]*Id.*
[137]316 U.S. 52 (1942).
[138]*See, e.g.*, Near v. Minnesota, 283 U.S. 697, 713 (1931).
[139]376 U.S. at 265.
[140]316 U.S. at 55.
[141]*Id.* at 54.
[142]376 U.S. at 265.

vertising' and that the protest against official action had been added
only to evade the ordinance."[143] In contrast, "The publication here
was not a 'commercial' advertisement in the [same] sense," the
Court concluded, because "Heed Their Rising Voices" communicated
information, opinion, grievances and protest on "matters of the highest public interest and concern."[144]

Yet the Court in *Sullivan* failed to explain why the communiqué at
issue in *Valentine* was not also an expression of grievance and protest, at the very least. Moreover, the unexplored distinction between
the nature of the speech on the handbills and the content of "Heed
Their Rising Voices" is determinative.[145] In *Sullivan*, the fact that
the libel occured in a paid advertisement is immaterial to the Court's
protection of robust political dialogue. Certainly a price promotion
for a submarine visit to which a business owner's annoyance with
city bureaucracy is affixed differs from an editorial commentary on
racism and oppression. But the Court in *Sullivan* fails to explain, or
even address, why this difference alone justifies diametrically opposed constitutional protections for the two.

Justice Brennan's majority opinion also cited Court decisions
striking down a state law prohibiting the peaceful display of red flags
associated with the American Communist Party[146] and laws banning
leafleting[147] to conclude that the First Amendment protects free political discussion to promote the security and stability of the nation[148]
and to provide a means of communication for non-publishers.[149] But
while the decisions highlighted the political value of pamphlets as
"historic weapons in the defense of liberty"[150] and "effective instru-
ments in the dissemination of opinion,"[151] neither case concluded
that the First Amendment protected the right of the disenfranchised
broadly to express their ideas.

The Court, nevertheless, relied on additional prior restraint decisions to establish fundamental First Amendment principles to apply
to libel law. For example, both the majority opinion and Justice
Goldberg's concurrence turned to *Associated Press v. United*

---

[143]*Id.* at 265–66.
[144]*Id.* at 266.
[145]*Valentine*, 316 U.S. at 52, 54.
[146]*See* Stromberg v. California, 283 U.S. 359, 369 (1931).
[147]*See* Schneider v. New Jersey, 308 U.S. 147, 164 (1939); Lovell v. Griffin , 303
U.S. 444, 452 (1938).
[148]*Sullivan*, 376 U.S. at 269, 284, 301.
[149]*Id.* at 266.
[150]*Lovell*, 303 U.S. at 452.
[151]*Schneider*, 308 U.S. at 164.

States[152] to establish that the First Amendment limits libel judgments to protect the "breathing space" necessary to the widest possible dissemination of information and the robust discussion of public officials and issues.[153] *Associated Press* actually established that the Constitution bars private monopolies that fetter free expression[154] because surely "[f]reedom of the press from governmental interference under the First Amendment does not sanction repression of that freedom by private interests."[155]

The *Sullivan* decision cited *NAACP v. Button*[156] to support its claim that public discussion of the civil rights movement was a matter of the greatest public concern. In *NAACP*, the Court held that the First Amendment prevented a state from banning attorneys from soliciting test desegregation cases. The *NAACP* opinion also held that government could not require groups to disclose their list of members and affiliates particularly when, as the Court noted, the organization was associated with an "unpopular cause" by "militant Negro[es ... that] has engendered the intense resentment and opposition of the politically dominant white community."[157]

The Court, in *NAACP,* acknowledged the importance of equal treatment under the law and the fact that "litigation may well be the sole practicable avenue open to a minority to petition for redress of grievances"[158] that "makes possible the distinctive contribution of a minority group to the ideas and beliefs of our society."[159] It also noted that the state law could too easily become a "weapon of oppression" that "could well freeze out of existence all such activity on behalf of the civil rights of Negro citizens."[160] However, the Court did not recognize any paramount importance of the civil rights movement or public discussion about it. To the contrary, the Court noted:

> That the petitioner happens to be engaged in activities of expression and association on behalf of the rights of Negro children to equal opportunity is constitutionally irrelevant to the ground of our decision. The

---

[152]326 U.S. 1, 20 (1945).

[153]376 U.S. at 271; *id.* at 298 (Goldberg, J., concurring) (citing NAACP v. Button, 371 U.S. 415, 433 (1963)).

[154]*See id.* at 266.

[155]*Associated Press,* 326 U.S. at 20.

[156]371 U.S. 415 (1963).

[157]*Id.* at 435.

[158]*Id.* at 430.

[159]*Id.* at 431.

[160]*Id.* at 436.

course of our decisions in the First Amendment area makes plain that its protections would apply as fully to those who would arouse our society against the objectives of the petitioner.[161]

Thus, although the Court handed down its decisions in *NAACP* and *Sullivan* in 1963 and 1964, at the peak of civil rights activity and violence, only *Sullivan* overtly indicates a willingness of the Court to consider the social implications of denying protection to the movement. As Justice Black noted in his concurrence, the *Sullivan* case cannot be removed from context: libel law was a means to target and eliminate the civil rights movement.[162]

The Court said *Speiser v. Randall*[163] and *NAACP* stood for the premise that the First Amendment does not condition its guarantees on a test of the truth of the ideas expressed.[164] But the question of truth was central only to the determination of who bore the burden of proof in *Speiser*, a case in which the Court invalidated a state law that conditioned tax exemptions upon the signing of an oath, swearing non-advocacy of illegal acts.[165] *Speiser* did, as Justice Brennan wrote in *Sullivan,* find that the Constitution requires government to draw clear lines between protected and unprotected speech so that speakers will not "steer far wider [than necessary] of the unlawful zone."[166]

Both the majority and Justice Goldberg referenced *Cantwell v. Connecticut*[167] and *NAACP* to establish that error and excess are inevitable in free expression and necessarily receive constitutional protection.[168] However, while *Cantwell* explicitly extended constitutional protection to false statements to assure the full religious and political debate needed in a democracy,[169] *NAACP* did not claim that "erroneous statement is inevitable ...and ... must be protected."[170] Instead, it held that the Constitution protects vigorous advocacy as well as abstract discussion.[171]

---

[161]*Id.* at 444.
[162]376 U.S. 254, 294–95 (1964) (Black, J., concurring).
[163]357 U.S. 513 (1958).
[164]376 U.S. at 271.
[165]357 U.S. at 525–26.
[166]376 U.S. at 285, 279 (quoting Speiser v. Randall, 357 U.S. 513, 526 (1958)).
[167]310 U.S. 296 (1940).
[168]376 U.S. at 271; *id.* at 305 (Goldberg, J., concurring).
[169]310 U.S. at 310.
[170]376 U.S. at 271–72.
[171]371 U.S. at 433.

Contempt

The Court in *New York Times v. Sullivan* also leaned upon its prior rulings limiting the power of judges to use contempt citations to punish extra-judicial publications. The Court relied on the quartet of cases of *Bridges v. California*,[172] *Pennekamp v. Florida*,[173] *Craig v. Harney*[174] and *Wood v. Georgia*[175] to establish the legal presumption that public officials are expected to be "men [sic] of fortitude able to thrive in a hardy climate"[176] of robust discussion and criticism.[177] In each of the four decisions, the Court had ruled that judges had failed to justify contempt citations by demonstrating that sanctioned extra-judicial comments posed a clear and present danger to the administration of justice. These cases hold that "concern for the dignity and reputation of the courts does not justify the punishment as criminal contempt of criticism of the judge."[178] However, the *Sullivan* assertion that "[i]njury to official reputation affords no more warrant for repressing speech that would otherwise be free than does factual error"[179] does not rest on these holdings. This is a new idea, and the rhetorical turn in *Sullivan* seems to broadly assert that government may not punish false statements that damage individual reputation. Yet this long had been the core doctrine of defamation law.

The *Sullivan* Court used contempt rulings to establish a history of providing constitutional protection to false speech that injured official reputations. But the cases it called upon involved neither defamatory content nor falsity. *Bridges* and *Wood* focused on statements of opinion critical of judicial performance, and the Court made no determination as to the accuracy of the criticisms.[180] The question presented in *Bridges* was not whether editorials criticizing judicial performance damaged the reputation of the judges but whether they engendered "disrespect for the judiciary,"[181] a nebulous and insufficiently substantial concern the Court said "wrongly appraises the character of American public opinion."[182] The Court reasoned that the public, well aware of the tendency to exaggerate in the heat of the

---

[172] 314 U.S. 252 (1941).
[173] 328 U.S. 331 (1946).
[174] 331 U.S. 367 (1947).
[175] 370 U.S. 375 (1962).
[176] *Times v. Sullivan*, 376 U.S. 254, 273 (1964).
[177] *Id.* at 273. *See also id.* at 298 (Goldberg, J., concurring).
[178] *Id.* at 272–73.
[179] *Id.* at 272.
[180] *Wood*, 370 U.S. at 376; *Bridges*, 314 U.S. 252, 266 n.11 (1941).
[181] 314 U.S. at 270.
[182] *Id.*

moment, was capable of differentiating hyperbole from fact.[183] *Bridges* established strong protection for exuberant and pointed criticism of judges, but it hardly dictated untrammeled First Amendment protection to "speak one's mind," as Brennan wrote in *Sullivan*.[184]

Similar difficulties arise from the Court's application of *Pennekamp*[185] and *Craig*.[186] *Craig* involved news coverage that did "not ... [demonstrate] good reporting"[187] and included "intemperate," "unfair" "inaccuracies" and "omissions,"[188] but the Court did not find the stories to be objectively and demonstrably false. Similarly, although the Supreme Court in *Sullivan* characterized the newspaper editorials and cartoons impugning the court in *Pennekamp* as "half-truths" and "misinformation,"[189] the Court in *Pennekamp* said only that the publications were "inaccurate" and did not tell "the full and objective truth."[190] The *Sullivan* opinion's transformation of these statements into blanket constitutional protection for false statements about public officials belies a willingness to encourage critical voices.

Objectionable Speech

Finally, the Court in *Sullivan* selected portions of disparate decisions dealing with a variety of forms of objectionable speech—illegal advocacy, fighting words, caustic public commentary and obscenity—to claim constitutional protection for libel. The Court did not assert parallels between these types of expression and libel—such as they all cause harm—but instead claimed these cases limned the only acceptable exclusions to a virtually unfettered right to speak caustically, vehemently and offensively.

The cases themselves provide a somewhat less consistent or expansive position on protected expression. Only through hindsight, for example, can *Abrams v. United States*[191] be said to support the constitutional invalidity of the Espionage or Sedition Acts.[192]

---

[183]*Id.* at 278.
[184]376 U.S. at 269. *See also id.* at 298 (Goldberg, J., concurring).
[185]328 U.S. 331 (1946).
[186]331 U.S. 367 (1947).
[187]*Id.* at 374.
[188]*Id.* at 376.
[189]376 U.S. at 272, 273.
[190]328 U.S. at 344.
[191]250 U.S. 616 (1919).
[192]*See* 376 U.S. at 276.

Abrams, of course, is well known for Justice Oliver Wendell Holmes' eloquent dissenting opinion elaborating on the marketplace of ideas theory of free speech.[193] In contrast, the Court in *Abrams* upheld espionage convictions for the printing and distribution of anti-draft leaflets.

Nor is it clear that, as the *Sullivan* decision asserts, the decision in *Whitney v. California*[194] affirming conviction for union activities stands for the principle that repression breeds instability.[195] It was in a stirring concurrence, not the majority opinion, that Justice Louis Brandeis expressed the core value of protecting the broadest possible range of free speech.[196] And it demands a rather creative reading for the Court in *Sullivan* to assert that *Whitney* established a nearly absolute privilege to criticize government.[197] In fact, while both *Whitney* and *Terminiello v. Chicago*[198] present rousing endorsements of the founders' belief in the fundamental value of free speech, *Whitney* says nothing about immunity from damages for citizen-critics and expressly rejects an absolute right to speak.[199]

Decisions in *De Jonge v. Oregon,*[200] *Chaplinsky v. New Hampshire*[201] and *Terminiello* help the Court in *Sullivan* define categories of offensive expression protected by the First Amendment but say virtually nothing about libel because they recognize defamation as a category of its own.[202] These cases establish constitutional protection for stirring advocacy, caustic commentary and upsetting speech that does not qualify as incitement or fighting words; they also clearly hold that when speech crosses the line and causes proscribable harms, it may be prosecuted.[203] These cases, therefore, offer almost no insight into the constitutionally correct treatment of defamation. It is only through the prism of the violent racial clashes in the South in the 1960s that one can follow the *Sullivan* Court's correlations between an arguably libelous full-page advocacy ad in a

---

[193]250 U.S. at 630 (Holmes, J., dissenting).

[194]274 U.S. 357 (1927).

[195]376 U.S. at 301 (citing *Whitney,* 274 U.S. at 375).

[196]274 U.S. at 375–77 (Brandeis, J., concurring).

[197]376 U.S. at 282 (citing *Whitney,* 274 U.S. at 375).

[198]337 U.S. 1 (1949).

[199]274 U.S. at 371 (noting that "the Constitution does not confer an absolute right to speak, without responsibility, whatever one may choose, or an unrestricted and unbridled license giving immunity for every possible use of language").

[200]299 U.S. 353 (1937).

[201]315 U.S. 568 (1942).

[202]376 U.S. at 296 (Black, J., concurring) (citing *Chaplinsky,* 315 U.S. 568).

[203]*See, e.g., DeJonge,* 299 U.S. at 365.

remote newspaper and the controversial comments of a speaker at a political rally that arouse a hostile and violent crowd outside.[204]

The trio of obscenity cases mentioned by the Court in *Sullivan* might provide equally insubstantial legal support for the decision. However, passing references to *Roth v. United States,*[205] *Smith v. California*[206] and *Bantam Books v. Sullivan*[207] do more than distinguish unprotected obscenity from protected speech. First, the Court uses the cases to support its contention that payment alone does not automatically establish the commercial nature of speech.[208] Second, the cases serve to affirm that civil penalties may pose "greater hazards" to free speech than does criminal law.[209] Finally, the Court uses the cases to assert that as *scienter* is required to hold booksellers liable for obscenity, so guilty knowledge should be required for libel damages.[210]

The Court employed an extremely loose, postmodern interpretation of these cases to support its central *Sullivan* reasoning. In addition, the Court reframed the issue before it from the application of libel law to the right of citizens freely to criticize government. In so doing, the Court shifted the decision's rationale away from libel precedent and toward the justices' perception of the "true" meaning of the First Amendment. Legal scholar Jerome Barron has called the Court's ruling "bewildering. It is an example of judicial law making"[211] in which the Court used its own vision of the Constitution to "soften" libel law "to encourage newspapers to be more adventurous and daring on matters of public concern."[212]

The decision is less bewildering if one focuses on Justice Brennan's strong tendency to view free speech as a means to advance other important societal interests. In one of his last opinions for the Court, Justice Brennan demonstrated his continued commitment to equal opportunity and a functionalist reading of free speech. Writing for the majority in 1990, Brennan concluded that minority broadcast ownership preferences advanced, rather than violated, the First Amendment because they served the Constitution's primary free speech objectives.[213] Accepting that the FCC's rules disadvantaged

---

[204]376 U.S. at 270 (referencing *Terminiello,* 337 U.S. at 4).

[205]354 U.S. 476 (1957).

[206]361 U.S. 147 (1959).

[207]372 U.S. 58 (1963).

[208]376 U.S. at 266.

[209]*Id.* at 278.

[210]*Id.*

[211]BARRON, *supra* note 4, at 11.

[212]*Id.* at 340.

[213]*See* Metro Broad. v. FCC, 497 U.S. 547 (1990).

some non-minority candidates, Brennan nonetheless found the program constitutional because

> A broadcasting industry with representative minority participation will produce more variation and diversity than will one whose ownership is drawn from a single racially and ethnically homogeneous group. The predictive judgment about the overall result of minority entry into broadcasting is not a rigid assumption about how minority owners will behave in every case but rather … [a] conclusion … that greater admission of minorities would contribute, on average, to the robust exchange of ideas.[214]

IMMEDIATE REACTIONS TO THE RULING

Leaders of news organizations praised the Supreme Court ruling in *New York Times v. Sullivan* but carefully avoided discussing its connections to issues of race. Herbert Bruckner, president of the American Society of Newspaper Editors, said the Court had revived "the most fundamental of our liberties. This is the right to oppose the conduct of public officials with outspoken vigor."[215] Creed C. Black, who chaired the American Society of Newspaper Editors' Freedom of Information Committee, said, "By forcefully restating the right to criticize the conduct of public officials, the court has protected and reinforced the traditional role of the press as a critic of government and an open forum for the exchange of ideas and opinions on public affairs."[216] V. M. Newton Jr., the former Freedom of Information chairman for Sigma Delta Chi (now the Society of Professional Journalists), declared: "It took the Anglo Saxons 400 years to win the right to criticize the politicians, and this decision simply cements that right."[217] None of the published comments referred to the content of the *Times* ad or the fact that it dealt with institutionalized oppression not of Anglo Saxons but of Americans of African descent.

The *Times*'s own editorial the day after the ruling fairly described the advertisement and its context. But without referring to other then-pending lawsuits against the paper and a reporter, the editorial asserted: "It is an increasingly important function of the press—and must be, if the press is to live up to its proper responsibilities—to en-

---

[214]*Id.* at 579 (internal quotations omitted).
[215]*Editors Hail High Court's Libel Ruling,* EDITOR & PUBLISHER, Mar. 21, 1964, at 54.
[216]*Id.*
[217]*Id.*

courage the free give-and-take of ideas and, above all, to be free to express criticism of public officials and public policies."[218] The
Washington Post's editorial that same day made no reference to the
content of advertisement and sidestepped the racial issue, describing
the other defendants as "four Alabama citizens." The *Post,* while
praising the Court's support for public discussion of issues, ended
the editorial on a cautionary note:

> Among private citizens and the media which serve them, these opin-
> ions will be read with a new sense of the responsibility that our system
> imposes upon citizens themselves and the media through which they
> speak, for fairness and restraint and for conformity to the truth, in the
> presentation of public issues. As the area of freedom of public utter-
> ance, in our society, is great, so is the responsibility to use that freedom
> with care and discretion.[219]

Anthony Lewis, who covered the Supreme Court arguments in the
Sullivan case, observed that the *Sullivan* suit was not the only instance in which southern officials tried to use libel law to stifle reporting about race relations. In fact, a brief to the Court submitted
for Ralph Abernathy said the *Sullivan* lawsuit represented a "further refinement" of "a concerted, calculated program to carry out a
policy of punishing, intimidating and silencing all who criticize and
seek to change [the South's] notorious political system of enforced
segregation."[220] In the decision itself, the Court also commented that
pending libel suits intended to punish or discourage media coverage
of civil rights totaled $6 million.[221] "The *Times* fortunately had the
money and the patience to take the case to the Supreme Court, which
found the award unconstitutional," Lewis wrote. "But there were
many similar cases in the South—against other newspapers, wire
services, television networks—and they continued. They had been
brought not really in the hope of collecting any damages but to discourage aggressive race-relations reporting by harassment."[222]
A major target of the harassing lawsuits was Lewis' colleague at
the *Times*, Harrison Salisbury, who had been sued for stories he
wrote about the racial conflict in Birmingham in 1960.[223] Salisbury

---

[218]Editorial, *Free Press and Free People*, N.Y. TIMES, Mar. 10, 1964, at 36.
[219]Editorial, *Criticizing Public Servants*, WASH. POST, Mar. 10, 1964, at A16.
[220]Quoted in ROSENBERG, *supra* note 60, at 237.
[221]376 U.S. 254, 278 (1964). *See also* ROSENBERG, *supra* note 60, at 236.
[222]LEWIS, *supra* note 52, at 294.
[223]*See* SALISBURY, *supra* note 43, at 382.

saw firsthand the effect of the Court's ruling in the *Sullivan* case. Noting that news organizations faced libel actions totaling almost $300 million by March of 1964, Salisbury wrote in his memoir: "Had the Supreme Court's verdict gone in the other direction, the burden of censorship and official intimidation might well have enabled the 'southern judicial strategy' to prolong lawlessness as a final barrier against the revolution in civil rights."[224] The libel suit filed against Salisbury and the *Times* by T. Eugene Connor, police commissioner of Birmingham, was not dismissed until 1966, when the Fifth Circuit Court of Appeals concluded that Connor could not collect damages because, under the *Sullivan* rule, he had failed to show the *Times* acted with reckless disregard for the truth. The ruling, Salisbury wrote, "stripped Connor and the whole range of southern officials of the ability to intimidate the press through the power of the purse and the libel law."[225] Smolla summed up the impact of post-*Sullivan* news coverage: "The movement needed the *New York Times*, it needed the infant news broadcasts of CBS, NBC, and ABC, it needed the constant, virile, unsuppressed attention of a national press, in order to appeal to a national conscience."[226]

Lewis drew a similar conclusion at a February 2004 conference marking the fortieth anniversary of the court's ruling. The Court's decision not only introduced a new doctrine of libel law, Lewis said, "[I]t gave new meaning, a broader meaning, to the constitutional protection of free speech and freedom of the press. And it removed a serious threat to the civil-rights movement whose success in the 1960s so greatly changed this country."[227] First Amendment attorney Floyd Abrams offered a parallel assessment in May 2004: "Without the ruling in the Sullivan case, all reporting on the civil rights movement in the South would have been constricted in a fashion unrecognizable today."[228]

Other commentators saw impact beyond civil rights coverage. Archibald Cox, best known as the special prosecutor during Water-

---

[224]*Id.* at 388–89. Justice Black's opinion refers to eleven libel suits against the *Times* seeking $5.6 million and five similar lawsuits against CBS seeking $1.7 million in damages. 376 U.S. at 295 (Black, J., concurring)). Lewis's account of the decision in the *Times* refers to Alabama libel suits against his paper for $5 million and against CBS for $1.5 million. Anthony Lewis, *High Court Curbs Public Officials in Libel Actions,* N.Y. TIMES, Mar. 10, 1964, at 1.

[225]*Id.* at 390.

[226]SMOLLA, *supra* note 82, at 42.

[227]J. Balloch, *Ruling on Libel Uniquely U.S.,* KNOXVILLE NEWS-SENTINEL, Feb. 28, 2004, at B1.

[228]E-mail message from Floyd Abrams, Cahill Gordon & Reindel, to Kenton Bird, University of Idaho (May 23, 2004, 11:12 a.m. PDT) (on file with authors).

gate, saw in *Sullivan* and subsequent rulings, greater latitude for the reporting on wrongdoing in government. Writing in 1975, just months after President Richard M. Nixon resigned, he observed: "The American press is now in a greatly improved position to pursue investigations into corruption and other abuses of public position. It seems likely that much of the early reporting upon Watergate and related scandals would not have been attempted under the older [pre-*Sullivan*] law."[229]

Commenting on the twentieth anniversary of *Sullivan,* law professor Ellen Solender concluded that the ruling was vital to the continued existence of the *New York Times* and other "respected sources of information" critical of segregation.[230] She said:

> If the national press could not safely report the activities of officials who were engaged in practices which denied blacks their basic civil rights, these wrongs might never have been corrected. When there is a tyranny of the majority in a particular locale, other Americans need to be informed, so that they can help the minority to gain their rights. ... The U.S. Supreme Court understood that and so could not affirm the decision of the Alabama Supreme Court.[231]

CONCLUSION

The Court's decision in *New York Times v. Sullivan* was a product of the times. No single, signature event prompted the ruling. Rather, as the advertisement itself was a response to and reflection of the felony tax evasion charges pending against Dr. Martin Luther King, Jr., and the recent introduction of sit-in protests to the civil rights repertoire, so the Supreme Court's ruling both reflected and reinforced a growing public consensus in favor of racial equality. The willingness of the Court in *New York Times v. Sullivan* to "jettison[] older First-Amendment formulas" radically changed the law of libel and "eliminate[d] yet another weapon in the arsenal of segregationists in the South."[232] For legal realists, the decision "showed that in defamation law, as in other areas of law, legal rules could be adjusted to fit the needs of the particular cause at hand."[233] At best, the law was little more than a cob-

---

[229]COX, *supra* note 112, at 40.
[230]Ellen K. Sollender, *What If?,* COMM. LAWYER, Summer 1984, at 23.
[231]*Id.*
[232]ROSENBERG, *supra* note 60, at 246, 243.
[233]*Id.* at 233.

bled system of "fragmentation and contingency."[234] For critical scholars, the novel, new vision of the Court corrected a significant imbalance in the marketplace of ideas[235] as it prevented public officials from using libel law to put "a handicap upon the freedoms of expression"[236] and eliminated "the pall of fear and timidity [libel law had] imposed upon those who would give voice to public criticism."[237] The protective shadow cast by the umbrella of *New York Times v. Sullivan* "expanded ... news coverage [and] helped to create a milieu in which fundamental social problems became subjects of more intensive media–and ultimately public–concern."[238]

But within a decade, scholar S. Prakash Sethi would express alarm that the paid messages the *Sullivan* Court lauded as the essence of free speech posed a very real "danger of ... squeezing out alternative viewpoints from the public communication space and thereby impairing public access to information."[239] Such is the law of unintended consequences. By the mid-1980s, though, Rodney Smolla worried that an explosion of libel suits might "chill the courage of the press, and in that chill all of us suffer, for it threatens to make the press slavishly safe, pouring out a centrist, spiceless paste of consensus thought."[240]

Clearly, *New York Times v. Sullivan* changed libel law and embodied the judicial realism and social activism many observers condemn in the Warren Court. It also protected the financially struggling civil rights movement from crippling financial damages and encouraged the media to provide greater coverage and more caustic criticism of politicians and political and social debate over segregation. But, as legal scholar Paul Kahn has noted, the Court cannot and did not change the face or the nature of the nation:

> Judicial decisions do not in and of themselves reorder and reorganize society. Courts do not make us who we are. At best, they are a fair reflection of our values and beliefs, with all the tensions that we experience among these norms. ... [They are], therefore, no less problematic than our own history.[241]

---

[234]*Id.*
[235]*See* BARRON, *supra* note 4, at 10.
[236]*Times v. Sullivan*, 376 U.S. 254, 266 (1964).
[237]*Id.* at 278.
[238]ROSENBERG, *supra* note 60, at 246.
[239]SETHI, *supra* note 7, at 4.
[240]SMOLLA, *supra* note 82, at 257.
[241]PAUL W. KAHN, THE CULTURAL STUDY OF LAW 136 (1999).

FROM *SULLIVAN* TO *NIKE*: WILL THE NOBLE PURPOSE OF THE LANDMARK FREE SPEECH CASE BE SUBVERTED TO IMMUNIZE FALSE ADVERTISING?

ROBERT L. KERR*

In deciding not to rule in Nike, Inc. v. Kasky, *the Supreme Court of the United States passed up an ideal opportunity to answer an urgent question that derives from two legacies of* New York Times v. Sullivan: *When speech implicates both the commercial speech doctrine and the political speech doctrine, how should that speech be assessed in terms of First Amendment protection? This analysis focuses upon the essential principles emphasized in* Sullivan's *landmark assessment of the societal value in protecting some false speech in the discussion of public issues. Concerns over the* Nike *case's implications for corporate expression must be weighed against the societal interest in preventing false commercial speech from being immunized by attaching it to a public issue.*

The most anticlimactic moment in the term of the Supreme Court of the United States that ended in June 2003 came when the justices announced that they would not, after all, decide the momentous First Amendment question presented by *Nike, Inc. v. Kasky*.[1] The Court had granted *certiorari* in the case six months earlier, accepted a total of thirty-four briefs (thirty-one from *amici curiae*), and heard oral arguments. On the last day of the term, however, it handed down a one-sentence, unsigned order dismissing the writ of *certio-*

---

*Assistant Professor, Gaylord College of Journalism and Mass Communication, University of Oklahoma.

[1]123 S. Ct. 2554 (2003).

rari as improvidently granted. A concurring opinion by Justice John Paul Stevens, joined by two other justices, attributed the dismissal to procedural problems that would make adjudication by the high Court premature,[2] but those assertions were challenged at length in a dissenting opinion by Justice Stephen Breyer.[3]

The facts of the case had presented the Court with what appeared to be an ideal opportunity to provide an answer to a question that has snowballed in significance ever since the Court opened the door to First Amendment protection for commercial speech in *New York Times Co. v. Sullivan.*[4] Over the four decades since that pronouncement, the activities of courts, regulators and commercial speakers have repeatedly tested the nature and extent of the holding, producing a commercial speech doctrine that requires laws restricting advertising to survive an intermediate level of scrutiny.[5] Yet, a doctrine that demands restrictions on political speech must survive the most rigorous level of constitutional scrutiny is also grounded in the way the Court articulated its ruling in *Sullivan*—declaring the fullest protection for speech involving "debate on public issues."[6] The question at the heart of the *Nike* case derives from the crossroads of those two *Sullivan* legacies: When speech potentially implicates both the commercial speech doctrine and the political speech doctrine, how should the speech be assessed in terms of First Amendment protection? Answering such a difficult and momentous question requires returning to *Sullivan* and deeply considering how the Court's fundamental purpose and reasoning can be applied to resolve the current doctrinal clash that its landmark decision set in motion forty years ago.

The speech at issue in the *Nike* case involved a public relations and advertising campaign launched by Nike, Inc., in response to allegations of unsafe and abusive working conditions in factories where its athletic shoes and apparel are manufactured.[7] Mark Kasky, one of several activists working to pressure the multinational corporation to improve the allegedly substandard working conditions, sued Nike in 1998 for unfair and deceptive practices under California's Unfair Competition Law[8] and False Advertising Law,[9] alleging the commu-

---

[2]*Id.* at 2555 (Stevens, J., concurring).

[3]*Id.* at 2560–69 (Breyer, J., dissenting).

[4]376 U.S. 254, 265–66 (1964).

[5]*See* Central Hudson Gas and Elec. Corp. v. Pub. Serv. Comm'n, 447 U.S. 557 (1980); Virginia State Bd. of Pharmacy v. Virginia Citizens Consumer Council, 425 U.S. 748 (1976).

[6]376 U.S. at 270.

[7]Kasky v. Nike, Inc., 45 P.3d 243, 247–48 (Cal. 2002).

[8]Cal. Bus. & Prof. Code Ann. § 17200 et seq. (West 1997).

[9]*Id.* at § 17500 et seq.

nications campaign made false and misleading statements.[10] The case reached the California Supreme Court on the question of whether the Nike messages were subject to regulation under California's commercial speech laws, as Kasky contended, or were protected as political speech on a subject of public debate, as Nike maintained. The California court ruled for Kasky,[11] and Nike appealed to the Supreme Court.[12]

Scholars have criticized the effort to maintain a distinction between commercial and noncommercial speech in terms of First Amendment Protection;[13] articulated arguments for maintaining a subordinate status for commercial speech in First Amendment jurisprudence;[14] or embraced a middle, less dichotomous approach to the

---

[10]45 P.3d at 247, 249.

[11]*Id.* at 262–63.

[12]Nike, Inc. v. Kasky, 537 U.S. 1009 (2003) (cert. granted).

[13]*See, e.g.*, Leo Bogart, *Freedom to Know or Freedom to Say?*, 71 TEX. L. REV. 815 (1993); R. H. Coase, *Advertising and Free Speech*, 6 J. LEGAL STUD. 1 (1977); Michael W. Field, *On Tap, 44 Liquormart, Inc. v. Rhode Island: Last Call For The Commercial Speech Doctrine*, ROGER WILLIAMS U. L. REV. 57 (1996); Daniel Halberstam, *Commercial Speech, Professional Speech, and the Constitutional Status of Social Institutions*, 147 U. PA. L. REV. 771 (1999); Alex Kozinski & Stuart Banner, *The Anti-History and Pre-History of Commercial Speech*, 71 TEX. L. REV.747 (1993); Alex Kozinski & Stuart Banner, *Who's Afraid of Commercial Speech*, 76 VA. L. REV. 627 (1990); Martin H. Redish, *First Amendment Theory and the Demise of the Commercial Speech Distinction: The Case of the Smoking Controversy*, 24 N. KY. L. REV. 553 (1997); Martin H. Redish, *The Value of Free Speech*, 130 U. PA. L. REV. 591, 630–35 (1982); Rodney A. Smolla, *Information, Imagery, and the First Amendment: A Case for Expansive Protection of Commercial Speech*, 71 TEX. L. REV. 777 (1993); Kathleen M. Sullivan, *Cheap Spirits, Cigarettes, and Free Speech: The Implications of 44 Liquormart*, 1996 SUP. CT. REV. 123; Brian J. Waters, *A Doctrine in Disarray: Why the First Amendment Demands the Abandonment of the Central Hudson Test for Commercial Speech*, 27 SETON HALL L. REV. 1626 (1997);

[14]*See, e.g.*, C. Edwin Baker, *Commercial Speech: A Problem in the Theory of Freedom*, 62 IOWA L. REV. 1 (1976); C. Edwin Baker, *Realizing Self-Realization: Corporate Political Expenditures and Redish's "The Value of Free Speech,"* 130 U. PA. L. REV. 646 (1982); Vincent Blasi, *The Pathological Perspective and the First Amendment*, 85 COLUM. L. REV. 449 (1985); Lillian R. BeVier, *The First Amendment and Political Speech: An Inquiry into the Substance and Limits of Principle*, 30 STAN. L. REV. 299 (1978); Ronald K.L. Collins & David M. Skover, *Commerce and Communication*, 71 TEX. L. REV. 697 (1993); Ronald K.L. Collins & David M. Skover, *The Psychology of First Amendment Scholarship: A Reply*, 71 TEX. L. REV. 819 (1993); Thomas H. Jackson & John Calvin Jeffries, Jr., *Commercial Speech: Economic Due Process and the First Amendment*, 65 VA. L. REV. 1 (1979); Sut Jhally, *Commercial Culture, Collective Values, and the Future*, 71 TEX. L. REV. 805, 809 (1993); Bruce Ledewitz, *Corporate Advertising's Democracy*, 12 B.U. PUB. INT'L. L.J. 389 (2003); R. Moon, *Lifestyle Advertising and Classical Freedom of Expression Doctrine*, 36 MCGILL L.J. 76 (1991); Tamara R. Piety, *"Merchants of Discontent": An Exploration of the Psychology of Advertising, Addiction, and the Implications for Commercial Speech*, 25 SEATTLE U. L. REV. 377 (2001); Robert Post, *The Constitutional Status of Commercial Speech*, 48 UCLA L. REV. 1 (2000).

question.[15] Scholars have contended that the California court's decision in *Kasky v. Nike, Inc.* will bar corporations from speaking publicly on issues of concern and have criticized the Supreme Court for
its failure to decide the case in favor of Nike.[16] The body of literature
issued to date in the wake of the case has focused on concern for the
implications of the case for corporations. Amber McGovern wrote
that the California Supreme Court should not have "taken a paternalistic approach towards protecting the public against potential
false or misleading speech" because "corporations should not be re-
stricted from speaking their mind because they are economically involved."[17] Michelle Dobrusin declared that the California ruling will
leave corporations "unable to defend themselves without fear of aggressive and unmerciful prosecution."[18] Victoria Dizik Teremenko
predicted that the decision means "corporate attorneys will advise
their corporate clients not to speak at all if they are at risk of being
sued every time they may answer a public concern."[19] J. Wesley
Earnhardt concluded that "[b]ecause nearly all corporations or businesses of any kind will likely fall under the broad umbrella of the California test, corporations will have an incentive to remain silent on
important political and business related issues."[20]

This article considers the issues involved in the *Nike* case from a different perspective: the broader context of the *Sullivan* legacy and its
landmark justification of the societal value in protecting *some* false

---

[15]*See, e.g.*, Ronald A. Cass, *Commercial Speech, Constitutionalism, Collective
Choice*, 56 U. CIN. L. REV. 1317 (1988); Edward J. Eberle, *Practical Reason: The
Commercial Speech Paradigm*, 42 CASE W. RES. L. REV. 411 (1992); Daniel Hays
Lowenstein, *"Too Much Puff": Persuasion, Paternalism, and Commercial Speech*,
56 U. CIN. L. REV. 1205 (1988); Frederick Schauer, *Categories and the First Amendment: A Play in Three Acts*, 34 VAND. L. REV. 265 (1981); Frederick Schauer, *Commercial Speech and the Architecture of the First Amendment*, 56 U. CIN. L. REV. 1181
(1988); Steven Shiffrin, *The First Amendment and Economic Regulation: Away
from a General Theory of the First Amendment*, 78 NW. U. L. REV. 1212 (1983); Nat
Stern, *In Defense of the Imprecise Definition of Commercial Speech*, 58 MD. L. REV.
55 (1999).

[16]*See* Michelle Dobrusin, *Crass Commercialism: Is it Public Debate or Sheer
Profit? The Controversy of Kasky v. Nike*, 24 WHITTIER L. REV. 1139 (2003); J. Wes-
ley Earnhardt, *Nike, Inc. v. Kasky: A Golden Opportunity to Define Commercial
Speech—Why Wouldn't the Supreme Court Finally "Just Do It™"?*, 82 N.C. L. REV.
797 (2004); Amber McGovern, *Kasky v. Nike, Inc.: A Reconsideration of the Com-
mercial Speech Doctrine*, 12 DEPAUL-LCA J. ART & ENT. L. 333 (2002); Victoria
Dizik Teremenko, *Corporate Speech Under Fire: Has Nike Finally Done It?*, 2
DEPAUL BUS. & COMM. L.J. 207 (2003).

[17]McGovern, *supra* note 16, at 333, 346.

[18]Dobrusin, *supra* note 16, at 1166.

[19]Teremenko, *supra* note 16, at 244.

[20]Earnhardt, *supra* note 16, at 807.

speech in discussion of public issues when doing so serves a greater good. Do the implications of the *Nike* case justify extending First Amendment protection to *all* false commercial speech that includes any discussion of a public issue? The *Nike* case brought that question front and center. The falsity that Kasky alleged in Nike's communication campaign has not been established in a court of law, because that issue was never assessed in the California litigation. The California Supreme Court considered only whether the speech in question should be considered commercial or noncommercial at trial for consideration of First Amendment protection.[21] Because false commercial speech receives no constitutional protection,[22] that court's ruling meant that a crucial issue at trial would have been whether the statements in question were false or misleading. Under California statutes, advertising is subject to misdemeanor punishment if it is "untrue or misleading, and ... is known, or which by the exercise of reasonable care should be known, to be untrue or misleading."[23] The case never reached trial, however, because three months after the Supreme Court declined to decide the appeal, Nike announced that the company and Kasky had settled the case out of court.[24] Thus, the *Nike* case itself will not be returning to the Court. Nevertheless, given the stakes and intense interest in the question, it seems likely another case will present the issue in a manner that will ultimately make its way back to the nation's highest court for resolution.

Through analysis of *Sullivan* and commercial speech case law, with emphasis on the Supreme Court's First Amendment holdings and rationale concerning falsity in advertising, this article asserts that *Sullivan* still offers relevant context for considering the critical question presented by *Nike*. The concerns expressed by scholars over the implications for corporate expression must be weighed against the societal interest in preventing corporations from immunizing false commercial speech by attaching it to a public issue.[25] From that perspective, as will be discussed, the California Supreme Court's decision is consistent with the *Sullivan* Court's effort to protect political speech, without denying that protection arbitrarily because of the

[21]45 P.3d 243, 262 (Cal. 2002).

[22]*See, e.g.,* Central Hudson Gas and Elec. Corp. v. Pub. Serv. Comm'n, 447 U.S. 557, 563 (1980); Virginia State Bd. of Pharmacy v. Virginia Citizens Consumer Council, 425 U.S. 748, 776–777 (1976) (Stewart, J., concurring).

[23]Cal. Bus. & Prof. Code Ann. § 17500 et seq. (West 1997).

[24]*See* Adam Liptak, *Nike Move Ends Case Over Firms' Free Speech*, N.Y. Times, Sept. 13, 2003, at A8.

[25]*See* Bolger v. Youngs Drug Products, 463 U.S. 60, 67–68 (1983) (quoting Central Hudson Gas and Elec. Corp. v. Pub. Serv. Comm'n, 447 U.S. 557, 563 (1980)).

mere *presence* of commercial speech. To that end, the California
court developed a limited-purpose test that carefully balances that
interest against the deeply established interest in protecting consumers from false advertising and not allowing such falsity to be immunized by attaching it to a public issue.[26]

It is important at this point to emphasize a distinction that is critical
to understanding the specific area of law focused upon in this article as
well as the terminology that will be used in discussing it. Over roughly
the same time period—particularly the past three decades—that the
Supreme Court has developed its doctrine determining the extent of
First Amendment protection for *commercial* speech, it has also developed a doctrine determining the extent of First Amendment protection for what is most precisely referred to as *corporate* speech. This
article focuses upon commercial speech questions, and the relevant
case law will be discussed in detail. Those questions are distinct from
the Court's considerations in its corporate speech cases, the first of
which, *First National Bank of Boston v. Bellotti*,[27] established First
Amendment protection for speech by corporations that is designed to
influence political and social outcomes, rather than to promote products.[28] In a series of rulings since then, the Court has narrowly distinguished what once appeared a more expansive precedent in the course
of defining the parameters within which political speech by corporations can be regulated by government. Those cases include *Federal
Election Commission v. National Right to Work Committee*,[29] *Federal
Election Commission v. National Conservative Political Action Committee*,[30] *Federal Election Commission v. Massachusetts Citizens for
Life, Inc.*[31] and *Austin v. Michigan State Chamber of Commerce*.[32] The
last of those most fully articulates the Court's doctrine that coalesced
in those cases to prevent actual and potential corruption of the political marketplace of ideas through wealth generated *via* the significant,
state-conferred advantages of the corporate form (such as perpetual
life, limited liability and special tax advantages)[33] in the economic
marketplace. That doctrine "aims at a different type of corruption in
the political arena: the corrosive and distorting effects of immense ag-
gregations of wealth that are accumulated with the help of the corpo-

---

[26]45 P.3d at 256–259.
[27]435 U.S. 765 (1978).
[28]*Id*. at 776–78.
[29]459 U.S. 197 (1982).
[30]470 U.S. 480 (1985).
[31]479 U.S. 238 (1986).
[32]494 U.S. 652 (1990).
[33]*See* United States v. Morton Salt Co., 338 U.S. 632, 652 (1950).

rate form and that have little or no correlation to the public's support for the corporation's political ideas," the Court said in *Austin*.[34] Thus it confuses the discussion not only semantically but doctrinally to refer to the two—corporate speech and commercial speech—as if they are interchangeable.[35]

The next section of this article will examine the threshold commercial speech question from *New York Times Co. v. Sullivan* in context to the purpose emphasized in its holding and rationale for protecting a degree of falsity in public debate. That will be followed by a section devoted to analysis of the Supreme Court's commercial speech cases and sections focusing upon analysis of the California Supreme Court's decision in *Kasky v. Nike, Inc.*, and the Supreme Court's decision not to rule on the *Nike* appeal. The acticle then weighs the *Nike* case's implications for corporate expression against the societal interest in preventing all false commercial speech from being immunized simply by attaching it to a public issue.

SULLIVAN'S NOBLE PURPOSE

New York Times Co. v. Sullivan arrived at the Supreme Court on appeal from the Alabama Supreme Court, which had affirmed a jury verdict awarding a civil libel judgment of $500,000 to L. B. Sullivan, one of the three elected commissioners of the City of Montgomery.[36] Sullivan, whose responsibilities included supervision of the city's police and fire departments, brought the libel action against the four clergymen and the *New York Times* concerning statements in a full-page advertisement published in the *Times* on March 29, 1960, titled "Heed Their Rising Voices." It stated, in part, that "thousands of Southern Negro students ... engaged in widespread non-violent demonstrations" against segregation were being met by "an unprecedented wave of terror." The text also described related events and concluded with an appeal for funds to support the student movement

---

[34]494 U.S. at 660.

[35]All corporate speech is not commercial, of course, and neither is all commercial speech corporate. To be most precise, one would need to utilize terminology such as "corporate commercial speech" and "non-corporate commercial speech." For although the Nike speech in question is—at least according to Kasky and the California Supreme Court—*commercial* speech by a corporation, other cases discussed in this article involve commercial speech by non-corporate entities. In the context of this article, however, there would be no significant purpose served by adding those cumbersome terms to the discussion.

[36]*See* New York Times Co. v. Sullivan, 144 So. 2d 25 (Ala. 1962).

and related civil rights efforts. Below the text were the names of numerous persons well known for their activities.[37]

While it was undeniably true that the students in question had experienced violent repression of their efforts, some of the statements in the message were not accurate. Although students had demonstrated on the State Capitol steps, they sang the National Anthem and not "My Country, 'Tis of Thee." Although nine students had been expelled by the State Board of Education, it was for demanding service at a lunch counter in the Montgomery County Courthouse, not for leading the demonstration at the Capitol. Most of the student body—though not all, as the text stated—had protested the expulsion by boycotting classes for one day, rather than by refusing to register for school at Alabama State College in Montgomery. The college dining hall was never padlocked, as the text had stated, and only a few students were barred from eating there, those for failing to have completed appropriate applications or requested temporary meal tickets. Although large numbers of police were deployed near the campus on three occasions, they did not go so far as to "ring" the campus. Dr. Martin Luther King, Jr., leader of the movement, had not been arrested seven times, but only four; and an alleged assault on him during one arrest had been disputed by one of the officers involved.[38]

Although Sullivan was not named in the text, he contended that charges concerning police activity could be understood to refer to him. A former employer testified that he doubted he would want to associate with someone who "would be a party to such things that are stated in that ad," and that if he believed the statements, he would not hire Sullivan again.[39]

For a cost of approximately $4,800, the *Times* had published the message as an advertisement upon request from a New York advertising agency that provided a letter from one of the clergymen who "was known to the *Times*' Advertising Acceptability Department as a responsible person" certifying the persons whose names appeared in the message had given their permission. The manager of that department testified that he had approved the advertisement for publication because he had no reason to believe it was false and because was endorsed by "a number of people who are well known and whose reputation" he "had no reason to question."[40] The jury rendering the verdict was in-

---

[37]New York Times Co. v. Sullivan, 376 U.S. 254, 256–58 (1964).

[38]*Id.* at 258–59.

[39]*Id.* at 260.

[40]*Id.* at 261.

structed by the trial judge that under Alabama law a publication was libelous *per se* if it tended to injure the plaintiff "in his public office, or impute misconduct to him in his office, or want of official integrity, or want of fidelity to a public trust,"[41] and that general damages were presumed without a showing of "actual intent" to harm or "gross negligence and recklessness."[42]

The Alabama Supreme Court affirmed the verdict, but the U.S. Supreme Court reversed, holding that the rule of law applied was constitutionally deficient in providing sufficient First Amendment protection "in a libel action brought by a public official against critics of his official conduct."[43] The Court declared that "compelling the critic of official conduct to guarantee the truth of *all* his factual assertions—and to do so on pain of libel judgments virtually unlimited in amount" leads to self-censorship.[44] The Court concluded, therefore, that "constitutional guarantees require ... a federal rule that prohibits a public official from recovering damages for a defamatory falsehood relating to his official conduct unless he proves that the statement was made with 'actual malice'—that is, with knowledge that it was false or with reckless disregard of whether it was false or not."[45]

The Threshold Commercial Speech Question

Before the Court could reach that conclusion, however, it had to dispose of Sullivan's assertion that the First Amendment's guarantees did not apply to the speech in question because it appeared in a paid advertisement.[46] That argument was based upon the Court's ruling in *Valentine v. Chrestensen*,[47] in which it had held unanimously that a "purely commercial advertisement" merited no First Amendment protection from government regulation.[48] As presented in *Sullivan*, however, the Court found the argument "wholly misplaced."[49] The Court held that the fact that the *New York Times* had been paid for the "Heed Their Rising Voices" advertisement was "immaterial in this connection."[50] The Court thus declared that in

---

[41]*Id*. at 267.
[42]*Id*. at 262.
[43]*Id*. at 264.
[44]*Id*. at 279 (emphasis added).
[45]*Id*. at 279–80.
[46]*Id*. at 265.
[47]316 U.S. 52 (1942).
[48]*Id*. at 54.
[49]376 U.S. at 265.
[50]*Id*. at 266.

the context of the facts of that case, the advertising format alone could not bar the speech involved from First Amendment protection. The Court distinguished the *Sullivan* context from that of *Valentine*, with emphasis on the fact that the latter involved not simply an advertisement but one in which the purpose of the political speech it contained was "to evade the ordinance" regulating handbills.[51] In *Sullivan*, by contrast, the purpose was not evading a law held to legitimately serve the public interest but advancing the cause of "a movement *whose existence and objectives are matters of the highest public interest and concern.*"[52] Clearly, the Court did consider the motive of the actual speaker involved—the supporters of the civil-rights movement—a material fact. What it deemed *not* material was the motive of the medium that conveyed the speech.

Nothing in the *Sullivan* opinion suggests that the Court considered the *Times'* motive to be the same as that of the civil rights supporters who paid for the ad—which of course it wasn't. The *Times'* motive in selling the advertising space for that message was no different than its motive in selling space to all the other advertisers on its pages. In the manner in which the Court distinguished the *Sullivan* context from that of *Valentine*, it deemed the motive of the speaker who was most closely linked to the content of the speech to be material to the question of First Amendment protection—and the motive of the speaker *not* so connected to be immaterial. In so doing, the *Sullivan* Court was engaging for practical purposes in the nuanced sort of test—although it did not articulate it as such—that the *Bolger v. Youngs Drug Products Corp.*[53] Court would employ some years later, and which the California Supreme Court would rely upon in *Kasky v. Nike, Inc.*[54] Both those cases, which will be discussed in detail, focused on the question of the appropriate level of constitutional protection to be applied to the commercial speech at issue, but both involved significantly different fact sets from *Sullivan*.

The Court in *Sullivan* emphasized that the consequence of not protecting the seller of the advertising space in that case would be to discourage such sellers from making their space available to "persons who do not themselves have access to publishing facilities."[55] With such language, the Court stressed its ultimate purpose of pro-

---

[51]*Id.*
[52]*Id.* (emphasis added).
[53]463 U.S. 60 (1983).
[54]45 P.3d 243 (Cal. 2002).
[55]376 U.S. at 266.

tecting the speech rights of citizens. Throughout the *Sullivan* opinion, that overriding purpose resonates. "[A] privilege for criticism of official conduct is appropriately analogous to the protection accorded a public official when he is sued for libel by a private citizen," the Court declared.[56] It characterized this principle as grounded in the most fundamental principles that drove the founders' efforts to ensure that the "structure of the government dispersed power in reflection of the people's distrust of concentrated power, and of power itself at all levels."[57] Nothing is more consistent in the language of *Sullivan* than its priority on how the decision is intended, above all, to help maintain the sovereignty of the people—a process that requires protecting citizens from concentrations of power that threaten fundamental rights. The *Sullivan* opinion did, of course, discuss the consistency of its holding with the nation's historical antipathy toward seditious libel.[58] The Court did not, however, go on to require proof of actual malice against public officials merely by citing that antipathy without any further explanation of the reasoning involved. It did so on the clearly articulated basis of the potential threat that would be represented by further empowering already powerful public officials with sweeping authority to easily punish their critics through the courts.

Protecting the People from Concentrations of Power

Focusing upon that reasoning is crucial in considering how *Sullivan* should apply to cases like *Nike* in which defendants invoke *Sullivan* to justify heightened First Amendment protection in circumstances involving significantly different fact sets.[59] Perfunctorily granting *Sullivan*'s protection for "the people" to Nike, Inc., represents a preposterous inversion of that reasoning. It requires considering a plaintiff such as Kasky to possess power of the same magnitude as that of a government official like Sullivan, simply because Kasky brought his suit in a government court. If that were the standard established by *Sullivan*, for example, the actual-malice test would be required of *every* libel plaintiff, even private citizens, because they too must bring their suits in government courts.

---

[56]*Id.* at 282.

[57]*Id.* at 274.

[58]*Id.* at 273–77.

[59]*See* Brief for Appellant at 2, 26, Nike, Inc. v. Kasky, 123 S. Ct. 2554 (2003) (No. 02–575).

The threat addressed specifically in *Sullivan* was excessive power of government to punish criticism of government officials by citizens. The Court's focus on addressing such threats is pronounced in both its framing of the question before it and in its statement of the essential holding. "The question before us is whether this rule of liability, as applied to an action brought by a public official against critics of his official conduct, abridges the freedom of speech and of the press that is guaranteed by the First and Fourteenth Amendments," the Court declared.[60] That emphasis on protecting criticism of government was reiterated in the Court's holding that "the rule of law applied by the Alabama courts is constitutionally deficient for failure to provide the safeguards for freedom of speech and of the press that are required by the First and Fourteenth Amendments in a libel action brought by a public official against critics of his official conduct."[61]

Yet, the Court consistently articulated its rationale most broadly throughout *Sullivan* in terms of the great necessity of maintaining the peoples' speech rights against encroachment by more powerful influences. "[D]ebate on public issues should be uninhibited, robust, and wide-open, and … it may well include vehement, caustic, and sometimes unpleasantly sharp attacks on government and public officials," the Court declared.[62] It drew upon a federal appellate case that affirmed the dismissal of a libel suit by a member of Congress who had been called anti-Semitic by a newspaper: "Cases which impose liability for erroneous reports of the political conduct of officials reflect the obsolete doctrine that the governed must not criticize their governors."[63] Additionally, in asserting the justification for establishing the actual malice standard of liability for libel cases brought by public officials, the Court noted that some state courts had already adopted such a standard, one of which had been upheld by the Kansas Supreme Court in a libel suit brought by the state attorney general during a reelection campaign.[64] *Sullivan*'s repeated emphasis on preventing government punishment of its critics accentuates another key distinction between it and the *Nike* case: It did not involve punishment of criticism of government. Thus, even if *Sullivan* could be viewed as establishing *only* that the actual-malice

---

[60]376 U.S. at 268.

[61]*Id.* at 264.

[62]*Id.* at 270.

[63]*Id.* at 272 (quoting Sweeney v. Patterson, 128 F.2d 457, 458 (D.C. Cir. 1942)).

[64]*Id.* at 281 (citing Coleman v. MacLennan, 78 Kan. 711, 723 (1908)). The official, who was also a member of a commission that managed and controlled the state school fund, sued a newspaper for criticism relating to his official conduct involving a school-fund transaction.

standard be applied to protect any criticism of government, then it could not provide authority for corporate parties in cases such as *Nike*. And neither can *Sullivan* be relied upon for that purpose if it is understood more broadly as protecting citizens from concentrations of power that threaten fundamental rights.

In the structure and emphasis of its discourse, the *Sullivan* opinion provides more support for the latter understanding. Other elements of the opinion are not as closely linked to the *Sullivan* holding in factual context, language or reasoning. For example, the discussion of protection for the *Times* and the other defendants *via* the actual malice standard was rather brief and focused almost exclusively on considering whether the record in the case indicated that the standard had been met by the public official who brought the suit. No evidence was presented that the individual defendants had any prior knowledge of falsity in the statements at issue. It was determined at trial that the *Times* advertising department could have checked articles by *Times* reporters concerning at least some of what turned out to be minor errors in the ad. Nevertheless, the newspaper was dealing with subject matter occurring completely outside the bounds of its own business operation (another distinction between *Sullivan* and the relationship of Nike, Inc., to the subject matter in the California case). The Court concluded "the evidence against the *Times* supports at most a finding of negligence in failing to discover the misstatements, and is constitutionally insufficient to show the recklessness that is required for a finding of actual malice."[65] Thus, the Court concluded that in the context of the greater purpose that it had articulated at length, falsity warranted protection when disseminated without either knowledge of the falsehood or recklessness concerning its verification.

Similarly, the Court's discussion of the "unfettered exchange of ideas" is not articulated so broadly as to imply establishing that condition as an absolute standard. The Court invoked the phrase as part of its broader discussion of protecting speech rights of "the people," certainly not in any proximity to its holding or even its discussion of commercial speech: "The general proposition that freedom of expression upon public questions is secured by the First Amendment has long been settled by our decisions. The constitutional safeguard, we have said, 'was fashioned to assure unfettered interchange of ideas for the bringing about of political and social changes desired by the people.'"[66] At that point, the Court already had completed its discus-

---

[65]*Id.* at 286–88.
[66]*Id.* at 269 (quoting Roth v. United States, 354 U.S. 476, 484 (1957)).

sion of the commercial speech question and was well into its discussion on the larger question of whether the Alabama liability standard was constitutional as applied to libel suits brought in response to criticism of government officials.

This analysis asserts that on balance the Court's emphasis in *Sullivan* reflects the greatest concern with maintaining the sovereignty of the people from encroachment by centers of concentrated power—in that case represented by the power of government officials to bring libel actions for criticism of their official activities. To the extent that *Sullivan* protected commercial speech, it went no farther—and clearly intended to go no farther—than to establish that the advertising format alone could not bar the speech involved from First Amendment protection. Further, the Court unequivocally linked that holding with the motive of the speaker involved in relation to the "movement whose existence and objectives are matters of the highest public interest and concern."[67] Nor did the Court in any way suggest that commercial speech should be similarly protected in other contexts where different facts and different societal interests were at stake. Thus, *Sullivan* in its reasoning and principles is not at odds with efforts by later Courts to distinguish between commercial and noncommercial speech for the purposes of resolving very different cases. Despite the many significant Supreme Court rulings that have shaped the evolution of the commercial speech doctrine, the holdings have not gone beyond protecting truthful commercial speech to also protect false commercial speech simply because it was attached to discussion of public issues.

THE TRUTH SETS COMMERCIAL SPEECH (ALMOST) FREE

Even though *Valentine v. Chrestensen* is typically thought of today as merely a decision long since abandoned in commercial speech doctrine, the Supreme Court has never in fact rejected the holding that commercial speech should not be able to "to achieve immunity from the law's command" by appending to it "a civic appeal, or a moral platitude."[68] The Court has never gone any farther than protecting *truthful* commercial speech in First Amendment cases.[69] To take the

---

[67]*Id.* at 266.

[68]*Valentine*, 316 U.S. 52, 55 (1942).

[69]Numerous articles discuss more broadly the development of the commercial speech doctrine. *See, e.g.*, Soontae An, *From a Business Pursuit to a Means of Expression: The Supreme Court's Disputes Over Commercial Speech from 1942 to 1976*, 8 COMM. L. & POL'Y 201 (2003); Sean P. Costello, *Strange Brew: The State of Commercial Speech Jurisprudence Before and After 44 Liquormart, Inc. v. Rhode Island*,

giant step of providing constitutional protection to false commercial speech in such as case as *Nike, Inc. v. Kasky* would require a complete departure from well established case law.

Valentine not only represents the Court's first statement on commercial speech, but the facts involved highlight the deep roots of efforts by commercial speakers to attach commercial speech to statements on public issues. *Valentine* involved a promoter who owned a submarine previously belonging to the U.S. Navy and which he wanted to exhibit from a New York pier. When F.J. Chrestensen attempted to distribute a handbill advertising twenty-five-cent tours of the craft, Police Commissioner Lewis J. Valentine informed him that such distribution of commercial and business advertising matter on New York City streets would be in violation of section 318 of the Sanitary Code, an anti-littering measure. After Chrestensen printed a message of protest on the back of his handbills concerning a dispute between him and the City of New York over wharfage facilities at a city pier and was told the handbills still violated the city ordinance, he challenged the matter in court, leading to the Supreme Court's first pronouncement on First Amendment protection for commercial speech.[70]

The Court disposed of the question quickly and unanimously. Less than two weeks after hearing oral arguments, it issued a four-page opinion declaring that although government was limited in the degree to which it could regulate freedom of speech on public streets, "We are equally clear that the Constitution imposes no such restraint on government as respects purely commercial advertising."[71] The Court also declared that it did not consider a message printed on the back of a handbill "inextricably attached" to an ad on the front of the handbill. It observed that future cases could well involve more complicated questions related to distinguishing commercial speech from political speech, but that the question before it did not rise to the level of requiring the Court's attention at that time. "It is enough for the present purpose that the stipulated facts justify the conclu-

47 CASE W. RES. L. REV. 681 (1997); Michael Feldman, *Survey of the Literature: Commercial Speech and Commercial Speakers,* 2 CARDOZO L. REV. 659 (1981); Arlen W. Langvardt, *The Incremental Strengthening of First Amendment Protection for Commercial Speech: Lessons from Greater New Orleans Broadcasting,* 37 AM. BUS. L.J. 587 (2000); Mary B. Nutt, *Trends in First Amendment Protection of Commercial Speech,* 41 VAND. L. REV. 173 (1988); Peter J. Tarsney, *Regulation of Environmental Marketing: Reassessing the Supreme Court's Protection of Commercial Speech,* 69 NOTRE DAME L. REV. 533 (1994);
[70]316 U.S. at 54.
[71]*Id.* at 55.

sion that the affixing of the protest against official conduct to the advertising circular was with the intent, and for the purpose of evading the prohibition of the ordinance,"[72] the court held.

While the *Valentine* Court's cavalier dismissal of commercial speech as meriting no restraint from government regulation would indeed be rendered obsolete in future case law, the refusal to countenance the blending of political and commercial speech in order to "achieve immunity from the law's command"[73] would firmly endure. The evolution of the Court's commercial speech doctrine began twenty-two years after *Valentine* with *New York Times Co. v. Sullivan*'s pronouncement that advertising format alone could not bar the speech involved from First Amendment protection.[74] That began the Court's long journey through the many challenges in later cases that would present constitutional questions concerning the extent of protection for commercial speech.

As early as *Pittsburgh Press Co. v. Pittsburgh Commission on Human Relations*[75] in 1973, the newspaper challenging a city regulation barring help-wanted advertisements segregated according to male or female interest asked the Court to "abrogate the distinction between commercial and other speech."[76] The Court observed that whatever the merits for such a holding might be in other contexts, it was not warranted by the facts of *Pittsburgh Press*, because "[d]iscrimination in employment is not only commercial activity, it is illegal commercial activity."[77] Acknowledging that, since *Sullivan*, "[S]peech is not rendered commercial by the mere fact that it relates to an advertisement,"[78] the *Pittsburgh Press* Court drew upon the reasoning of the *Sullivan* Court to reject the argument that the ads should not be considered commercial speech. In their "crucial respects," the newspaper's help-wanted ads resembled the speech in *Valentine* more than that of *Sullivan*, the *Pittsburgh Press* Court concluded.[79] The Court declared that the help-wanted ads included no statements on "whether, as a matter of social policy, certain positions ought to be filled by members of one or the other sex, nor does any of them criticize the Ordinance or the Commission's enforcement practices. Each is no more than a proposal of possible employ-

---

[72]*Id.*
[73]*Id.* at 52, 55.
[74]376 U.S. 254, 266 (1964).
[75]413 U.S. 376 (1973).
[76]*Id.* at 388.
[77]*Id.*
[78]*Id.* at 384 (citing 376 U.S. 254 (1964)).
[79]*Id.* at 385.

ment. The advertisements are thus classic examples of commercial speech."[80]

In *Bigelow v. Virginia*,[81] two years later, the Court declared Sullivan had rendered "untenable" any holding that "all statutes regulating commercial advertising are immune from constitutional challenge."[82] In declaring unconstitutional a Virginia statute that banned publication in the state of any advertisement for abortion services, the Court distinguished the ad in question from those in *Pittsburgh Press*. The ad that had run afoul of the Virginia statute contained truthful information for a service that was legal in the state (New York) where the services were offered and contained material of public interest in the state where the commercial message was published.[83] While holding that the commercial speech in question was thus not without First Amendment protection, the Court declined to decide "the precise extent to which the First Amendment permits regulation of advertising that is related to activities the State may legitimately regulate or even prohibit."[84]

Freeing the Flow of Commercial Information

One year later, the Court, for the first time, established that even speech that does "no more than propose a commercial transaction" is not completely without First Amendment protection.[85] In striking down a state statute prohibiting pharmacists from advertising the price of prescription drugs in *Virginia State Board of Pharmacy v. Virginia Citizens Consumer Council*, the Court emphasized the restraint that the First Amendment places on government against denying truthful information to citizens. "Virginia is free to require whatever professional standards it wishes of its pharmacists. ... But it may not do so by keeping the public in ignorance of the entirely lawful terms that competing pharmacists are offering," the Court declared.[86] It grounded that assertion in terms of the public good served by consumers receiving accurate commercial information: "So long as we preserve a predominantly free enterprise economy, the allocation of our

---

[80]*Id.*

[81]421 U.S. 809 (1975).

[82]*Id.* at 820–21.

[83]*Id.* at 821–23 (citing Pittsburgh Press Co. v. Pittsburgh Commission on Human Relations, 413 U.S. 376 (1973)).

[84]*Id.* at 824–25.

[85]Virginia State Bd. of Pharmacy v. Virginia Citizens Consumer Council, 425 U.S. 748, 762 (1976) (quoting *Pittsburgh Press,* 413 U.S. at 385).

[86]*Id.* at 770.

resources in large measure will be made through numerous private economic decisions. It is a matter of public interest that those decisions, in the aggregate, be intelligent and well informed. To this end, the free flow of commercial information is indispensable."[87]

Concurring, Justice Potter Stewart wrote to assert that the holding did not similarly restrict government's right to regulate false or deceptive advertising. The *Sullivan* principles "suggest that government may take broader action to protect the public from injury produced by false or deceptive price or product advertising than from harm caused by defamation," Justice Stewart declared.[88] He emphasized as critical to that distinction the advertiser's greater relative access to the truth or falsity of its factual statements:

> In contrast to the press, which must often attempt to assemble the true facts from sketchy and sometimes conflicting sources under the pressure of publication deadlines, the commercial advertiser generally knows the product or service he seeks to sell and is in a position to verify the accuracy of his factual representations before he disseminates them. The advertiser's access to the truth about his product and its price substantially eliminates any danger that governmental regulation of false or misleading price or product advertising will chill accurate and nondeceptive commercial expression. There is, therefore, little need to sanction "some falsehood in order to protect speech that matters."[89]

Two years later in *Ohralik v. Ohio State Bar Association*,[90] the Court reinforced that assertion by refusing to invalidate on First Amendment grounds a lawyer's suspension from practice for face-to-face solicitation of business and declaring that "[t]o require a parity of constitutional protection for commercial and noncommercial speech alike could invite dilution, simply by a leveling process, of the force of the Amendment's guarantee with respect to the latter kind of speech."[91] The correctness of Justice Stewart's assertion that

---

[87]*Id*. at 765.

[88]*Id*. at 776–77 (1976) (Stewart, J., concurring).

[89]*Id*. at 777–78 (quoting Gertz v. Robert Welch, Inc., 418 U.S. 323, 340 (1974)).

[90]436 U.S. 447 (1978).

[91]*Id*. at 456. A year before that, in another case involving regulation of advertising by attorneys, the Court ruled that the First Amendment barred a *total* ban on such advertising, but emphasized why untruthful commercial speech in the same context was completely subject to regulation:

> [W]e, of course, do not hold that advertising by attorneys may not be regulated in any way. ... Advertising that is false, deceptive, or misleading of course is subject to restraint. Since the advertiser knows his product and has a commercial interest in its dis-

false commercial speech would remain completely subject to government regulation was borne out most unequivocally two years after that when the Court established a four-part test for assessing the constitutionality of advertising regulations under intermediate scrutiny in *Central Hudson Gas and Electric. v. Public Service Commission*.[92] The threshold question in that test was established as whether the speech in question concerns lawful activity and is not misleading—with failure to survive that prong of the test denying the speech any further consideration of First Amendment protection.[93] Because First Amendment protection for commercial speech is based on the informational function of advertising, "Consequently, there can be no constitutional objection to the suppression of commercial messages that do not accurately inform the public about lawful activity."[94] The Court also again emphasized the "extensive knowledge" that commercial speakers have "of both the market and their products."[95]

In *Metromedia, Inc. v. City of San Diego*,[96] a year later, the Court struck down a city ban on most outdoor signs, finding that the regulation survived the *Central Hudson* test but still was unconstitutional because it permitted signs advertising goods or services available on sites where the sign was located but did not permit other messages on those signs.[97] The failure to include an exception for noncommercial speech on such onsite signs meant the regulation was unconstitutional on its face, the Court said, because, "Insofar as

---

semination, we have little worry that regulation to assure truthfulness will discourage protected speech. And any concern that strict requirements for truthfulness will undesirably inhibit spontaneity seems inapplicable because commercial speech generally is calculated. Indeed, the public and private benefits from commercial speech derive from confidence in its accuracy and reliability. Thus, the leeway for untruthful or misleading expression that has been allowed in other contexts has little force in the commercial arena.

Bates v. State Bar of Arizona, 433 U.S. 350, 383 (1977) (citing Virginia State Bd. of Pharmacy v. Virginia Citizens Consumer Council, 425 U.S. 748, 771–72 n.24 (1976)).

[92] 447 U.S. 557 (1980).

[93] *Id.* at 566 ("At the outset, we must determine whether the expression is protected by the First Amendment. For commercial speech to come within that provision, it at least must concern lawful activity and not be misleading. Next, we ask whether the asserted governmental interest is substantial. If both inquiries yield positive answers, we must determine whether the regulation directly advances the governmental interest asserted, and whether it is not more extensive than is necessary to serve that interest."). The Court struck down a state ban on advertising that promoted use of electricity after determining that the ban failed the fourth prong of the test.

[94] *Id.* at 563.

[95] *Id.* at 564.

[96] 453 U.S. 490 (1981).

[97] *Id.* at 503–17.

the city tolerates billboards at all, it cannot choose to limit their content to commercial messages; the city may not conclude that the
communication of commercial information concerning goods and
services connected with a particular site is of greater value than the
communication of noncommercial messages."[98] The Court emphasized, however, that its ruling was not a departure from *Central
Hudson*, holding that, on the contrary, the San Diego regulation had
"invert[ed]" the doctrine of "recent commercial speech cases [that]
have consistently accorded noncommercial speech a greater degree
of protection than commercial speech" by "affording a greater degree
of protection to commercial than to noncommercial speech."[99]

The Court provided its most substantial guidance for distinguishing between commercial and noncommercial speech in 1983's
Bolger v. Youngs Drug Products Corp.[100] In order to determine
whether a condom manufacturer's flyers and pamphlets promoting
its products—but also discussing venereal disease and family plan-
ning—could be considered commercial messages subject to federal
regulation, the Court developed a three-part test that considered
the combination of the advertising format of the messages, reference to a specific product, and the economic motivation for disseminating the messages.[101] Declaring that none of those three factors
alone would necessarily prove dispositive, the combination of all of
them "provides strong support for the ... conclusion that the informational pamphlets are properly characterized as commercial
speech ... notwithstanding the fact that they contain discussions of
important public issues. ... We have made clear that advertising
which 'links a product to a current public debate' is not thereby entitled to the constitutional protection afforded noncommercial
speech."[102] Further, the Court emphasized advertisers' ability to
separate commercial messages from noncommercial messages: "A
company has the full panoply of protections available to its direct
comments on public issues, so there is no reason for providing similar constitutional protection when such statements are made in the
context of commercial transactions."[103]

---

[98]*Id*. at 513.
[99]*Id*.
[100]463 U.S. 60 (1983).
[101]*Id*. at 62–63, 65–68.
[102]*Id*. at 67–68 (1983) (quoting Central Hudson Gas and Elec. Corp. v. Pub. Serv.
Comm'n, 447 U.S. 557, 563 (1980)).
[103]*Id*. at 68.

In 1993's *Cincinnati v. Discovery Network*,[104] the Court ruled unconstitutional a city ban on use of news racks on city streets to distribute commercial handbills.[105] In doing so, it emphasized that the ban's distinction between commercial and noncommercial speech bore "no relationship whatsoever to the particular interests [in maintaining esthetics] that the city has asserted" because commercial news racks "are no greater an eyesore than the [noncommercial] newsracks permitted."[106] Thus, the city had offered no permissible interest in preventing "commercial harms," which the Court stressed as "the typical reason why commercial speech can be subject to greater governmental regulation than noncommercial speech."[107] Yet, the Court also asserted the holding as a narrow one, declaring, "[W]e do not reach the question whether, given certain facts and under certain circumstances, a community might be able to justify differential treatment of commercial and noncommercial newsracks. We simply hold that on this record Cincinnati has failed to make such a showing."[108]

In a concurring opinion, Justice Harry Blackmun stated that he would have gone further than the rest of the majority in deciding the case by holding that "truthful, noncoercive commercial speech concerning lawful activities is entitled to full First Amendment protection."[109] It is important to note, however, Justice Blackmun's particular emphasis on greater protection for *truthful* commercial speech, declaring as he did that "[t]he very fact that government remains free, in my view, to ensure that commercial speech is not deceptive or coercive … greatly reduces the risk that protecting truthful commercial speech will dilute the level of First Amendment protection for speech generally."[110] Even though Blackmun wrote that he hoped the Court would ultimately "abandon *Central Hudson*'s analysis entirely," he recommended it be replaced with "one that affords full protection for truthful, noncoercive commercial speech about lawful activities."[111]

The same year, in *Edenfield v. Fane*,[112] the Court ruled unconstitutional a state ban on certified public accountants' personal solicita-

---

[104]507 U.S. 410 (1993).
[105]*Id*. at 430–31.
[106]*Id*. at 424–25.
[107]*Id*. at 426.
[108]*Id*. at 427.
[109]*Id*. at 436 (Blackmun, J., concurring).
[110]*Id*. at 438 (Blackmun, J., concurring).
[111]*Id*. (Blackmun, J., concurring).
[112]507 U.S. 761 (1993).

tion of prospective clients,[113] declaring the state had not demonstrated that the regulation advanced the interests asserted to justify it.[114] To the contrary, the Court found the rule threatened citizens' access to complete and accurate commercial information, because the speech in question sought "to communicate no more than truthful, nondeceptive information proposing a lawful commercial transaction."[115] Also in 1993, the Court in *United States v. Edge Broadcasting*[116] upheld a federal law prohibiting lottery advertising by radio stations located in states where lotteries are not legal,[117] applying the *Central Hudson* test to conclude that the regulation advanced North Carolina's antigambling policy without unduly interfering with lotteries sponsored by nearby States.[118]

Extending Protection for Truthful Commercial Speech

In *Rubin v. Coors*[119] in 1995, the Court held a federal law prohibiting beer labels from advertising alcohol content to be unconstitutional[120] because it failed both the third and fourth prongs of the *Central Hudson* test.[121] The Court held that the regulation did not advance the government's interest in combating "strength wars" between beer companies because of "the overall irrationality of the Government's regulatory scheme," which allowed and in some instances required that the alcohol content be included in labels on wine and other spirits.[122] Additionally, the regulation failed the Court's application of the fourth prong, the Court concluded, because there were less restrictive alternatives that would have advanced the government's interest, such as directly limiting the alcohol content of beer or prohibiting marketing that emphasized strong alcohol content.[123] Thus, as in *Edenfield*, the Court emphasized that it could find no basis for failing to protect the dissemina-

---

[113]Id. at 767.
[114]*Id.* at 770–73. The State of Florida declared those interests to be preventing fraud, protecting the privacy of accountants' potential clients, and maintaining the fact and appearance of accountants' independence. *Id.* at 768–70.
[115]*Id.* at 765.
[116]509 U.S. 418 (1993).
[117]*Id.* at 436.
[118]*Id.* at 426–35.
[119]514 U.S. 476 (1995).
[120]*Id.* at 480.
[121]*Id.* at 486–91.
[122]*Id.* at 488.
[123]*Id.* at 490–91.

tion of the truthful, factual information in question from government regulation.[124]

Three years after Justice Blackmun expressed support for full constitutional protection of truthful commercial speech in his concurring opinion in *Cincinnati v. Discovery Network*,[125] Justice Clarence Thomas offered similar support in a concurring opinion in *44 Liquormart v. Rhode Island*.[126] In that case, the Court struck down two Rhode Island statutes that prohibited the advertisement of alcohol prices anywhere in Rhode Island except at the point of purchase.[127] Members of the Court were splintered in their reasoning, however, with no more than four justices agreeing on what test should be applied to the commercial speech regulations, and a majority agreeing only on the judgment and the application of the Twenty-first Amendment to the issue. The nine justices aligned themselves into five groups with varied memberships of three or four justices each to join selected parts of the eight-part principal opinion. On the question of the Twenty-first Amendment's grant to states of broad regulatory power over the commerce of alcohol, the Court held that the "Twenty-first Amendment does not qualify the constitutional prohibition against laws abridging the freedom of speech embodied in the First Amendment."[128]

Only two justices joined the part of Justice Stevens' opinion in which he argued that more rigorous scrutiny than the *Central Hudson* intermediate scrutiny should be applied to regulations that entirely prohibit "the dissemination of truthful, nonmisleading commercial messages for reasons unrelated to the preservation of a fair bargaining process."[129] Justice Sandra Day O'Connor's concurring opinion, joined by three other justices, specifically rejected any such departure from the *Central Hudson* test for considering First Amendment protection of the commercial speech involved.[130] In that concurrence, Justice O'Connor argued that the regulation would fail the fourth prong of the *Central Hudson* test because it was more extensive than necessary to serve its stated interest.[131]

No one joined Justice Thomas in his concurring opinion arguing that when government denies "legal users of a product" information

---

[124]*Id*. at 484.
[125]507 U.S. 410, 431–38 (1993) (Blackmun, J., concurring).
[126]517 U.S. 484, 518–28 (1996) (Thomas, J., concurring).
[127]*Id*. at 516.
[128]*Id*.
[129]*Id*. at 501.
[130]*Id*. at 528, 532. (O'Connor, J., concurring).
[131]*Id*. at 529–32. (O'Connor, J., concurring).

in order to "manipulate their choices in the marketplace" in the manner of the regulation challenged in the case, that interest "can no more justify regulation of 'commercial' speech than it can justify regulation of 'noncommercial' speech."[132] Justice Thomas's concurrence seemed to suggest his continued support for regulation of commercial speech that is false or misleading or proposes illegal transactions,[133] and Justice Stevens declared unequivocal support for that proposition: "When a State regulates commercial messages to protect consumers from misleading, deceptive, or aggressive sales practices, or requires the disclosure of beneficial consumer information, the regulation's purpose is consistent with the reasons for according constitutional protection to commercial speech and therefore justifies less than strict review."[134]

In *Lorillard Tobacco v. Reilly*,[135] the Court noted how petitioners challenging state regulations on outdoor tobacco advertising urged the Court to "reject the *Central Hudson* analysis and apply strict scrutiny"[136] on the grounds that several justices had "expressed doubts about the *Central Hudson* analysis and whether it should apply in certain cases."[137] Pointing out that petitioners had made the same argument in *Greater New Orleans Broadcasting v. United States* two years earlier, the *Lorillard* Court said that, as in that case, it saw "no need to break new ground. *Central Hudson*, as applied in our more recent commercial speech cases, provides an adequate basis for decision."[138] So, in *Lorillard* the Court held that the regulations involving advertising of cigars and smokeless tobacco failed the *Central Hudson* test as more extensive than necessary to advance the

---

[132]*Id*. at 518. (Thomas, J., concurring). For discussion of Justice Thomas's arguments for greater protection of commercial speech, *see* David L. Hudson, Jr., *Justice Clarence Thomas: The Emergence of a Commercial-Speech Protector*, 35 CREIGHTON L. REV. 485 (2002).

[133]*Id*. at 520 (Thomas, J., concurring).

[134]*Id*. at 501.

[135]533 U.S. 525 (2001).

[136]*Id*. at 554.

[137]*Id*. For further discussion of the Court's recent consideration of its Central Hudson test, *see, e.g.*, Elizabeth Blanks Hindman, *The Chickens Have Come Home to Roost: Individualism, Collectivism and Conflict in Commercial Speech Doctrine*, 9 COMM. L. & POL'Y 237 (2004); Susan Dente Ross, *Reconstructing First Amendment Doctrine: The 1990s Revolution of the Central Hudson and O'Brien Tests*, 23 HASTINGS COMM. & ENT. L.J. 723 (2001); Brian J. Waters, *A Doctrine in Disarray: Why the First Amendment Demands the Abandonment of the Central Hudson Test for Commercial Speech*, 27 SETON HALL L. REV. 1626 (1997).

[138]533 U.S. at 554–55 (citing 527 U.S. 173, 184 (1999)). In *Greater New Orleans Broadcasting* the Court ruled unconstitutional federal regulations that prohibited casino gambling advertisements broadcast by stations located in states where such gambling was legal. *Id*. at 195–96.

government's substantial interest in preventing underage tobacco use,[139] while the regulations on advertising of cigarettes were found to be preempted[140] by the Federal Cigarette Labeling and Advertising Act.[141]

The Court declared that while the government interest in preventing use of tobacco by minors is "substantial, and even compelling ... it is no less true that the sale and use of tobacco products by adults is a legal activity. We must consider that tobacco retailers and manufacturers have an interest in conveying truthful information about their products to adults, and adults have a corresponding interest in receiving truthful information about tobacco products."[142] Even while asserting in a concurring opinion that he would subject all of the advertising regulations in question to strict scrutiny rather than *Central Hudson*'s intermediate scrutiny, Justice Thomas qualified his argument specifically to apply when "the government seeks to restrict truthful speech in order to suppress the ideas it conveys ... whether or not the speech in question may be characterized as 'commercial.'"[143]

Thus, although justices have expressed disagreement about the appropriate level of constitutional protection for commercial speech, the Court's holdings have never wavered on the government's power to regulate false or deceptive speech. The holdings have emphasized preventing government from denying citizens truthful information, especially when it involves using speech restrictions to discourage activities that government otherwise makes legal.[144] Such a doctrine places a priority on protecting truth in commercial speech, a principle completely antithetical to the notion of allowing false commercial speech to be immunized by attaching it to discussion of a public issue.

---

[139]*Id.* at 566–66.

[140]*Id.* at 550–51.

[141]15 U.S.C. § 1331 et seq. (1966).

[142]533 U.S. at 564.

[143]*Id.* at 572 (Thomas, J., concurring).

[144]For further discussion of the Court's developing doctrine limiting government's right to restrict non-misleading commercial communication about lawful products and services, *see, e.g.*, Nicholas P. Consula, *The First Amendment, Gaming Advertisements, and Congressional Inconsistency: The Future of the Commercial Speech Doctrine after Greater New Orleans Broadcasting Association v. United States*, 28 Pepp. L. Rev. 353 (2001); Michael Hoefges, *Protecting Tobacco Advertising Under the Commercial Speech Doctrine: The Constitutional Impact of Lorillard Tobacco Co.*, 8 Comm. L. & Pol'y 267(2003); Michael Hoefges & Milagros Rivera-Sanchez, *"Vice" Advertising under the Supreme Court's Commercial Speech Doctrine: The Shifting Central Hudson Analysis*, 22 Hastings Comm. & Ent. L.J. 345 (2000); Timothy R. Mortimer, *44 Liquormart, Inc. v. Rhode Island: A Toast to the First Amendment*, 32 New Eng. L. Rev. 1049 (1998).

To the contrary, the Court has repeatedly asserted its refusal to countenance such an interpretation of the First Amendment.

KASKE V. NIKE, INC. AT THE CALIFORNIA SUPREME COURT

In making its decision in *Kasky v. Nike, Inc.*, the California Supreme Court followed well-established law that false or misleading commercial speech receives no protection under the First Amendment. To that end, the court developed a limited-purpose test that carefully balanced the interest in protecting discussion of public issues against the interest in protecting consumers from false advertising and not allowing such falsity to be immunized by attaching it to a public issue. "[T]he regulations in question do not suppress points of view but instead suppress false and misleading statements of fact," the court concluded. "[T]o the extent Nike's speech represents expression of opinion or points of view on general policy questions such as the value of economic 'globalization,' it is noncommercial speech subject to full First Amendment protection. Nike's speech loses that full measure of protection only when it concerns facts material to commercial transactions—here, factual statements about how Nike makes its products."[145]

The case was begun by Mark Kasky, an activist critical of Nike's alleged treatment of workers at factories that manufacture its products. In April 1998, Kasky sued Nike for unfair and deceptive practices under California's Unfair Competition Law[146] and False Advertising Law.[147] Nike, the Oregon-based, multinational corporate manufacturer of athletic shoes and apparel with sales in excess of $9.2 billion at the time, had been for several years the subject of considerable public criticism for alleged inhumane working conditions in many of its overseas factories.[148] The suit alleged that Nike had deceived the public in a public relations and advertising campaign about conditions in its foreign plants in order to aid its sales. Nike responded to the suit with a demurrer contending that the messages in question were protected by the First Amendment because they concerned an issue of public concern and therefore were not subject to regulation as commercial speech.[149]

---

[145]45 P.3d 243, 261 (Cal. 2002).
[146]Cal. Bus. & Prof. Code Ann. § 17200 et seq. (West 1997).
[147]*Id.* at § 17500 et seq.
[148]45 P.3d at 247–48.
[149]*Id.* at 248.

The trial court and California Court of Appeals agreed with Nike in focusing solely on the issue of whether Nike's allegedly false and misleading statements were commercial or noncommercial for purposes of analyzing the protections afforded by the First Amendment, ruling that the statements were noncommercial speech and therefore constitutionally protected.[150] The California Supreme Court reversed on the commercial-speech question, applying a limited-purpose test to conclude that the speech at issue was commercial for the purposes of the proceedings against it and remanding the case for further proceedings.[151]

Kasky alleged that Nike made false and misleading statements for the purpose of maintaining and increasing profits in response to adverse publicity concerning the factories where its products are manufactured. Most of Nike's goods are produced by subcontractors in China, Vietnam and Indonesia, where most of the workers are women under the age of 24. Nike had since 1993 assumed responsibility under a memorandum of understanding with its subcontractors for compliance with the applicable local regulations concerning minimum wage, overtime, occupational health and safety, and environmental protection. Beginning in the mid 1990s, numerous media accounts reported allegations that workers in Nike factories were subjected to a variety of wrongs, including dangerous working conditions that violated local regulations; wages below applicable minimums; forced overtime; and physical, verbal and sexual abuse.[152]

Nike countered with a campaign that included press releases, letters to newspapers and to university presidents and athletic directors, other documents distributed for public relations purposes, and full-page newspaper advertisements. Among the messages communicated were statements that workers in the factories that make Nike products were protected from physical and sexual abuse, paid in accordance with applicable local laws and regulations and on average double the applicable local minimum wage, given free meals and health care, and provided working conditions in compliance with applicable health and safety laws and regulations.[153] Some of the messages also publicized a report prepared under a contract with Nike by former U.S. Ambassador to the United Nations Andrew Young as chairman of Goodworks International, a consulting group based in Atlanta, stating that no evidence of illegal or unsafe working condi-

---

[150]Kasky v. Nike, Inc., 79 Cal. App. 4th 165, 178 (1st Dist. 2000).
[151]45 P.3d at 262–63.
[152]*Id*. at 247–48.
[153]*Id*. at 248.

tions was found at Nike factories in China, Vietnam and Indonesia.[154] Kasky alleged that the statements in those messages were
false and misleading and were made with knowledge of falsity or
reckless disregard for California's laws prohibiting such statements.[155] After both the trial and appellate courts identified the
dispositive issue as whether the speech in question was commercial
or noncommercial and then granted Nike's demurrer on the basis
that the speech was noncommercial and fully protected by the First
Amendment, the California Supreme Court granted Kasky's petition
for review.[156]

That court concluded that Nike's statements were commercial
speech for purposes of applying California laws designed to prevent
false advertising and other commercial deception "[b]ecause in the
statements at issue here Nike was acting as a commercial speaker,
because its intended audience was primarily the buyers of its products, and because the statements consisted of factual representations about its own business operations."[157] In rejecting Nike's
contention that its statements were not commercial speech because
they were part of "an international media debate on issues of intense
public interest,"[158] the court emphasized the Supreme Court's assertion in *Bolger v. Youngs Drug Products Corp.* that advertisers like
Nike "may not 'immunize false or misleading product information
from government regulation simply by including references to public
issues.'"[159] Nike's allegedly false and misleading messages "all relate
to the commercial portions of the speech in question—the description of actual conditions and practices in factories that produce
Nike's products—and thus the proposed regulations reach only that
commercial portion," the California court declared. It further relied
on the Supreme Court's assertion in *Board of Trustees, State University of New York v. Fox* that "commercial and noncommercial messages are not 'inextricable' unless there is some legal or practical
compulsion to combine them."[160] The California court pointed out
that "[n]o law required Nike to combine factual representations
about its own labor practices with expressions of opinion about economic globalization, nor was it impossible for Nike to address those

---

[154]*Id.*
[155]*Id.*
[156]*Id.* at 248–49.
[157]*Id.* at 259.
[158]*Id.*
[159]*Id.* at 260 (quoting 463 U.S. 60, 68 (1983)).
[160]*Id.* (quoting 492 U.S. 469, 474 (1989)).

subjects separately."[161] The court did not consider the issue of whether Nike's speech actually was false or misleading.[162]

The California court drew even more extensively on *Bolger* in formulating its limited-purpose test for distinguishing commercial from noncommercial speech in its *Kasky* decision. Making such a distinction for the purposes of considering whether the speech in question could be subjected to laws regulating false advertising, the court concluded, requires consideration of three elements: the speaker, the intended audience and the content of the message.[163] The court first cited the Supreme Court's discussion in *Central Hudson Gas and Electric v. Public Service Commission* and other cases of commercial speech as speech proposing a commercial transaction, which implies that such communication is usually between speakers and target audiences that both engage in such transactions.[164] The court also stressed *Bolger*'s holding that advertising format and economic motivation are relevant considerations, both of which also imply speakers and audiences seeking to engage in commercial transactions, although advertising format alone neither always establishes that a message is commercial in character nor is always necessary to the characterization of speech as commercial.[165]

Regarding the California court's third element for distinguishing between commercial and noncommercial speech—that the factual content of the message should be commercial in character—it said "this typically means that the speech consists of representations of fact about the business operations, products, or services of the speaker (or the individual or company that the speaker represents), made for the purpose of promoting sales of, or other commercial transactions in, the speaker's products or services."[166] The court asserted this as consistent with the *Bolger* holding of product references as a relevant consideration in reaching such determinations.[167] It said that it found the Supreme Court's commercial speech doctrine construed that element as including not only "statements about the price, qualities, or availability of individual items offered for sale" but also "statements about the manner in which the products are manufactured, distributed, or sold, about repair or warranty services that the seller provides to purchasers of the product, or about the

---

[161]*Id*. at 260–61.
[162]*Id*. at 262.
[163]*Id*. at 256.
[164]*Id*. (citing 447 U.S. 557, 562 (1980)).
[165]*Id*. (citing 463 U.S. 60, 66–67 (1983)).
[166]*Id*.
[167]*Id*. at 256–57.

identity or qualifications of persons who manufacture, distribute, sell, service, or endorse the product" and also "statements about the education, experience, and qualifications of the persons providing or endorsing the services."[168]

Such a broad definition is necessary, the California court declared, "to adequately categorize statements made in the context of a modern, sophisticated public relations campaign intended to increase sales and profits by enhancing the image of a product or of its manufacturer or seller."[169] Further, the court said, its understanding of the content element is consistent with the Supreme Court's holdings on the reasons for denying First Amendment protection to false or misleading commercial speech—"because the truth of commercial speech is 'more easily verifiable by its disseminator' and because commercial speech, being motivated by the desire for economic profit, is less likely than noncommercial speech to be chilled by proper regulation."[170] That explanation, in the California court's view, "assumes that commercial speech consists of factual statements and that those statements describe matters within the personal knowledge of the speaker or the person whom the speaker is representing and are made for the purpose of financial gain."[171]

In applying its limited-purpose test to the Nike messages, the California court declared that the first element (commercial speaker) was satisfied because the speakers—the corporation, its officers and directors—were engaged in commerce. The second element (intended commercial audience) was also satisfied, the court said, because Nike's letters to university presidents and directors of athletic departments were targeted at actual and potential purchasers of its products, and its press releases and letters to newspaper editors were also intended to ultimately "reach and influence actual and potential purchasers of Nike's products." The court noted that plaintiff Kasky in support of that assertion had submitted a letter to a newspaper editor from Nike's communications director that discussed Nike's labor policies and practices and observed that "[c]onsumers are savvy and want to know they support companies with good products and practices" and that "[d]uring the shopping season, we encourage shoppers to remember that Nike is the industry's leader in improving factory conditions."[172]

---

[168]*Id.* at 257.
[169]*Id.*
[170]*Id.* (citing Virginia State Bd. of Pharmacy v. Virginia Citizens Consumer Council, 425 U.S. 748, 772 n.24 (1976)).
[171]*Id.* at 257.
[172]*Id.* at 258.

Regarding the third element (representations of fact of a commercial nature), the court said Nike made factual representations about its own business operations, addressing consumers on working conditions, wages and other labor practices "within its own knowledge. ... Nike was in a position to readily verify the truth of any factual assertions it made on these topics."[173] Further, the court said, the speech by Nike was "particularly hardy or durable" and that "regulation aimed at preventing false and actually or inherently misleading speech is unlikely to deter Nike from speaking truthfully or at all about the conditions in its factories."[174] To the contrary, the court said, "To the extent that application of these laws may make Nike more cautious, and cause it to make greater efforts to verify the truth of its statements, these laws will serve the purpose of commercial speech protection by 'insuring that the stream of commercial information flow[s] cleanly as well as freely.'"[175]

As in its holding and reasoning, the majority on the California court in its responses to the dissenting justices in Kasky grounded its assertions and language in an effort to follow well-established law that false or misleading commercial speech receives no protection under the First Amendment. The majority characterized Justice Janice Rogers Brown's dissent[176] as an effort "to find the magic formula or incantation that will transform a business enterprise's factual representations in defense of its own products and profits into noncommercial speech exempt from our state's consumer protection laws."[177] The majority declared that when such representations are aimed at potential customers in order to maintain sales and profits, they "may be regulated to eliminate false and misleading statements because they are readily verifiable by the speaker and because regulation is unlikely to deter truthful and nonmisleading speech."[178] Rather than prohibiting business enterprises from speaking on issues of public importance or defending their own labor practices, the court declared that its decision in *Kasky* will only require that such enterprises speak truthfully when they make factual representations about their own products or operations in order to promote sales and profits.[179] "Unlike our dissenting colleagues, we do not consider this

---

[173]*Id.*

[174]*Id.*

[175]*Id.* (quoting Virginia State Bd. of Pharmacy v. Virginia Citizens Consumer Council, 425 U.S. at 772 (1976)).

[176]*Id.* at 268–80 (Brown, J., dissenting).

[177]*Id.* at 262.

[178]*Id.*

[179]*Id.* at 247.

a remarkable or intolerable burden to impose on the business community," the court said.[180]

In response to dissents by Justice Brown[181] and Justice Ming W. Chin[182] that Nike's speech should not be categorized as commercial speech because the statements dealt with subjects that had already become a matter of public interest and public debate, the majority declared the contention to be based upon a false assumption. That assumption—that speech relating to a matter of significant public interest or controversy cannot be categorized as commercial speech—is contradicted by Supreme Court holdings that commercial speech quite commonly concerns such matters, the court said.[183] In support of that assertion, the California court cited *Virginia State Board of Pharmacy v. Virginia Citizens Consumer Council's* assertion that consumer interest in product and service information "may be as keen, if not keener by far, than his interest in the day's most urgent political debate," and the *Greater New Orleans Broadcasting v. United States* observation that the commercial speech in question clearly concerned "an activity that is the subject of intense debate in many communities."[184]

Regarding the dissents' reliance on *Thomas v. Collins*[185] and *Thornhill v. Alabama*[186] in support of the argument that speech on issues of public importance or controversy must be considered noncommercial speech, the majority pointed out that those decisions were issued some three decades before the Supreme Court developed its current commercial speech doctrine and that neither decision addressed the constitutionality of a law prohibiting false or misleading speech. "To the extent they hold that truthful and nonmisleading speech about commercial matters of public importance is entitled to constitutional protection, they are consistent with the modern commercial speech doctrine and with the decision we reach today," the court declared.[187] The court also emphasized the holding in *National Commission on Egg Nutrition v. Federal Trade Commission*,[188] in which false statements on health risks associated with eating eggs

---

[180]*Id.*

[181]*Id.* at 271–72 (Brown, J., dissenting).

[182]*Id.* at 265 (Chin, J., dissenting).

[183]*Id.* at 259.

[184]*Id.* (quoting 425 U.S. 748, 763 (1976); 527 U.S. 173, 184 (1999)).

[185]323 U.S. 516 (1945).

[186]310 U.S. 88 (1940).

[187]45 P.3d at 259–60.

[188]570 F.2d 157 (7th Cir. 1977). The appellate court sustained a final order by the Federal Trade Commission directing petitioners to cease and desist from disseminating advertisements containing statements to the effect that no scientific evi-

were declared commercial speech subject to federal regulation, despite the fact that the subject concerned debate on a matter of public interest.[189] In that case, the U.S. Court of Appeals for the Seventh Circuit declared that "the right of government to restrain false advertising can hardly depend upon the view of an agency or court as to the relative importance of the issue to which the false advertising relates."[190] The commercial speech in question had been argued to be more like the paid political advertisements in *Sullivan*.[191]

The *Kasky* majority stated in conclusion that the dissenting justices were correct "that the identity of the speaker is usually not a proper consideration in regulating speech that is entitled to First Amendment protection, and that a valid regulation of protected speech may not handicap one side of a public debate."[192] But the "very first question" that must be considered in deciding whether a law regulating speech violates the First Amendment is "whether the speech that the law regulates is entitled to First Amendment protection at all," the court said.[193] In light of the well established law that commercial speech that is false or misleading merits no protection under the First Amendment, "a law that prohibits only such unprotected speech cannot violate constitutional free speech provisions."[194]

THE SUPREME COURT DECIDES NOT TO DECIDE

The Supreme Court accepted Nike's appeal but after hearing oral arguments and receiving thirty-four briefs from the litigating parties and *amici curiae*, issued a *per curiam* order dismissing the writ of *certiorari* as improvidently granted.[195] A concurring opinion by Justice John Paul Stevens, joined by Justice Ruth Bader Ginsburg in whole and Justice David Souter in part, declared the dismissal justified by "three independently sufficient reasons:" the judgment entered by the California Supreme Court decision was not sufficiently final; neither party had standing to invoke federal court jurisdiction because neither had as of yet suffered a constitutionally cognizable injury; and the "reasons for avoiding the premature adjudication of

---

dence existed to indicate that eating eggs increases the risk of heart and circulatory disease.

[189]45 P.3d at 260.
[190]570 F.2d at 163.
[191]*Id.*
[192]45 P.3d at 261.
[193]*Id.*
[194]*Id.*
[195]Nike, Inc. v. Kasky, 123 S. Ct. 2554 (2003).

novel constitutional questions apply with special force to this case."[196] Those questions particularly concerned the way "the speech at issue represents a blending of commercial speech, noncommercial speech and debate on an issue of public importance," Justice Stevens wrote.[197] If, on one hand, the speech at issue contained significant factual misstatements, "The regulatory interest in protecting market participants from being misled by such misstatements is of the highest order."[198] On the other hand, Justice Stevens continued, if Nike was truly participating in a debate about important public issues extending beyond its own labor practices to those of other multinational corporations, "[T]he interest in protecting such participants from the chilling effect of the prospect of expensive litigation is ... also a matter of great importance."[199]

Thus, Justice Stevens sketched the parameters of why the central question in *Nike* makes it such a hard case, but contended that neither he nor the Court should move forward in answering it at that time. Whether the sort of broad protection *Sullivan* provided for misstatements made about public officials without actual malice should be extended by the Court "to cover corporate misstatements made about the corporation itself, or whether we should presume that such a corporate speaker knows where the truth lies" are among the questions that might yet be decided in *Nike*, Justice Stevens wrote.[200] Answering such questions correctly would be "more likely to result from the study of a full factual record than from a review of mere unproven allegations in a pleading," he declared, but with such a record yet to be developed, the Court had "wisely decided not to address the constitutional questions."[201]

Justice Anthony Kennedy's dissent from the order dismissing the writ of *certiorari* consisted of one sentence offering no arguments.[202] Justice Stephen Breyer's dissent, joined by Justice O'Connor, however, ran eleven pages and questioned whether it was indeed wise for the Court to delay answering the crucial questions presented in *Nike*.[203] For Justice Breyer, the questions before the Court directly concerned "the freedom of Americans to speak about public matters in public debate, no jurisdictional rule prevents us from deciding

---

[196]*Id.* at 2555 (Stevens, J., concurring).
[197]*Id.* at 2558 (Stevens, J., concurring).
[198]*Id.* (Stevens, J., concurring).
[199]*Id.* at 2559. (Stevens, J., concurring).
[200]*Id.* (Stevens, J., concurring).
[201]*Id.* (Stevens, J., concurring).
[202]*Id.* (Kennedy, J., dissenting).
[203]*Id.* at 2559–70 (Breyer, J., dissenting).

those questions now, and delay itself may inhibit the exercise of constitutionally protected rights of free speech without making the issue
significantly easier to decide later on."[204] Justice Breyer contended
that the mere fact that Nike had to defend the case presented a cognizable injury—the risk of chilling protected speech—and thus the Article III case-or-controversy requirement,[205] to show "injury in fact"
that is "fairly traceable" to actions of the opposing party and likely to
be redressed by a favorable decision, in no way barred the Court from
hearing the case.[206] While recognizing the same potentially conflict-
ing doctrinal issues outlined by Justice Stevens, Justice Breyer was
willing to take the next step and find that the *Nike* speech in question
warranted greater protection than provided by the commercial-speech doctrine, and that under a form of heightened constitutional scrutiny the California regulations in question could not
survive.[207]

Beyond the disagreement over dismissing *Nike*, both Justice
Stevens and Justice Breyer seemed to anticipate seeing the crucial
questions that the case presented before the Court again. That would
seem a likely proposition, but the questions will not return *via* the
Nike case, because Nike announced in late 2003 that it had agreed to
pay $1.5 million to a worker rights organization to settle the case.[208]
As part of the settlement, Nike consented to make the donation to
the Fair Labor Association, a Washington-based group that monitors
corporate labor practices abroad and helps educate workers. Marc
Kasky and Nike said in a joint statement that supporting such pro-
grams was preferable to continued litigation.[209] Other terms of the
settlement were not disclosed. Jim Carter, general counsel for Nike
told reporters that the Supreme Court's decision not to rule "left us
with no satisfactory comfort that we could get back to the Supreme
Court."[210]

Yet, given the attention and comment generated by the Nike case,
combined with the way questions over the extent of protection for
commercial speech have grown more urgent ever since *New York
Times Co. v. Sullivan* first opened the door to such protection, it

---

[204]*Id*. at 2560 (Breyer, J., dissenting).

[205]U.S. CONST. art. 3, § 2.

[206]123 S. Ct. at 2560–61 (Breyer, J., dissenting) (quoting Bennett v. Spear, 520
U.S. 154, 162 (1997)).

[207]*Id*. at 2565 (Breyer, J., dissenting).

[208]*See* Adam Liptak, *Nike Move Ends Case Over Firms' Free Speech*, N.Y. TIMES,
Sept. 13, 2003, at A8.

[209]*Id*.

[210]*Id*.

would seem probable that a similar case will reach the Supreme
Court in the not-too-distant future.

NIKE AND THE SULLIVAN LEGACY

The California Supreme Court gave its full attention to the question of how to address allegedly deceptive speech in the sort of highly
sophisticated corporate marketing campaign that is increasingly
characteristic of commercial communication today. Given the broad
definition it applied to declare the speech in question commercial,
the First Amendment question of whether such a deceptive-speech
regime could pass constitutional muster would inevitably have required resolution by the Supreme Court. Because Nike chose to settle its litigation with Kasky rather than pursue the case further, the
ultimate question from that case remains yet to be answered. If the
Court must one day choose between embracing a broader definition
of false/misleading commercial speech or providing constitutional
protection to such speech—the ultimate dilemma presented by *Nike,
Inc. v. Kasky*—the greater societal ill would be the latter choice.

As the Court's holdings have repeatedly acknowledged, even under a standard of accountability for factual claims such as California's, the relative hardiness of commercial speech would ensure its
continued vigor in the very manner in which *Virginia Pharmacy* envisioned: "The First Amendment, as we construe it today, does not
prohibit the State from insuring that the stream of commercial information flow[s] cleanly as well as freely."[211] The standard to which advertising is held in California is hardly as draconian as to put
commercial speakers "at risk of being sued every time they may answer a public concern," as portrayed by some scholars.[212] That standard simply makes it a misdemeanor to disseminate advertising that
is "untrue or misleading, and which is known, or which by the exercise of reasonable care should be known, to be untrue or misleading."[213] In contrast, consider the inestimable societal cost represented by the nightmare scenario of a consumer market in which any
false/misleading-speech regulation at all could be evaded merely by
linking commercial messages to an issue of public interest.

For the Court to decide the commercial/noncommercial speech
question highlighted in *Nike, Inc. v. Kasky* in such a way as to pro-

---

[211]425 U.S. 748, 772 (1976).
[212]Victoria Dizik Teremenko, *Corporate Speech Under Fire: Has Nike Finally
Done It?*, 2 DEPAUL BUS. & COMM. L.J. 207, 244 (2003).
[213]Cal. Bus. & Prof. Code Ann. § 17500 et seq. (West 1997).

vide constitutional protection for false commercial speech would be at odds with the Court's relevant body of case law. Despite some disagreement on the high Court over the appropriate level of constitutional protection for truthful commercial speech, the holdings have never wavered on the government's fundamental authority to regulate false or misleading commercial speech. Even those justices who have argued for a more rigorous level of scrutiny concerning regulation of commercial speech have not extended their argument to include false or misleading commercial speech. The Court has continued to hold that the *Central Hudson* intermediate-scrutiny test for determining the constitutionality of advertising regulations is the appropriate test for considering such questions. To survive the threshold test of *Central Hudson* scrutiny, the speech in question cannot be misleading; otherwise it merits no First Amendment consideration.[214] Further, the Court's decisions that have found specific advertising regulations to be unconstitutional always have emphasized denying government the power to deprive citizens of truthful information concerning legal activity, advancing the public good served by consumers receiving accurate commercial information.[215]

Most relevant to the critical question in *Nike*, the Court has repeatedly asserted its long-established holding that advertisers must not be allowed to immunize false commercial speech by linking a product "to a current public debate.'"[216] When faced with its most significant case involving commercial speech that included discussion of a public issue, *Bolger v. Youngs Drug Products Corp.*, the Court—much like the California Supreme Court in *Nike*—developed a limited-purpose test through which it concluded the speech remained commercial for purposes of government regulation.[217] Indeed, during oral arguments for *Nike, Inc. v. Kasky*, the questioning reflected some doubt as to whether the speech at question in *Nike* could be distinguished from the speech deemed commercial in *Bolger*.[218] For a future Court to decide a case like *Nike* in favor of protecting false or deceptive speech from regulation would mean for the first time allowing the immunization that the

---

[214]447 U.S. 557, 566 (1980).

[215]*See, e.g.,* Lorillard Tobacco v. Reilly, 533 U.S. 525, 564 (2001); 44 Liquormart v. Rhode Island, 517 U.S. 484, 501 (1996); Rubin v. Coors, 514 U.S. 476, 484 (1995); Edenfield v. Fane, 507 U.S. 761, 765 (1993); Virginia State Bd. of Pharmacy v. Virginia Citizens Consumer Council, 425 U.S. 748, 770 (1976).

[216]Bolger v. Youngs Drug Products Corp., 463 U.S. 60, 67–68 (1983) (quoting *Central Hudson,* 447 U.S. at 563).

[217]*Id.* at 62–63, 65–68.

[218]Oral Arguments at 8–11, *Nike, Inc. v. Kasky,* 123 S. Ct. 2554 (2003) (No. 02–575).

Court has consistently denied to date. That would completely contradict the purpose for which the *Sullivan* Court first declared that a commercial format alone was not sufficient to deprive a message of constitutional protection.[219]

The Court was correct in the way it considered and decided that question in *Sullivan*, and the manner in which it did so continues to offer guidance on the subject. In the manner in which the Court distinguished the context that *Sullivan* involved, the Court deemed the motive of the speaker who was most closely linked to the content of the speech to be material to the question of whether the speech could be eligible for First Amendment protection. The higher purpose that the Court emphasized in distinguishing the speech involved—advancing the cause of "a movement whose existence and objectives are matters of the highest public interest and concern"—derived from the civil rights leaders who placed the ad, not the commercial entity that merely conveyed the speech.[220] By the same token, the party with the greatest access to the truth of the speech in question was not the commercial entity that conveyed the speech. The importance of a commercial speaker's access to the truth of its factual representations was emphasized even more clearly in later commercial speech cases. In *Virginia State Board of Pharmacy v. Virginia Citizens Consumer Council*, the Court stated that "[t]he advertiser's access to the truth about his product and its price substantially eliminates any danger that governmental regulation of false or misleading price or product advertising will chill accurate and nondeceptive commercial expression." There is, therefore, little need to sanction "some falsehood in order to protect speech that matters."[221] In *Central Hudson Gas and Electric. v. Public Service Commission*, the Court again emphasized the "extensive knowledge" that commercial speakers have "of both the market and their products."[222] Yet, in *Nike, Inc. v. Kasky*, the commercial motive and the greatest access to the truth of the message were not located in separate entities but in the same entity: Nike.

The California Supreme Court reflected the significance of that distinction in its observation that a fundamental assumption of commercial speech doctrine is that "commercial speech consists of factual statements and that those statements describe matters within

---

[219]376 U.S. 254, 266 (1964).

[220]*Id*. at 266.

[221]425 U.S. 748, 777–78 (1976) (Stewart, J., concurring) (quoting Gertz v. Robert Welch, Inc., 418 U.S. 323, 340 (1974)).

[222]447 U.S. 557, 564 (1980).

the personal knowledge of the speaker or the person whom the speaker is representing and are made for the purpose of financial gain."[223] Thus, a holding that protected false commercial speech in a case like *Nike* would also be inconsistent with the emphasis of the Supreme Court's commercial speech holdings on providing citizens with more access to truthful information. Rather than denying citizens truthful information, the California Supreme Court's decision offers a mechanism whereby untruthful commercial information may be reduced, *increasing* the relative flow of truthful commercial information to consumers. The *Sullivan* Court found that, in order to protect a cause "of the highest public interest and concern," it was justified to bar punishment for falsehoods made without knowledge or reckless disregard of their falsity.[224] To invert that reasoning in order to deny citizens truthful commercial information would be to render the noble purpose of *Sullivan* meaningless. *Sullivan* provides a basis for considering when false speech warrants protection—not for perfunctorily protecting falsity in any message attached to any public issue, regardless the context, regardless the purpose.

As Justice Stewart wrote in *Virginia Pharmacy*, "government may take broader action to protect the public from injury produced by false or deceptive price or product advertising than from harm caused by defamation."[225] In seeking to limit government's authority to punish criticism of government, the *Sullivan* Court sought to prevent the threat to the sovereignty of the people from the sort of excessive concentration of power that such authority would represent. Citizens subject to such punishment from government officials would be disadvantaged in a manner contradictory to the most fundamental principles of the American Constitution. To provide immensely powerful corporate speakers such as Nike with constitutional protection for false commercial speech would similarly threaten citizens. Society's ability to "insur[e] that the stream of commercial information flow[s] cleanly as well as freely"[226] would be jeopardized to an extent never before deemed constitutional by the Supreme Court.

Preventing false commercial speech from being immunized by attaching it to a public issue is also consistent with the way the Court's case law reflects its unwillingness to extend the *Sullivan* actual malice standard too broadly. *Sullivan* established the rule of law that

---

[223]45 P.3d 243, 257 (Cal. 2002).
[224]376 U.S. at 266.
[225]425 U.S. 748, 776–77 (1976) (Stewart, J., concurring).
[226]*Id.* at 772.

public officials may not recover damages for defamatory statements made relating to their official conduct absent showing with convincing clarity that the statements were knowingly false or made with reckless disregard of whether they were false.[227] Seven years after *Sullivan*, the Court briefly appeared to extend that protection to "all discussion and communication involving matters of public or general concern," regardless the identity of the defamed, in *Rosenbloom v. Metromedia*.[228] Three years after *Rosenbloom*, however, that plurality holding was rejected in *Gertz v. Robert Welch, Inc*.[229] The Court said that the interest in preventing self-censorship in discussion of public issues had to be balanced against what it declared the greater interest in protecting private individuals from the "harm inflicted on them by defamatory falsehood."[230] Therefore, the Court concluded, it was constitutional to condition the actual malice requirement on the identity of the defamed and to require only the lesser fault standard of negligence in libel actions by private individuals.[231]

Possibly the Supreme Court would have been able to dispose of the *Nike* case without deciding the commercial/noncommercial speech issue, instead overturning the California court's action on issues raised by Nike over California allowing the suit to be brought by a private citizen without establishing the suffering of actual injury.[232] Kasky initiated the suit against Nike through a provision in the California False Advertising Law that permits actions for violations of the law to be brought either by a state prosecutor or by "any person acting for the interests of itself, its members or the general public."[233] Justice Breyer also criticized that aspect of the case in his dissenting opinion in *Nike*.[234] On the other hand, questioning in oral arguments seemed to suggest some skepticism on that point, with the question arising as to whether a plaintiff like Kasky could establish actual injury simply by showing he had purchased a pair of Nike

---

[227]376 U.S. at 279–80.

[228]403 U.S. 29, 43–44 (1971).

[229]418 U.S. 323 (1974).

[230]*Id*. at 341. The latter interest was greater, the Court said, because public officials and figures voluntarily expose themselves to comment and criticism by their involvement in public affairs and have greater access to channels of mass communication through which to respond to negative statements made about them.

[231]*Id*. at 348–51.

[232]Brief for Appellant at 20, 47–50, Nike, Inc. v. Kasky, 123 S. Ct. 2554 (2003) (No. 02–575).

[233]Cal. Bus. & Prof. Code Ann. § 17535. (West 1997).

[234]123 S. Ct. 2554, 2560, 2566–69 (2003) (Breyer, J., dissenting).

shoes that he wouldn't have purchased if he had not been misled by the allegedly deceptive advertising in question.[235]

At the very least, it would be a remarkable stroke of jurisprudential irony to make such considerations dispositive in *Nike* when none of the plaintiffs in the landmark *Virginia Pharmacy* case that established constitutional protection for purely commercial speech had themselves suffered any injury—as Justice William Rehnquist pointed out at the time.[236] The regulation in question barred pharmacists from advertising the prices of prescription drugs, but it placed no such restrictions on the consumer group that brought the suit. Nothing in the regulation, Justice Rehnquist wrote, would have prevented the group from

> collecting and publishing comparative price information as to various pharmacies in an area. Indeed they have done as much in their briefs in this case. Yet ... the Court finds that they have standing to protest that pharmacists are not allowed to advertise. ... Here, the only group truly restricted by this statute, the pharmacists, have not even troubled to join in this litigation and may well feel that the expense and competition of advertising is not in their interest.[237]

It would provide greater clarity if the Court were to decide a future case like *Nike* on a broader basis. That would mean weighing, as the Court did in *Sullivan,* the greater societal balance at stake and rendering a decision that protects the sovereignty of citizens against the encroachment of concentrated power. Enabling immense *corporate* commercial entities like Nike to immunize false commercial speech from regulation by attaching it to a public issue represents a particularly dangerous concentration of power. The Supreme Court in its corporate speech cases[238] has articulated a doctrine focused upon preventing actual and potential corruption of the political market-

---

[235]Oral Arguments at 12–15, 21–28, *Nike, Inc. v. Kasky*, 123 S. Ct. 2554 (2003) (No. 02–575).

[236]Virginia State Bd. of Pharmacy v. Virginia Citizens Consumer Council, 425 U.S. 748, 781–84 (1976) (Rehnquist, J., dissenting).

[237]*Id*. at 783–84 (Rehnquist, CJ, dissenting).

[238]*See* Austin v. Michigan State Chamber of Commerce, 494 U.S. 652 (1990); Federal Election Commission v. Massachusetts Citizens for Life, Inc., 479 U.S. 238 (1986); Federal Election Commission v. National Conservative Political Action Committee, 470 U.S. 480 (1985); Federal Election Commission v. National Right to Work Committee, 459 U.S. 197 (1982). "Corporate speech" in this context refers to speech by corporations that is designed to influence political and social outcomes, rather than to promote products, and the related case law defines the parameters within which political speech by corporations can be regulated by government.

place of ideas through wealth generated via the significant, state-conferred advantages of the corporate form in the economic marketplace.[239] Just as the Court has sought to protect the political marketplace from the dangers of concentrated power represented by the corporate form, so too it would do well to protect the economic marketplace from the threat of false commercial speech immunized by linkage to public debate.

CONCLUSION

The Supreme Court let the opportunity pass to answer the significant question at the heart of *Nike, Inc. v. Kasky*, yet it is all but inevitable that a similar set of circumstances will come again. The question has grown ever more urgent since the Court opened the door to First Amendment protection for commercial speech in *New York Times Co. v. Sullivan*. Whether, for purposes of regulation, commercial speech can ultimately be distinguished from speech disseminated by a commercial speaker concerning matters of public debate is a question that will continue to demand an answer from the high Court. The *Sullivan* legacy provides relevant context for considering the implications of the *Nike* case. Whether the interest in protecting public debate justifies extending First Amendment protection to any false commercial speech attached to a public issue, a future Court must decide. Such a holding, however, would not only represent the most significant change of course in the commercial speech case law since *Sullivan* itself, it would subvert the most fundamental principles by which that historic First Amendment decision was decided.

---

[239]Those advantages include particularly perpetual life, limited liability and special tax advantages. *See* United States v. Morton Salt Co., 338 U.S. 632, 652 (1950).

A KEY INFLUENCE ON THE DOCTRINE OF ACTUAL MALICE: JUSTICE WILLIAM BRENNAN'S JUDICIAL PHILOSOPHY AT WORK IN CHANGING THE LAW OF SEDITIOUS LIBEL

CARLO A. PEDRIOLI*

Much of the scholarship on Justice William Brennan's landmark opinion in New York Times Co. v. Sullivan *has focused on the actual malice doctrine and its implications. In light of the historic change in the law of seditious libel in the United States as a result of the case and the need for further exploration of the human factors behind the case, this article explains how Justice Brennan's instrumentalist judicial philosophy had an important influence on changing the course of legal protection for speech critical of the government. The article concludes that the outcome of the case likely would have differed notably if a justice with a formalist, Holmesian or natural law philosophy had authored the opinion for the Court.*

Judicial self-restraint, which defers too much to the sovereign powers of the states and reserves judicial intervention for only the most revolting cases, will not serve to enhance Madison's priceless gift of "the great rights of mankind secured under this Constitution."[1]

We may try to see things as objectively as we please. Nonetheless, we can never see them with any eyes except our own.[2]

---

*Member, State Bar of California; Ph.D. student, Department of Communication, University of Utah.

[1] William J. Brennan, *The Bill of Rights and the States*, 36 N.Y.U. L. REV. 761, 778 (1961).

[2] BENJAMIN N. CARDOZO, THE NATURE OF THE JUDICIAL PROCESS 13 (1921).

The profound impact of the actual malice doctrine that Justice William Brennan laid out in *New York Times Co. v. Sullivan*,[3] which constitutionalized libel law, an area of the law traditionally left to the states, and "held that the 'central meaning' of the First Amendment is to protect criticism of the government,"[4] has become apparent in the years since 1964.[5] The opinion by Justice Brennan[6] for the Supreme Court of the United States aided the news media in informing the U.S. public, without fear of legal retaliation, about the South's resistance to civil rights advocates like Martin Luther King, Jr.[7] This national awareness of resistance in the South helped King gain support for his cause and influenced passage of the 1964 Civil Rights Act fewer than four months after the Court ruled in *Times v. Sullivan*.[8] Additionally, the actual malice doctrine has had a major impact on the news, political and otherwise, that people in the United States receive every day since, without the case, news organizations would

---

[3]376 U.S. 254 (1964). The doctrine of actual malice specifically states that a public official can prevail in a libel suit related to the official's public status only if the official shows that the defendant acted "with knowledge that [the statement] was false or with reckless disregard of whether [the statement] was false or not." *Id.* at 280–81. Because this doctrine raises the level of proof for public officials in lawsuits, one impact is to open the door to greater criticism of government officials.

[4]W. Wat Hopkins, *Justice Brennan, Justice Harlan, and* New York Times Co. v. Sullivan: *A Case Study in Supreme Court Decision Making*, 1 COMM. L. & POL'Y 469, 471 (1996).

[5]For an idea of the general scholarly agreement of the historic status that *Times v. Sullivan* has among Supreme Court decisions on free speech jurisprudence, *see, e.g.*, MATTHEW D. BUNKER, CRITIQUING FREE SPEECH: FIRST AMENDMENT THEORY AND THE CHALLENGE OF INTERDISCIPLINARITY 146 (2001); W. WAT HOPKINS, MR. JUSTICE BRENNAN AND FREEDOM OF EXPRESSION 83 (1991); KIM ISAAC EISLER, A JUSTICE FOR ALL: WILLIAM J. BRENNAN, JR., AND THE DECISIONS THAT TRANSFORMED AMERICA 185 (1993); Clay Calvert, *When First Amendment Principles Collide: Negative Political Advertising & the Demobilization of Democratic Self-Governance*, 30 LOY. L.A. L. REV. 1539, 1546 (1997). Hopkins has called the decision "the most important libel opinion ever written and the most important free-expression opinion in U.S. jurisprudence" because the case changed both the law and the language of libel. *Supra* note 4, at 471. Calvert has labeled the decision "seminal," at 1546.

[6]Chief Justice Earl Warren asked Justice Brennan to write the majority opinion, perhaps because Brennan already had demonstrated his ability to craft opinions that could command a Court in difficult cases. For instance, Brennan had done so in *Baker v. Carr*, 369 U.S. 186 (1962), in which the Court held that federal courts can hear suits by voters who claim that legislative apportionment has denied the voters equal protection of the law. *See* ANTHONY LEWIS, MAKE NO LAW: THE SULLIVAN CASE AND THE FIRST AMENDMENT 166 (1991). Also, while Brennan, like other justices, often asked his law clerks to write initial drafts of opinions, Brennan himself drafted the opinion in *Times v. Sullivan*. *Id.* at 166.

[7]*See* HUNTER R. CLARK, JUSTICE BRENNAN: THE GREAT CONCILIATOR 232 (1995).
[8]*See id.*

have to be much more careful about avoiding potential libel suits.[9] In the wake of the September 11, 2001, terrorist attacks on the United States and President George W. Bush's war on terror,[10] the case once again stands as a firm reminder that citizens have a fundamental right to criticize the government when they do not approve of its conduct.[11] This right to criticize the government, formerly not a right but the crime of seditious libel,[12] is a key part of representative democracy, regardless of whether the members of government fully appreciate it.[13]

---

[9]*See* STEPHEN L. SEPINUCK & MARY PAT TREUTHART, THE CONSCIENCE OF THE COURT: SELECTED OPINIONS OF JUSTICE WILLIAM J. BRENNAN JR. ON FREEDOM AND EQUALITY 4 (1999).

[10]*See, e.g., President Bush Addresses Congress*, ONLINE NEWSHOUR (Sept. 20, 2001), http://www.pbs.org/newshour/bb/military/terroristattack/bush_speech_9_20 .html (last visited Feb. 6, 2004) ("Our war on terror begins with al-Qaida, but it does not end there. It will not end until every terrorist group of global reach has been found, stopped, and defeated.").

[11]Many citizens opted to exercise their rights under *Times v. Sullivan* and protest the Bush Administration's 2003 war against Iraq. Some individuals even protested the war months before it began. *See, e.g., Protesting War with Iraq*, ONLINE NEWSHOUR (Nov. 25, 2002), http://www.pbs.org/newshour/bb/military/july_dec02/ antiwar_11_25.html (last visited Feb. 6, 2004); *Background: Protesting War*, ONLINE NEWSHOUR (Jan. 20, 2003), http://www.pbs.org/newshour/bb/politics/jan_ june03/background_protesting_1_20.html (last visited Feb. 6, 2004); *Anti-War Protests Continue with Large Crowds in N.Y.*, ONLINE NEWSHOUR (Mar. 22, 2003), http://www.pbs.org/newshour/updates/protests_03_22_03.html (last visited Feb. 6, 2004).

[12]*See* DWIGHT L. TEETER ET AL., LAW OF MASS COMMUNICATIONS: FREEDOM AND CONTROL OF PRINT AND BROADCAST MEDIA 25 (1998) (defining *seditious libel* "as expression attacking government's form, laws, institutions, or officers"). The traditional justification for criminalizing speech critical of the government was that such speech would tarnish necessary respect for the government. *See* William T. Mayton, *Seditious Libel and the Lost Guarantee of a Freedom of Expression*, 84 COLUM. L. REV. 91, 91 (1984). More recently, the justification has been that speech critical of the government might bring about illegal acts. *Id.* For the early seventeenth century origin of the crime of seditious libel in England, *see* Irving Brant, *Seditious Libel: Myth And Reality*, 39 N.Y.U. L. REV. 1 (1964) (arguing that Sir Edward Coke had essentially no precedent upon which to base a claim that seditious libel had become well established in the English common law by Coke's own time). For more on the genesis of seditious libel, *see* Philip Hamburger, *The Development of the Law of Seditious Libel and the Control of the Press*, 37 STAN. L. REV. 661, 691–97 (1985).

[13]In his opinion for the Court, Brennan wrote, "'It is a prized American privilege to speak one's mind, although not always with perfect good taste, on all public institutions.'" *Times v. Sullivan*, 376 U.S. 254, 269 (1964) (quoting Bridges v. California, 314 U.S. 252, 270 (1941)). The notion of free speech as an important component of democracy goes back at least as far as ancient Greece. *See* Judith Schenck Koffler & Bennett L. Gershman, *The New Seditious Libel*, 69 CORNELL L. REV. 816, 879–80 (1984). *See also* David J. Vergobbi, *Freedom of Expression, Western Historical Foundations of, in* 2 ENCYCLOPEDIA OF INT'L MEDIA & COMMUNICATIONS 41, 41–43 (Donald H. Johnston ed., 2003). Unfortunately for 60% of the population in ancient Athens, free speech rights only attached to citizenship, and this fact left "males un-

Nonetheless, despite the memory of a cultural legacy of free expression that many individuals in the United States may have today,
for much of its history the United States experienced a cultural legacy of suppression. As this article will demonstrate, from soon after
the ratification of First Amendment until the middle of the twentieth
century, the legal basis for protecting criticism of the government
was generally quite feeble. The protection for this type of speech
changed with *Times v. Sullivan*, in which the Court offered a re-
sounding defense for speech critical of the government.

Perhaps not surprisingly, much of the scholarship on Brennan's
opinion for the Court has focused on the actual malice doctrine and
its implications. Some of this scholarship has defended the actual
malice rule in a democratic society,[14] evaluated the rule in the context of contemporary political campaigning,[15] considered whether
the economic impacts of the rule would justify modifying the rule,[16]
proposed a standard lower than actual malice in cases without damages at stake,[17] looked at the rule in the context of the corporation as
a defamation plaintiff,[18] and even questioned whether the Supreme
Court made a prudent decision in *Times v. Sullivan*.[19] Also, this
scholarship has compared the rule in *Times v. Sullivan* with a similar rule in Australian law.[20]

The doctrinal components of the case are worthy of study, but so
are other aspects. In light of this point, some research has given at-

---

der eighteen, women, resident aliens, [and] slaves" without such rights. James G.
McLaren, *The "Primacy" of the First Amendment: Does It Have a Justification in
Natural Law, History, and Democracy?*, 5 USAFA J. LEG. STUD. 45, 47 (1994/1995).
Justice Louis Brandeis, echoing the work of Pericles, picked up on the better aspects
of this Greek understanding of the relationship between free speech and democracy
with the concurring opinion in *Whitney v. California*, 274 U.S. 357, 375 (1927). *See*
Koffler & Bennet, *supra* at 880 n.297.

[14]*See* Harry Kalven, *The* New York Times *Case: A Note on "The Central Meaning
of the First Amendment,"* 1964 SUP. CT. REV. 191.

[15]*See* Thomas Kane, *Malice, Lies, and Videotape: Revisiting* New York Times v.
Sullivan *in the Modern Age of Political Campaigns*, 30 RUTGERS L.J. 755 (1999).

[16]*See* Kristian D. Whitten, *The Economics of Actual Malice: A Proposal for Legislative Change to the Rule of* New York Times v. Sullivan, 32 CUMB. L. REV. 519
(2001).

[17]*See* Pierre N. Leval, *The No-Money, No-Fault Libel Suit: Keeping* Sullivan *in Its
Proper Place*, 101 HARV. L. REV. 1287 (1988).

[18]*See* D. Mark Jackson, *The Corporate Defamation Plaintiff in the Era of
SLAPPs: Revisiting* New York Times v. Sullivan, 9 WM. & MARY BILL RTS. J. 491
(2001).

[19]*See* Richard A. Epstein, *Was* New York Times v. Sullivan *Wrong?*, 53 U. CHI. L.
REV. 782 (1986).

[20]*See* Russell L. Weaver & Kathe Boehringer, *Implied Rights and the Australian
Constitution: A Modified* New York Times, Inc. v. Sullivan *Goes Down Under*, 8
SETON HALL CONST. L.J. 459 (1998).

tention to various human factors behind the actual malice rule. For instance, research has focused on the interpersonal and group dynamics of the members of the Court who decided the case[21] and considered *Times v. Sullivan* in the context of Brennan's views on free speech.[22] However, such research has not given sufficient attention to the broad judicial philosophy that guided Brennan's understanding of free speech. Given that humans make the rules of constitutional law by which citizens in the United States live and that different justices might establish differing rules of law in the same case, additional research on the human factors behind *Times v. Sullivan* is necessary to foster a better understanding of this vitally important case and its impact on changing the course of the law.

In light of the historical change in the law of seditious libel that *Times v. Sullivan* prompted and the need for further exploration of the human factors behind the case, this article gives attention to Brennan's judicial philosophy at work in the case. It defines judicial philosophy as a system of guiding principles upon which a judge calls in the process of legal decision-making.[23] Specifically, the article explains how, through *Times v. Sullivan,* Brennan's instrumentalist judicial philosophy had an important influence on changing the course of legal protection for criticism of the government in the United States.[24] To advance this central point, the article will present a short history of criticism of the government in the United States before *Times v. Sullivan*, an overview of Brennan and his judicial philosophy, a summary of *Times v. Sullivan*, and an application of Brennan's judicial philosophy to the case.

---

[21]*See* Hopkins, *supra* note 4.

[22]*See* HOPKINS, *supra* note 5, at 83–90. Much of chapter five of this study focuses on *Times v. Sullivan*, but, as the title suggests, the book as a whole considers Brennan's views on free speech beyond this case.

[23]In the words of Benjamin Cardozo, a judicial philosophy is "a stream of tendency ... which gives coherence and direction to thought and action." CARDOZO, *supra* note 2, at 12. Factors like "inherited instincts, traditional beliefs, [and] acquired convictions" influence one's judicial philosophy. *Id.*

[24]Other factors likely influenced Brennan's decision in *Times v. Sullivan*, too. For instance, the other justices had their say in the decision. Also, the civil rights era of the 1950s and 1960s in which the Court issued *Times v. Sullivan* can help to account for the political context of the decision. *See* Clay Calvert, *Protecting the Cellular Citizen-Critic: The State of Political Speech from* Sullivan *to* Popa, 9 WM. & MARY BILL RTS. J. 353, 353 (2001). Additionally, law professor Herbert Wechsler coauthored the brief and argued the case for the New York Times Co.; Brennan adopted in the Court's opinion portions of Wechsler's argument. *See* Anthony Lewis, New York Times v. Sullivan *Reconsidered: Time to Return to "The Central Meaning of the First Amendment,"* 83 COLUM. L. REV. 603, 603–07 (1983). Regardless of these other influences, since Brennan himself ultimately authored the opinion for the Court, his judicial philosophy deserves careful attention.

CRITICISM OF THE GOVERNMENT BEFORE *TIMES V. SULLIVAN*

Prior to *Times v. Sullivan*, the United States had experienced a history of hostility towards criticism of the government. For example, several years after the ratification of the First Amendment, the Congress passed the Sedition Act of 1798, which criminalized:

> any false, scandalous and malicious writing or writings against the government of the United States, or either house of the Congress of the United States, or the President of the United States, with intent to defame the said government, or either house of the said Congress, or the said President, or to bring them, or either of them, into contempt or disrepute.[25]

Under the Sedition Act, one could face a fine of up to $2,000 and up to two years in prison.[26] The government successfully prosecuted fourteen journalists and publicists for criticizing the administration of John Adams.[27]

This approach to free speech continued into the nineteenth century. Before the Civil War, almost all southern states passed laws that limited speech critical of slavery, a government-sanctioned institution.[28] In addition, many postmasters in the South censored abolitionist literature that passed through the mails,[29] and southern academics who spoke out against slavery faced "a better than excellent chance of losing [their] job[s]."[30] Suppression of speech was not limited to the South. Some citizens, no matter where they lived, decided to take matters into their own hands regarding abolition.[31] In 1835, for example, a Boston mob dragged outspoken abolitionist Wil-

---

[25]1 Stat. 596 (1798).

[26]*Id.* at 597.

[27]*See* TEETER ET AL., *supra* note 12, at 31. Some of the Jeffersonian Republicans pointed out that the Sedition Act was a clear impediment to self-government. *Id.*

[28]*See* NAT HENTOFF, THE FIRST FREEDOM: THE TUMULTUOUS HISTORY OF FREE SPEECH IN AMERICA 89 (1980). *See also* Amy Reynolds, *The Impact of* Walker's Appeal *on Northern and Southern Conceptions of Free Speech in the Nineteenth Century*, 9 COMM. L. & POL'Y 73 (2004).

[29]*See id.* at 90.

[30]*Id.*

[31]*Id.* Unlike most of the examples of suppression of speech discussed herein, the pre-Civil War mob activity was not officially government action. Hence, it did not implicate the First Amendment since the Constitution generally limits government rather than private action. *See* WILLIAM COHEN & JONATHAN D. VARAT, CONSTITUTIONAL LAW: CASES AND MATERIALS 1107 (1998). Regardless, this mob activity did impact the right of citizens to speak out against the government policy that legitimized slavery.

liam Lloyd Garrison through the streets.[32] In other cases, mobs destroyed abolitionists' printing presses.[33]

During the Civil War, suppression of speech persisted. Congress passed a law that banned seditious conspiracy, and the government practiced censorship.[34] President Abraham Lincoln shut down New York City newspapers for printing material which reflected poorly on the government,[35] and some northern military commanders shut down newspapers.[36] President Lincoln also ordered that "[t]housands of suspected or known dissenters and suspected 'dangerous' men [be] thrown into military prisons without charges and without trial."[37] Additionally, the postmaster general banned certain types of papers from the mails.[38]

Despite earlier suppression of speech, the World War I era may have been the most oppressive toward speech critical of the government. Congress passed the Sedition Act of 1918, which criminalized criticism of the government, especially criticism which attempted to interfere with the draft or the armed forces.[39] Under the Sedition Act of 1918, one could face a fine of up to $10,000, up to twenty years in prison, or both.[40] The government used this legislation to prosecute about 1,900 individuals.[41] In the same spirit, the Supreme Court refused to allow opponents of the government to send anti-war leaflets through the post,[42] to criticize *via* newspapers the government's involvement in the war,[43] to deliver speeches against the government's involvement in the war,[44] or to distribute pro-anarchy circulars.[45] Essentially, the Court upheld the Sedition Act of 1918 and allowed a number of critics of the government to go to jail.

---

[32]*Id.*

[33]*Id.* at 91.

[34]*See* Margaret A. Blanchard, *"Why Can't We Ever Learn?" Cycles of Stability, Stress and Freedom of Expression in United States History*, 7 COMM. L. & POL'Y 347, 354 (2002).

[35]*See id.*

[36]*See* HENTOFF, *supra* note 28, at 94.

[37]Koffler & Gershman, *supra* note 13, at 829–30.

[38]*See* HENTOFF, *supra* note 28, at 94.

[39]40 Stat. 553–54 (1918). The Sedition Act of 1918 amended the Espionage Act of 1917. 40 Stat. 217 (1917).

[40]*Id.*

[41]*See* TEETER ET AL., *supra* note 12, at 33.

[42]*See* Schenck v. United States, 249 U.S. 47 (1919).

[43]*See* Frohwerk v. United States, 249 U.S. 204 (1919).

[44]*See* Debs v. United States, 249 U.S. 211 (1919).

[45]*See* Abrams v. United States, 250 U.S. 616 (1919). *But see* the dissent of Justice Oliver Wendell Holmes, 250 U.S. at 630 (noting "that the best test of truth is the power of the thought to get itself accepted in the competition of the market").

Shortly after World War I, the government pursued a wave of prosecutions of members of the Communist Party. The Supreme Court
upheld these convictions for both printing and distributing a manifesto that called for the overthrow of the government[46] and for simply attending a Communist Party meeting.[47] At this time in history,
individuals often went to jail for what they had communicated rather
than for what they had done.[48]

During World War II and the ensuing decade, the government
adopted a similar attitude towards criticism of the government. Congress established the House Committee on Un-American Activities,
which ultimately investigated a number of individuals believed to be
Communists.[49] In 1940, Congress passed the Alien Registration Act,
more commonly known as the Smith Act, which criminalized advocating the forcible overthrow of the government and carried a penalty of no more than $10,000, a prison sentence of no longer than ten
years, or both.[50] Under the Smith Act, the government fined or im-
prisoned approximately 100 people.[51] In one highly publicized case,[52]
the Supreme Court upheld under the Smith Act the prosecutions of
eleven Communists.[53]

As this brief review of history shows, the United States before
1964 had a long-standing legacy of hostility towards criticism of the
government.[54] Since shortly after the ratification of the Bill of

---

[46]*See* Gitlow v. New York, 268 U.S. 652 (1925). *But see* the dissent of Justice
Holmes, 268 U.S. at 672.

[47]*See* Whitney v. California, 274 U.S. 357 (1927). *But see* the concurrence of Justice Louis Brandeis, 274 U.S. at 375 (noting that "public discussion is a political
duty").

[48]*See* HENTOFF, *supra* note 28, at 119.

[49]*See* Blanchard, *supra* note 34, at 364.

[50]54 Stat. 670–71 (1940).

[51]*See* TEETER ET AL., *supra* note 12, at 34.

[52]*See* Dennis v. United States, 341 U.S. 494 (1951).

[53]*See* TEETER ET AL., *supra* note 12, at 35.

[54]This article does not advance the position that before 1964 the law in the United
States had in all cases been hostile to criticism of the government. *See, e.g.,* Yates v.
United States, 354 U.S. 298 (1957) (overturning fourteen Smith Act convictions of
Communist Party members who conspired to advocate and teach the overthrow of
the government and who organized the Communist Party as a means of so advocating and teaching); Bridges v. California, 314 U.S. 252 (1941) (upholding the right to
criticize the judiciary regarding pending cases); Near v. Minnesota, 283 U.S. 697
(1931) (condemning prior restraint of the press by the government). While these
cases extended protection for speech critical of the government, they did not go as
far rhetorically as did *Times v. Sullivan*. *Near* merely protected against governmental prior restraint; that case, unlike *Times v. Sullivan*, did not protect against libel
suits that could follow the printing of material critical of government officials. Also,
despite Justice Hugo Black's language in *Bridges* that "it is a prized American privilege to speak one's mind, although not always with perfect good taste, on all public

Rights, the government, sometimes assisted by private individuals, had taken a number steps to limit this speech. Accordingly, in 1964 the stage was set for Brennan's opinion in *Times v. Sullivan*.

JUDICIAL PHILOSOPHY AND JUSTICE BRENNAN

Justice William Brennan played a significant role on the Supreme Court between 1956, when he joined the Court, and 1990, when he retired. During that time, he wrote some 1,360 opinions—461 majority opinions, 425 dissents and a variety of other separate hybrid opinions.[55] Some of Brennan's major opinions ranged from legislative apportionment and voting rights,[56] to governmental interference with religion,[57] to school desegregation,[58] to public assistance funding,[59] to the death penalty,[60] to gender-based discrimination.[61]

Many of Brennan's most significant contributions, however, came in the area of free speech. During his tenure, the Court considered almost 300 cases on free speech.[62] Brennan wrote forty-two majority or plurality opinions in those cases, more than any other member of the Court, and seventy-five concurring or dissenting opinions.[63] *Times v. Sullivan* may be Brennan's most significant because, in resolving the case, the Court unanimously voted to expand the range of speech protected under the ambit of the First Amendment's Free Speech and Press clauses and made lawfully criticizing public officials much

---

institutions," 314 U.S. at 270, that language initially did not stand up when tested because, a decade later, the Court upheld convictions under the Smith Act for eleven Communists who had advocated the overthrow of the government. *See Dennis*, 341 U.S. at 494. Finally, while *Yates* granted protection for criticism of the government, unlike *Times v. Sullivan* it did not do so in "ringing or memorable words" that would set the standard for decades to come. Blanchard, *supra* note 34, at 372.

[55]*See* David H. Souter, *Justice Brennan's Place in Legal History, in* REASON AND PASSION: JUSTICE BRENNAN'S ENDURING INFLUENCE 301 (E. Joshua Rosenkranz & Bernard Schwartz eds., 1997).

[56]*See* Baker v. Carr, 369 U.S. 186, 186 (1962). Chief Justice Earl Warren called *Baker* "the most important case of my tenure on the Court." Lani Guinier & Pamela S. Karlan, *The Majoritarian Difficulty: One Person, One Vote, in* REASON AND PASSION: JUSTICE BRENNAN'S ENDURING INFLUENCE 207 (E. Joshua Rosenkranz & Bernard Schwartz eds., 1997).

[57]*See, e.g.,* Sherbert v. Verner, 374 U.S. 398 (1963). For limitations on *Sherbert*, *see* Employment Division v. Smith, 494 U.S. 872 (1990).

[58]*See, e.g.,* Green v. County School Board of New Kent County, 391 U.S. 430 (1968).

[59]*See* Goldberg v. Kelly, 397 U.S. 254 (1970).

[60]*See, e.g.,* Furman v. Georgia, 408 U.S. 238 (1972) (Brennan, J., concurring).

[61]*See* Craig v. Boren, 429 U.S. 190 (1976).

[62]*See* HOPKINS, *supra* note 5, at 13.

[63]*Id.* at 13, 14.

easier.[64] Perhaps in part because of Brennan's prolific nature and the prominent nature of cases like *Times v. Sullivan*, Justice Antonin Scalia, appointed by President Ronald Reagan, later called Brennan the most influential justice of the twentieth century.[65]

As do all justices, Brennan called upon his own understanding of the legal system to arrive at his conclusions. Both before and after *Times v. Sullivan,* he explained his judicial philosophy in speeches later published in law reviews, sources that can prove helpful in understanding a justice's philosophy on the law.[66]

Brennan's Philosophy and the Second Annual James Madison Lecture

In 1961, three years before the Supreme Court handed down *Times v. Sullivan*, Justice Brennan gave the Second Annual James Madison Lecture at the New York University School of Law.[67] In this speech, Brennan explained his belief in the doctrine of incorporation. Under the doctrine, the Bill of Rights would apply to the states so as to limit state restrictions on individual constitutional rights in situations where limitations already existed on federal restrictions on such rights.[68] The justice, who in 1961 had been on the Court a mere five years, explained how the result of the historical rejection of his position had been a failure to protect the rights of individuals. To make his case, Brennan traced the issue of incorporation to the founding of the nation, where the debate over federalism had begun,[69] through the seminal 1830s case of *Barron v.*

---

[64]Hopkins, *supra* note 4, at 471.

[65]*Justice Brennan Remembered*, available at ONLINE NEWSHOUR (July 24, 1997), http://www.pbs.org/newshour/bb/law/July_dec97/brennan_7_24.html (last visited Jan. 25, 2004).

[66]*See* John W. Poulos, *The Judicial Philosophy of Roger Traynor*, 46 HASTINGS L.J. 1643 (1995) (using a number of Traynor's speeches later published as articles to gain an understanding of Traynor's judicial philosophy). Unlike many majority opinions, speeches allow for clear expression of judges' philosophies because in speeches judges do not have to consider the philosophies of their colleagues and therefore can be more direct about personal preferences. The speeches cited in this article are representative of Brennan's speeches published mostly in law reviews from the early 1960s to roughly the end of his career.

[67]*See* Brennan, *supra* note 1. Justice Hugo Black gave the First Annual James Madison Lecture, in which he presented an absolutist understanding of the Bill of Rights and briefly expressed his support for the notion of total incorporation, by which the entire Bill of Rights applied to the states through the Fourteenth Amendment. *See* Hugo L. Black, *The Bill of Rights*, 35 N.Y.U. L. REV. 865 (1960).

[68]Brennan, *supra* note 1, at 761.

[69]*Id.* at 762. Federalism is the political arrangement by which the national and state governments share power. *See* LINDA R. MONK, THE WORDS WE LIVE BY: YOUR

Baltimore,[70] which had taken a conservative position on federalism,[71] and the post-Civil War years, during which demand for federal protection against abuse of state power had become stronger,[72] to the twentieth century debate over incorporation, noting that as of 1961 the Court had incorporated only several aspects of the Bill of Rights, including the Free Speech and Press clauses of the First Amendment.[73] In light of this history, Brennan called for much fuller incorporation of the Bill of Rights.

While the once-controversial debate over incorporation may be a fascinating matter for study, Justice Brennan's speech is of particular use to a historical study of *Times v. Sullivan* for at least three key philosophical insights that the justice offered. First, Brennan expressed his view of a living Constitution. Such a Constitution evolves with the times and is not stuck forever in the past, especially in the late eighteenth century.[74] Brennan's general view of incorporation was that even if the Bill of Rights did not apply to the states in 1833, it could apply to them in 1897, as in the case of the Takings Clause.[75] Some of Brennan's other examples, including the application of the Free Speech Clause to the states in 1925, served this point, too.[76] By giving examples in which the legal understanding of the Constitution had changed with time, and also by advocating for fuller incorporation of the Bill of Rights to the states, Brennan showed his preference for a living Constitution.

ANNOTATED GUIDE TO THE CONSTITUTION 118 (2003). Under the Tenth Amendment, powers not given to the federal government nor denied to the states belong to the states or the people. U.S. CONST. amend X.

[70]32 U.S. 243 (1833).

[71]Brennan, *supra* note 1, at 764. In *Barron v. Baltimore*, Chief Justice John Marshall held that the Bill of Rights applied only to the federal government and not to the states. 32 U.S. at 243. Hence, John Barron could not rely upon the Takings Clause of the Fifth Amendment to sue the city of Baltimore for damage to his wharf because at that time the Takings Clause did not apply to state and local governments. Under the Takings Clause, the government must provide fair compensation to a property owner whose property the government damages or acquires through ouster of the owner. BLACK'S LAW DICTIONARY 1467 (7th ed. 1999). In *Chicago, B. & Q. R. Co. v. Chicago*, 166 U.S. 226 (1897), the Court overturned *Barron* and absorbed for the first time a provision of the Bill of Rights, here the Takings Clause of the Fifth Amendment, into the Fourteenth Amendment.

[72]*Id.* at 765.

[73]*Id.* at 768–70. The Court addressed the incorporation of the Free Speech and Press clauses in *Gitlow v. New York*, 268 U.S. 652, 666 (1925).

[74]*See* Arlin M. Adams, *Justice Brennan and the Religion Clauses: The Concept of a "Living Constitution,"* 139 U. PA. L. REV. 1319, 1319 (1991).

[75]Brennan, *supra* note 1, at 764, 771.

[76]*Id.* at 770.

Second, Justice Brennan stated his belief in the critical importance of individual rights. As a matter of note, one point in the debate
over incorporation was that without incorporation state and local
governments might have the power to harm individual rights, even if
the federal government frequently did not have such power. In his
speech, Brennan stated that "case after case comes to the Court
which finds the individual battling to vindicate a claim under the Bill
of Rights," and the justice noted that checks are needed on the government's attempts at "whittling away the rights of the individual."[77] Brennan described the individual rights in the Bill of Rights
as the embodiment of "constitutional liberty"[78] and reminded his audience of the importance of "Madison's priceless gift of 'the great
rights of mankind secured under this Constitution.'"[79] Hence, individual rights were of critical importance to Brennan.

Third, Justice Brennan sketched out his view of the judiciary, both
at the federal and state levels, as the protector of individual rights.[80]
The justice said that "[j]udicial self-restraint which defers too much
to the sovereign powers of the states and reserves judicial intervention for only the most revolting cases will not serve to enhance Madison's priceless gift of 'the great rights of mankind secured under this
Constitution.'"[81] Brennan also observed that "[t]he Court has ...
compelling reasons for the application to the states of more of the
specifics of the Bill of Rights."[82] He then added, "Excessive emphasis
upon states' rights must not make the process of absorption 'a license to the judiciary to administer a watered-down, subjective version of the individual guarantees of the Bill of Rights when state
cases come before' the Court."[83] These comments suggest that the
courts, including the Supreme Court, have a key role to play in the

---

[77]*Id.* at 776.

[78]*Id.*

[79]*Id.* at 778.

[80]Critics of this perspective might describe it with the term *judicial activism*.
This term refers to an approach to judicial decision-making under which judges supposedly allow their views on public policy to guide their decisions. *See* BLACK'S LAW
DICTIONARY, *supra* note 71, at 850. In contrast, the term *judicial restraint* refers to
an approach to judicial decision-making under which judges supposedly refrain from
allowing their views on public policy to guide their decisions and instead look to precedent. *Id.* at 852.

[81]Brennan, *supra* note 1, at 778.

[82]*Id.* at 776.

[83]*Id.* at 777. The term *absorption* refers to application of the Bill of Rights to the
states. *See* BLACK'S LAW DICTIONARY, *supra* note 71, at 8. From a perspective that
adopts this language, the Due Process Clause of the Fourteenth Amendment would
absorb the provisions of the Bill of Rights for application to the states.

protection of individual rights. This was Brennan's view of the judiciary as protector of individual rights.

Brennan's Philosophy Expanded

In his James Madison Lecture, Justice Brennan expressed his belief in a living Constitution, the critical importance of individual rights, and the role of the judiciary as protector of such rights, but he focused most of his speech on incorporation. Hence, he was not necessarily as explicit in his argumentation about his macro-level judicial philosophy as he could have been had he selected a broader topic. In the years after the Court's decision in *Times v. Sullivan*, Brennan took a number of opportunities to explain his judicial philosophy more specifically. The philosophy Brennan expressed in the years following the opinion can be helpful in shedding light on the philosophy from which the opinion grew. Because the detail with which Brennan addressed his philosophy in his later speeches can provide for a richer understanding of the same philosophy that he merely sketched out in the 1961 Madison Lecture, looking at some of the key points in those subsequent speeches that mirror the key points in the Madison Lecture is now appropriate.

To begin with, throughout his judicial career Justice Brennan expressed his belief in a living Constitution.[84] "The genius of the Constitution resides not in any static meaning that it had in a world that is dead and gone," he said, "but in its adaptability to interpretations of its great principles that cope with today's problems and today's needs."[85] Law, "to be effective, must conform to the world in which it finds itself," Brennan stated.[86] For example, the justice maintained, "Equal protection of the laws means equal protection today, whatever else the phrase may have meant in other times."[87] To bolster his argument for a living Constitution, Brennan even went so far as to

---

[84]Justice Brennan adopted the metaphor which Justice Louis Brandeis had used to describe the Constitution. According to Brandeis, the Constitution "'is not a strait-jacket. It is a living organism.'" William J. Brennan, *Why [H]ave a Bill of Rights?*, 9 OXFORD J. LEG. STUDS. 425, 426 (1989).

[85]William J. Brennan, *Some Aspects of Federalism*, 39 N.Y.U. L. REV. 945, 956 (1964). *See also* William J. Brennan, *Constitutional Adjudication*, 40 NOTRE DAME LAWYER 559, 568 (1965); William J. Brennan, *Construing the Constitution*, 19 U.C. DAVIS L. REV. 2, 7 (1985); William J. Brennan, *State Constitutions and the Protection of Individual Rights*, 90 HARV. L. REV. 489, 495 (1977); William J. Brennan, *The Worldwide Influence of the United States Constitution as a Charter of Human Rights*, 15 NOVA L. REV. 1, 8 (1991).

[86]William J. Brennan, *"How Goes the Supreme Court?"*, 36 MERCER L. REV. 781, 788 (1985).

[87]Brennan, *Constitutional Adjudication, supra* note 85, at 567.

claim that "the Founding Fathers knew better than to pin down their descendants too closely."[88]

Justice Brennan maintained that the Constitution did not exist "to preserve a preexisting society but to make a new one."[89] He put his view of a living Constitution in this manner:

> We current Justices read the Constitution in the only way that we can: as Twentieth Century Americans. We look to the history of the time of framing and to the intervening history of interpretation. But the ultimate question must be, what do the words of the text mean in our time?[90]

Along these lines, the justice once noted with approval that "[l]aw is again coming alive as a living process responsive to changing human needs. The shift is to justice and away from fine-spun technicalities and abstract rules."[91] Again, this perspective accepted the need for the law, including the Constitution, to be relevant and adaptive to the concerns of the day.

Because he was not fond of the view that the Constitution is forever fixed in the past, Justice Brennan took a jab at individuals who held such a view.[92] "Those who would restrict claims of right to the values of 1791 specifically articulated in the Constitution," he declared, "turn a blind eye to social progress and eschew adaptation of overarching principles to changes of social circumstance."[93] From Brennan's vantage point, a Constitution fixed in the past would not be able to account for the evolution of the times.

Brennan also expressed a belief that individual rights were of critical importance. The jurist wrote that equality involved bringing "justice, equal and practical, to the poor, to the members of minority groups, to the criminally accused, to the displaced persons of the technological revolution, to alienated youth, to the urban masses, to the unrepresented consumers."[94] He added, "[T]he judicial pursuit of equality is in my view properly regarded to be the

---

[88]Brennan, *supra* note 86, at 789.

[89]Brennan, *Construing the Constitution*, *supra* note 85, at 7.

[90]*Id. See also* Brennan, *The Worldwide Influence*, *supra* note 85, at 8.

[91]Brennan, *Constitutional Adjudication*, *supra* note 85, at 563.

[92]For an example of a perspective different from the perspective which views the Constitution as a living document, *see* Edwin Meese, *Construing the Constitution*, 19 U.C. DAVIS L. REV. 22 (1985). Meese called the perspective that he and others held "a jurisprudence of original intention." *Id.* at 26.

[93]Brennan, *The Worldwide Influence*, *supra* note 85, at 8.

[94]William J. Brennan, *Address*, 6 U. HAW. L. REV. 1, 2 (1984). *See also* William J. Brennan, *The Equality Principle: A Foundation of American Law*, 20 U.C. DAVIS L. REV. 673, 674 (1987).

noblest mission of judges; it has been the primary task of judges since the repudiation of laissez faire capitalism as our central constitutional concern."[95] Beyond the principle of equality, Brennan stressed due process individual rights such as the rights of life and liberty.[96] For example, he expressed great concern for the right of criminal defendants in capital cases to life.[97] "As government acts ever more deeply upon those areas of our lives once marked 'private,'" he warned, "there is an even greater need to see that individual rights are not curtailed or cheapened in the interest of what may temporarily appear to be the 'public good.'"[98] Brennan viewed the Constitution as the "charter of [those] human rights" for which he had stated his concern.[99]

The jurist suggested that protection of individual rights promoted the human dignity of citizens. Specifically, he expressed his belief that the Constitution "is a sparkling vision of the supremacy of the human dignity of every individual,"[100] later adding, "The supreme value of democracy is the dignity and worth of the individual ... ."[101] Additionally, Brennan saw the protection of individual rights as a process that would help the United States set a worldwide example "as a shining city upon a hill."[102]

Although Justice Brennan maintained that he was a "believer in our concept of federalism," he would not allow federal deference to the rights of states to harm individual rights.[103] Hence, while states had a role in enforcing individual rights, so did the federal govern-

---

[95]*Id.* at 2.

[96]Brennan, *State Constitutions, supra* note 85, at 491–92.

[97]*See, e.g.,* William J. Brennan, *Constitutional Adjudication and the Death Penalty: A View from the Court,* 100 HARV. L. REV. 313 (1986); William J. Brennan, *Foreword: Neither Victims Nor Executioners,* 8 NOTRE DAME J.L. ETHICS & PUB. POL'Y 1 (1994).

[98]Brennan, *Construing the Constitution, supra* note 85, at 9.

[99]Brennan, *The Worldwide Influence, supra* note 85, at 2.

[100]Brennan, *Construing the Constitution, supra* note 85, at 8.

[101]William J. Brennan, *What's Ahead for the New Lawyer?,* 47 U. PITT. L. REV. 705, 707 (1986).

[102]Brennan, *The Equality Principle, supra* note 94, at 678. Of note, the "city upon a hill" metaphor has been a somewhat popular metaphor in U.S. rhetoric. John Winthrop, Ronald Reagan and other speakers have used the metaphor. *See* Amos Kiewe & Davis W. Houck, *The Rhetoric of Reaganomics: A Redemptive Vision,* 40 COMM. STUD. 97, 97, 107 (1989); Harold Mixon, *"A City Upon a Hill": John Cotton's Apocalyptic Rhetoric and the Fifth Monarchy Movement in Puritan New England,* 12 J. COMM. & RELIG. 1, 1 (1989). The metaphor dates back at least as far as Matthew's gospel. *Matthew* 5:14.

[103]Brennan, *State Constitutions, supra* note 85, at 502.

ment. "Federalism is not served when the federal half of that protection is crippled," he explained on more than one occasion.[104]

Furthermore, Justice Brennan expressed a strong belief that the judiciary should enforce the individual rights he believed to be of such critical importance. Noting "the American habit, extraordinary to other democracies, of casting social, economic, philosophical, and political questions in the form of actions at law and suits in equity,"[105] he pointed out that "important aspects of the most fundamental issues confronting our democracy end up ultimately in the Supreme Court for judicial determination."[106] Given this understanding of the legal system, the justice claimed, "'It is the duty of courts to be watchful for the constitutional rights of the citizen, and against any stealthy encroachments thereon.'"[107] Later, Brennan noted, "It will remain the business of judges to protect fundamental constitutional rights that will be threatened in ways not possibly envisaged by the Framers."[108] On this point, the justice quoted James Madison, who had declared, "'[T]he independent tribunals of justice will consider themselves in a peculiar manner the guardian of those rights.'"[109]

Brennan believed that both federal and state courts had a duty to protect the rights of individuals. "The fact that state courts have a duty to safeguard individual rights, and are honoring that duty," he pointed out, "cannot justify the Supreme Court in going on to limit the protective role of the federal judiciary."[110] According to Brennan, individual rights required protection from both levels of government.

As one can see, Brennan in his later speeches addressed some of the same key philosophical points that he addressed in his 1961 Madison Lecture. However, in later speeches Brennan was more specific about the same ideas, so consideration of the later speeches is helpful in attempting to develop a deeper understanding of some of the main ideas that influenced Brennan's decision in *Times v. Sullivan*.

---

[104]*Id.* at 503. *See also* William J. Brennan, *Color-Blind, Creed-Blind, Status-Blind, Sex-Blind*, 14 HUM. RTS. Q. 30, 37 (1987).

[105]Brennan, *Constitutional Adjudication*, *supra* note 85, at 560.

[106]*Id.*

[107]Brennan, *State Constitutions*, *supra* note 85, at 494 (quoting Boyd v. United States, 116 U.S. 616, 635 (1886)).

[108]Brennan, *supra* note 86, at 793.

[109]William J. Brennan, *The Bill of Rights and the States: The Revival of State Constitutions as Guardians of Individual Rights*, 61 N.Y.U. L. REV. 535, 552 (1986).

[110]Brennan, *supra* note 86, at 784.

Brennan's Judicial Philosophy As Instrumentalist

Broadly defined, Brennan's judicial philosophy is instrumentalist in nature.[111] Such a philosophy views the "law in functional terms as a means serving an end."[112] From an instrumentalist perspective, judges "see the judicial role primarily as an instrument to achieve justice in society."[113] Instrumentalist thinking adopts the belief "that people in ... society seek to use law to achieve practical social goals"[114] and that judges have an important role to play "in making and carrying out public policy."[115] Sometimes this perspective is seen as "social engineering."[116] In placing more emphasis on outcomes, instrumentalist judges place less emphasis on deference to the legislature and to precedent.[117] Frequently, an instrumentalist philosophy focuses on the protection and preservation of individual rights, especially those of minorities,[118] rather than on the technical legal process of determining those rights in the first place. Besides Brennan, Earl Warren, William Douglas, Thurgood Marshall and Harry Blackmun adopted instrumentalist philosophies.[119]

A succinct understanding of three other major philosophical approaches to judging—formalist, Holmesian and natural law approaches—can help to clarify Brennan's instrumentalist approach via contrast. To begin with, a formalist approach to judging emphasizes "the literal meaning of terms" in law[120] and looks for "clear, bright-line rules" of law that are capable of formal, logical, and predictable application.[121] Sometimes legal formalists consider evidence that sheds light on the specific intent of the framers of a constitu-

---

[111]Instrumentalist philosophy is frequently associated with the 1960s and the Warren Court. *See* Richard Delgado, *Rodrigo's Ninth Chronicle: Race, Legal Instrumentalism, and the Rule of Law*, 143 U. PA. L. REV. 379, 390–94 (1994).

[112]R. Randall Kelso & Charles D. Kelso, *How the Supreme Court is Dealing with Precedents in Constitutional Cases*, 62 BROOKLYN L. REV. 973, 980 (1996).

[113]*Id.*

[114]Willard Hurst, *The Unfinished Work of the Instrumentalists:* Instrumentalism and American Legal Theory *by Robert Samuel Summers*, 82 MICH. L. REV. 852, 853 (1984) (book review).

[115]*Id.* at 854.

[116]*Id.* at 853.

[117]*See* R. Randall Kelso, *Styles of Constitutional Interpretation and the Four Main Approaches to Constitutional Interpretation in American Legal History*, 29 VAL. U. L. REV. 121, 215, 217 (1994).

[118]*See* MARK SILVERSTEIN, JUDICIOUS CHOICES: THE NEW POLITICS OF SUPREME COURT CONFIRMATIONS 49 (1994).

[119]Kelso & Kelso, *supra* note 112, at 981.

[120]*Id.* at 977.

[121]*Id.* at 978.

tional provision,[122] but often law by itself is a sufficient basis for deciding cases.[123] Rather than tending to focus on outcomes and an understanding of social justice as would instrumentalists, adherents of legal formalism attempt to employ syllogistic-like logic, which they maintain helps them to arrive at "value-free" conclusions.[124] A legal formalist philosophy understands law as a science[125] that denies judges choices in the outcomes of cases.[126] Justices Antonin Scalia and Clarence Thomas are examples of justices who view the law in a formalist manner.[127]

Additionally, some judges adhere to a Holmesian approach to judging. While recognizing the importance of legal clarity and certainty so vital to formalist judges, Holmesian judges look beyond formalist considerations to extra-legal human experience that sheds light on the law and believe that citizens of a democracy should act upon this human experience through the passing of legislation.[128] Hence, Holmesian judges emphasize judicial restraint and frequently defer to the legislature and the executive for law-making purposes.[129] Instead of viewing the judiciary as an instrument of social justice, as do instrumentalist judges, Holmesian judges look to the other two branches of government for social progress. Justices Oliver Wendell Holmes, Felix Frankfurter and William Rehnquist have exemplified this perspective.[130]

Other judges subscribe to a natural law perspective. Under this approach, judges support "reasoned elaboration of the law over time."[131] This means that judges will look to moral principles in the Constitution or in other pre-existing laws and then attempt to interpret those principles in light of history.[132] Original intent and plain meaning of laws receive consideration, too.[133] In a way, this Enlight-

---

[122]*See id.* at 977.

[123]*See* David Lyons, *Legal Formalism and Instrumentalism—A Pathological Study*, 66 CORNELL L. REV. 949, 950 (1981).

[124]ROY L. BROOKS, STRUCTURES OF JUDICIAL DECISION-MAKING FROM LEGAL FORMALISM TO CRITICAL THEORY 39 (2002).

[125]*See* C.C. LANGDELL, SELECTION OF CASES ON THE LAW OF CONTRACTS viii (1879).

[126]*See* Frederick Schauer, *Formalism*, 97 YALE L.J. 509, 538 (1988).

[127]*See* Kelso & Kelso, *supra* note 112, at 978.

[128]*See id.* at 979.

[129]*See id.*

[130]*See id.* at 979, 980; Kelso, *supra* note 117, at 199.

[131]Kelso & Kelso, *supra* note 112, at 982.

[132]*See id.*

[133]*See* R. Randall Kelso, *The Natural Law Tradition on the Modern Supreme Court: Not Burke, But the Enlightenment Tradition Represented by Locke, Madison, and Marshall*, 26 ST. MARY'S L.J. 1051, 1058 (1995).

enment-oriented approach is about reviewing the terms of a social contract to make sure that they are current.[134] If necessary, judges will add glosses to pre-existing understandings of the Constitution, but such glosses frequently are based on precedent.[135] To more of an extent than instrumentalist judges, natural law judges tend to give great weight to precedent.[136] Justices John Marshall, Joseph Story, Sandra Day O'Connor and Anthony Kennedy are examples of justices on the Supreme Court who have adopted a natural law approach to judging.[137]

While these four major approaches to judging are helpful in organizing judicial thinking, it is important to note that the categories are not mutually exclusive.[138] For example, an instrumentalist judge likely will give some weight to precedent, and a formalist judge might avoid a close reading of a statute or other law if that would produce an absurd result.[139] Regardless of the limitations of these categories, they help to draw boundaries around judicial philosophies, and such boundaries are useful in studying judges and their approaches to the law.

TIMES V. SULLIVAN

Nearly four years before Brennan's judicial philosophy would help to resolve *Times v. Sullivan*, the events that ultimately led to the case began to unfold. On March 29, 1960, the *New York Times* published for the Committee to Defend Martin Luther King and the Struggle for Freedom in the South a full-page advertisement entitled "Heed Their Rising Voices."[140] The advertisement stated: "'As the whole world knows by now, thousands of Southern Negro students are engaged in widespread non-violent demonstrations in positive affirmation of the right to live in human dignity as guaranteed by the U.S. Constitution and the Bill of Rights.'"[141] The advertisement alleged that individuals opposed to the students' activities were spreading a "'wave of terror'" against the students.[142]

Two of the ten paragraphs of text were of particular note to the case. The third paragraph alleged that after students sang "My

---

[134]*See* Kelso & Kelso, *supra* note 112, at 982.
[135]*See* Kelso, *supra* note 133, at 1063.
[136]*See* Kelso & Kelso, *supra* note 112, at 984.
[137]*See id.* at 982, 983.
[138]*See* I CHARLES D. KELSO, MATERIALS ON CONSTITUTIONAL LAW 14 (2000).
[139]*See id.*
[140]*Times v. Sullivan*, 376 U.S. 254, 256, 257 (1964).
[141]*Id.* at 256.
[142]*Id.* at 256–57.

Country 'Tis of Thee" on the steps of the Alabama capitol building, student leaders were expelled and armed police surrounded the Alabama State College campus.[143] When students protested the police presence, the police allegedly padlocked the dining hall in order to starve them into submission.[144] The sixth paragraph alleged that the "Southern violators" had bombed the home of Martin Luther King, Jr., assaulted King and arrested him initially for trivial offenses and then for the felony of perjury.[145]

The name of Commissioner L. B. Sullivan, who supervised the city police department in Montgomery, Alabama, appeared nowhere in the advertisement.[146] However, Sullivan believed that since he was commissioner of police in Montgomery, readers would associate the references to police action and the "wave of terror" with him.[147] The *New York Times* distributed about 394 copies of this edition of the newspaper in Alabama, and approximately 35 copies went to subscribers in Montgomery County.[148]

No one involved in the case disputed that some of the statements were inaccurate. For instance, the students sang "The Star Spangled Banner" rather than "My Country 'Tis of Thee," and the students who were later expelled from school were expelled for requesting service at the county courthouse lunch counter rather than for leading the demonstration at the capitol building.[149] Also, the police did not come to Alabama State College in response to the protest on the steps of the capitol, nor did the police ever padlock the dining facilities at the university.[150] Additionally, the police had not been involved in the bombing of King's house, and the bombing had taken place before Sullivan assumed his job as commissioner.[151] Moreover, Sullivan was not responsible for charging King with perjury; several of King's arrests had occurred before Sullivan began his commissionership.[152]

In response to the advertisement in the *Times*, Sullivan sued four black Alabama clergymen, whose names appeared in the advertisement as names of endorsers, and the New York Times Company, publisher of the *Times*, for libel.[153] Under Alabama law, the state-

---

[143]*Id.* at 257.
[144]*Id.*
[145]*Id.* at 257–58.
[146]*Id.* at 256, 258.
[147]*Id.* at 257, 258.
[148]*Id.* at 260 n.3.
[149]*Id.* at 258–59.
[150]*Id.* at 259.
[151]*Id.*
[152]*Id.*
[153]*Id.* at 256, 286.

ments in the advertisement were libelous *per se* because they attacked a person's "'reputation, profession, trade or business, or charge[d] him with an indictable offense, or tend[ed] to bring the individual into public contempt,'" so the jury only had to find that the defendants had published the advertisement and that the statements were "'of and concerning'" Sullivan.[154] Sullivan received $500,000 in damages from the jury in Montgomery County, and Alabama's Supreme Court affirmed the award of damages.[155]

The Supreme Court granted certiorari in the case.[156] On January 6, 1964, the Supreme Court heard oral arguments; some two months later, on March 9, 1964, the Court issued its historic decision.[157] According to Brennan's opinion for the Court, one major issue emerged. Brennan asked whether the First and Fourteenth Amendment protections of free speech and press limit the power of a state to award damages in a libel action that a public official brings against critics of the official's conduct in office.[158]

BRENNAN'S JUDICIAL PHILOSOPHY AND *TIMES V. SULLIVAN*

To *New York Times Co. v. Sullivan,* Brennan brought his own judicial philosophy. As previously indicated, this philosophy was dedicated to a living Constitution, the critical importance of individual rights, and the judiciary as enforcer of individual rights.

A Living Constitution

In 1964 some states already had laws that offered individuals varying degrees of protection against defamation suits,[159] but the Constitution did not protect free speech and press interests from such defamation suits.[160] Indeed, while the First Amendment states that "Congress shall make no law ... abridging the freedom of speech, or of the press,"[161] the document is devoid of specifics and says nothing about defamation. The nature of free speech and press protection at the time of the creation of the Constitution remains somewhat nebu-

---

[154]*Id.* at 263 (quoting New York Times Co. v. Sullivan, 273 Ala. 656, 673 (1962)).

[155]*Id.* at 256.

[156]*Id.* at 264.

[157]*Id.* at 254.

[158]*Id.* at 256, 268.

[159]*See* W. WAT HOPKINS, ACTUAL MALICE: TWENTY-FIVE YEARS AFTER TIMES V. SULLIVAN 47–48 (1989).

[160]*See* TEETER, LE DUC & LOVING, *supra* note 12, at 206.

[161]U.S. CONST. amend I.

lous. Various authorities believe that at that time the Free Speech and Press clauses protected against governmental prior restraint and nothing else.[162] Other authorities believe the Free Speech and Press clauses stood for more than a prohibition on prior restraint and did away with the crime of seditious libel, thus opening the door to criticism of the government legally unknown before the colonies broke away from England.[163] In trying to resolve the matter, one might want to know what the framers of the First Amendment thought, but determining the exact framers and their collective intent proves difficult.[164] Thus, although through the years the Free Speech and Press clauses came to stand for much more than mere protection against prior restraint, if that is indeed what the clauses stood for in 1791, their origin is somewhat murky and hence disputed. Nonetheless, until 1964 the two clauses did not cover traditional defamation suits.[165]

Despite this historical background, Justice Brennan decided in *Times v. Sullivan* that a new rule of constitutional law to protect criticism of government officials was necessary.[166] The justice called upon *Coleman v. MacLennan*,[167] a case the Supreme Court of Kansas decided in 1908, for the legal principle that a public official can prevail in a libel suit related to the official's public status only if the public official shows "actual malice," which Brennan defined as acting "with knowledge that [the statement] was false or with reckless disregard of whether [the statement] was false or not."[168] In a long footnote, Brennan added that the "consensus of scholarly opinion

---

[162]*See, e.g.*, CASS R. SUNSTEIN, DEMOCRACY AND THE PROBLEM OF FREE SPEECH xiii–xiv (1995). *See also* HOPKINS, *supra* note 5, at 59; DON R. PEMBER, MASS MEDIA LAW 40 (2003).

[163]*See, e.g.*, ZECHARIAH CHAFEE, FREEDOM OF SPEECH IN THE UNITED STATES 21 (1941); Mayton, *supra* note 12, at 119–21. Also, at least one commentator has wondered how the founders could have ignored seditious libel, "the primary form of restraint on the press during the colonial period." David A. Anderson, *The Origins of the Press Clause*, 30 UCLA L. REV. 455, 534–35 (1983) (also noting several other problems with the argument that the First Amendment did not do away with seditious libel).

[164]*See* Erwin Chemerinsky, *History, Tradition, the Supreme Court, and the First Amendment*, 44 HASTINGS L.J. 901, 910 (1993).

[165]*See* LEWIS, *supra* note 6, at 153.

[166]As of 1964, some states already had adopted various versions of the actual malice rule, which offered differing levels of protection for defamation defendants. *See* HOPKINS, *supra* note 159, at 47–48. At that time, several states offered *Sullivan*-like protection for defamation defendants. *See cases cited* at *Times v. Sullivan*, 376 U.S. 254, 280 n.20 (1964).

[167]78 Kan. 711 (1908).

[168]*Times v. Sullivan*, 376 U.S. at 280–81.

apparently favors the rule that is here adopted."[169] While Brennan adopted the rule for public officials, he declined to state how far down the chain of command in government the rule would pertain.[170]

This judicial argumentation provided a clear case in which Justice Brennan saw the Constitution as a "living organism," as Justice Louis Brandeis once called it.[171] When the case began, defamation suits were beyond the scope of the First Amendment, but when the case came to a close, Brennan had written an opinion that brought defamation suits within the ambit of the First Amendment. In short, he brought centuries of the common law of defamation onto the federal constitutional scene and expanded the scope of constitutional protection of individual rights. With Brennan's opinion in *Times v. Sullivan*, the Constitution had continued to evolve and grow.

Justices with other judicial philosophies probably would not have been inclined to embrace the concept of a living Constitution the way Brennan did. For example, a formalist justice likely would not have accepted the newly articulated idea of "the central meaning of the First Amendment,"[172] no matter how much Justice Brennan's argument created the appearance that this "central meaning" had enjoyed widespread support in the United States for the better part of two centuries. Also, despite the passing claim Justice Holmes made in *Abrams v. United States* that the First Amendment abolished the crime of seditious libel,[173] developing a clear argument for that position given the somewhat murky origin of the First Amendment would be a difficult task.[174] Hence, in light of both little Supreme Court precedent to support the idea of "the central meaning of the First Amendment" and the relatively obscure original intent of the Amendment,[175] a formalist justice likely would have rejected Brennan's approach as activist and thus creating new law.

Other non-instrumentalists would have leaned toward the same result. For instance, if a Holmesian justice had favored a

---

[169]*Id.* at 280 n.20.

[170]*Id.* at 284.

[171]*See* Brennan, *supra* note 84, at 426.

[172]*Times v. Sullivan*, 376 U.S. at 273.

[173]250 U.S. 616, 630 (Homes, J., dissenting) (1919).

[174]On this point, the Sedition Act of 1918, which the Court upheld in a number of cases, was relatively similar to the Sedition Act of 1798. Hence, if the Sedition Act of 1798 had not expired of its own accord and prior to *Times v. Sullivan* the Court had heard a case on the Sedition Act of 1798, the Court could have found the original Sedition Act constitutional. Thus, the argument that the First Amendment did away with the crime of seditious libel becomes problematic. *See* Kalven, *supra* note 14, at 206-07.

[175]*See* Kelso & Kelso, *supra* note 112, at 977.

reinterpretation of the First Amendment, the justice would have been inclined to allow the legislative branch of government to take the step of introducing a constitutional amendment. This approach would have come from the respect that Holmesian justices have for the other branches of government and Holmesian justices' reluctance to engage in judicial activism such as reinterpreting an Amendment to develop its meaning.[176] Finally, given a great respect for precedent,[177] a natural law justice might have shied away from Brennan's discarding much of the legal thinking in cases like *Schenck v. United States*,[178] *Abrams v. United States*[179] and others. Thus, if a formalist, Holmesian, or natural law justice had authored the opinion for the Court, a result that embraced a living Constitution and allowed for the creation of the rule of actual malice would have been unlikely.

The Critical Importance of Individual Rights

Brennan's strong belief in the importance of individual rights manifested itself in his explanation in *Times v. Sullivan* of why free speech is of vital importance to citizens of the United States. Brennan wrote that the main purpose of the First Amendment is to allow for political and social changes which citizens of the country want[180] and that free speech and assembly are necessary because of the "'occasional tyrannies of governing majorities.'"[181] He also observed, "'It is a prized American privilege to speak one's mind, although not always with perfect good taste, on all public institutions.'"[182] Given this understanding of the individual right to free speech, the justice framed the Court's consideration of the case "against the background of a profound national commitment to the principle that debate on public issues should be uninhibited, robust, and wide-open."[183]

Justice Brennan wrote that the individual right of free speech is so important that it does not necessarily lose its First Amendment protection either because statements made are false or because they are

---

[176]*See id.* at 979.

[177]*See id.* at 984.

[178]249 U.S. 47 (1919).

[179]250 U.S. 616 (1919).

[180]*Times v. Sullivan*, 376 U.S. 254, 269 (1964).

[181]*Id.* at 270 (quoting Whitney v. California, 274 U.S. 357, 376 (1927) (Brandeis, J., concurring)).

[182]*Id.* at 269 (quoting Bridges v. California, 314 U.S. 252, 270 (1941)).

[183]*Id.* at 270.

defamatory.[184] First, Brennan cited a number of authorities to support the point that the First Amendment protects many false statements of fact: James Madison for the proposition that some degree of abuse is inherent in the operation of the press, prior Supreme Court case law for the recognition that "erroneous statement is inevitable in free debate," the U.S. Court of Appeals for the District of Columbia for the notion that in discussion of politics errors are inevitable, and John Stuart Mill for the idea that since faulty arguments are so often made in "perfect good faith," it is infrequently possible "to stamp the misrepresentation as morally culpable."[185] Second, Brennan came to the conclusion that statements do not necessarily lose their First Amendment protection because they are defamatory. The justice stated that public officials ought to be able to thrive in harsh political climates.[186] These points support a rigorous understanding of the individual right of free speech.

One matter of interpretation is important here. Sullivan ultimately lost his case against the *New York Times*. At first blush, this might seem like a case where the rights of an individual lost to the rights of a major media power.[187] However, re-framing the case can help in understanding how individual rights won out. One can view the *New York Times* as a conduit of the message that various individual social outsiders used to disseminate a message of social change that the powerful establishment, symbolized by Sullivan, did not want to hear. The Court protected the speech rights of individuals in the civil rights movement from the oppressive power of Alabama and state agents like Sullivan.[188] Framed in this way, the case was one about the individual right to free speech in a representative democracy.

Justices with other philosophies likely would have come to different results. A formalist justice who consulted the Court's precedent for

---

[184]*Id.* at 271.

[185]*Id.* at 271–72.

[186]*Id.* at 273. Later in his opinion, Brennan drew an analogy between the protection granted to public officials' job-related speech and the protection that Brennan sought to grant to citizens' political speech. *Id.* at 282–83 (citing Barr v. Matteo, 360 U.S. 564 (1959)). In short, both types of speech served democratic purposes. *Id.*

[187]Brennan even noted that "'occasional injury to the reputations of individuals must yield to the public welfare.'" *Id.* at 281 (quoting Coleman v. MacLennan, 78 Kan. 711, 724 (1908)). Given the civil rights struggle of a few social outsiders against the establishment out of which the *Times v. Sullivan* case grew, this quotation is probably not the most accurate way of explaining the outcome in the case.

[188]*See* Blanchard, *supra* note 34, at 374. Blanchard considers this point in the context of other cases from the civil rights era, but the idea applies just as well to *Times v. Sullivan* since it is a civil rights-era case, too. Also, Blanchard notes the Court's awareness of the need to promote individual rights during this time. *Id.*

"clear, bright-line rules" of law[189] would have had a difficult time finding a sturdy right to speak out against the government because, as noted above, precedent did not afford much of a right of that nature. Along the same lines, given the somewhat murky origins of the First Amendment previously outlined, a formalist justice who endeavored to discern the original intent of the founders would have had a difficult time arguing for a robust right to criticize the government.[190]

Also, a Holmesian justice would have been inclined to agree with a formalist justice on this matter. For example, upon not finding in First Amendment precedent and history a sturdy right to criticize the government, a Holmesian justice likely would have deferred to the legislature in the possible event of the creation of a new rule of law that provided for this right.[191] By doing so, the justice would have allowed the people's representatives to call upon social experience to enact new laws *via* the legislature and would have avoided the appearance of judicial activism.[192]

---

[189]Kelso & Kelso, *supra* note 112, at 977.

[190]*Id.* To the contrary, a formalist justice who looked at the actual text of the First Amendment and did not extensively consider other relevant legal rules or make an attempt to ascertain the original intent of the founders could come to the same conclusion about the right to criticize the government to which Brennan came since the plain words of the First Amendment by themselves do not allow any exceptions to the abridgment of speech or press. This point helps to explain how Justice Hugo Black, no instrumentalist himself, agreed with Brennan's conclusion in *Times v. Sullivan. See* Michael J. Gerhardt, *A Tale of Two Textualists: A Critical Comparison of Justices Black and Scalia*, 74 B.U. L. REV. 25, 28–29 (1994).

[191]*See* Kelso & Kelso, *supra* note 112, at 979. Ironically, the namesake of the Holmesian approach to judging, Oliver Wendell Holmes, did find such a right, but his initial argument for that right came only in passing at the end of his dissent in *Abrams v. United States.* 250 U.S. 616, 630 (1919) (Holmes, J., dissenting).

[192]Despite Kelso and Kelso's observations that Justices Tom Clark, Potter Stewart, Byron White and John Marshall Harlan held Holmesian judicial philosophies, these four justices joined Brennan's opinion for the Court in *Times v. Sullivan. See* KELSO, *supra* note 138, at 12; Charles D. Kelso & R. Randall Kelso, *A Review of Professor Lusky's Call for Judicial Restraint:* Our Nine Tribunes: The Supreme Court in Modern America, 5 SETON HALL CONST. L.J. 1289, 1320 (1995) (generally reviewing Lusky's book). This result may be a testimony to the consensus-building skills of Brennan, who had a reputation for crafting consensus among members of the Court but had a challenge getting and maintaining a majority in *Times v. Sullivan. See* Hopkins, *supra* note 4, at 494. *See also* LEWIS, *supra* note 6, at 164. Also, Sullivan's $500,000 jury award and the potential for chilling political speech that affirming the decision of the Alabama Supreme Court would have had may have loomed ominously for these four justices as well as for the other members of the Court. Whether each of the four Holmesian justices on the Court would have authored an opinion like Brennan's instead of merely going along with Brennan's opinion may be a different question. Regardless, these justices were not as consistent with following their philosophies as one might have expected them to be. A key point here is that judicial philosophies provide predictions rather than promises of what justices will do in any given case. Helpfully, Hopkins and Lewis have studied some of the interac-

Finally, a natural law justice would have looked to the Constitution, history, original intent of the founders and precedent in an attempt to find a sturdy right to criticize the government,[193] and, unless the justice had reasoned that such a right was found somewhere within these sources, the justice probably would not have created such a right. Given the absence of relatively compelling authority, whether constitutional, historical or otherwise, this individual right probably would not have appeared in the opinion of a natural law justice. Accordingly, the individual right to criticize the government would not have been likely to come from most formalist, Holmesian, and natural law readings of the case.

The Judiciary As Enforcer of Individual Rights

Justice Brennan's judicial philosophy had an important impact on the *Times v. Sullivan* decision through the ideas of a living Constitution and the critical importance of the individual right to free speech in a representative democracy. Furthermore, Brennan's philosophy had an impact on the case through the idea of judicial protection of the defendants' legal rights.

Accordingly, instead of merely introducing the Supreme Court's version of the actual malice doctrine, Justice Brennan used the Court to enforce the rights that this doctrine sought to protect. While Brennan might have stated the new rule of constitutional law and then remanded the case for further consideration, he instead opted to apply the rule and came to the conclusion that actual malice was lacking. This judicial step of passing judgment on the facts as well as the law was a highly unusual one for the Court.[194] The jurist noted there was no evidence at trial that the four individual defendants were aware of any falsity in the advertisement.[195] Furthermore, the editors at the *Times* said they believed the content of the advertisement was "substantially correct," and the *Times* relied upon the good reputations of many of the individuals named in the advertise-

---

tions among the justices, including Harlan's eventual acquiescence to Brennan despite Harlan's concerns that the Court's actual malice doctrine would violate the principle of federalism, during the formulation of Brennan's opinion in *Times v. Sullivan*. *See* LEWIS, *supra* note 6, at 164–82; Hopkins, *supra* note 4. Future research might seek to explain further why all four Holmesian justices on the Court in March 1964 embraced what appeared to be a judicially-created individual right rather than deferring to the Congress for the possible creation of such a right.

[193]*See* Kelso & Kelso, *supra* note 112, at 982, 984; Kelso, *supra* note 133, at 1058.

[194]*See* KERMIT L. HALL, THE MAGIC MIRROR: LAW IN AMERICAN HISTORY 316 (1989).

[195]*Times v. Sullivan*, 376 U.S. 254, 286 (1964).

ment.[196] At best, the *Times* was negligent in failing to discover the faulty statements in the advertisement.[197] Brennan added that the advertisement specifically did not name Sullivan and that several of the accusations in the advertisement did not even concern the police.[198] As to the accusations that did concern the police, Brennan found that Sullivan's witnesses at trial had not indicated that they thought Sullivan's reputation came under attack simply because Sullivan was the police commissioner.[199] In short, Sullivan did not muster enough evidence to demonstrate that either the individual defendants or the *New York Times* acted with actual malice. By not only proclaiming a new rule of First Amendment doctrine, the rule of actual malice, but also by applying the rule to come to the conclusion that the defendants were not liable to Sullivan, Brennan used the judiciary to enforce the free speech and press rights of the defendants.

Justices with other judicial philosophies probably would have shied away from judicial activism. For instance, many formalists are against an activist judiciary. They see the law as a scientific endeavor,[200] and the creation of rights *via* judicial activism tends not to be a part of that endeavor. Hence, a formalist justice probably would not have gone along with the opinion in *Times v. Sullivan*.[201] Along the same lines, a Holmesian justice, based on an inclination of judicial deference to the legislature,[202] likely would not have engaged in judicial activism of the sort found in Brennan's opinion.[203] Finally, unless a natural law justice had felt that a new gloss over previous understanding of the Free Speech and Press clauses was appropri-

---

[196]*Id.* at 286–87.

[197]*Id.* at 287.

[198]*Id.* at 288.

[199]*Id.* at 289.

[200]*See* LANGDELL, *supra* note 125, at viii. In some cases, Justice Hugo Black was an exception. He did not shy away from judicial enforcement of rights he believed to be within the Constitution because he saw the judiciary as the enforcer of the explicit rights in that text. *See* Gerhardt, *supra* note 190, at 56.

[201]Notably, Justice Black was against an activist judiciary when he could not find a given right in the text of the Constitution. However, in cases where he believed a right to be solidly grounded in the Constitution, Black did not hesitate to enforce the right *via* judicial activism. *See* Gerhardt, *supra* note 190, at 65–66. This information helps to explain why Black supported Brennan's conclusion in *Times v. Sullivan* but dissented the next year from Justice William Douglas' opinion for the Court in *Griswold v. Connecticut*, which established a constitutional right to privacy. 381 U.S. 479, 529 (1965) (Black, J., dissenting).

[202]*See* Kelso & Kelso, *supra* note 112, at 979.

[203]Ironically, the four Holmesian justices on the Court at the time of *Times v. Sullivan* joined Brennan's judicial activism. Perhaps future scholarship will attempt to explain this unlikely judicial behavior.

ate,[204] the natural law justice probably would have upheld precedent and avoided judicial activism due to a respect for established law.[205] Again, justices with non-instrumentalist philosophies likely would have been inclined to avoid the activism which Brennan's instrumentalist philosophy helped to bring about, so the outcome in *Times v. Sullivan* could have been quite different.

CONCLUSIONS

Justice William Brennan's judicial philosophy had an important influence on the Supreme Court's decision in *Times v. Sullivan* and hence on changing the direction of the law as it pertained to criticism of the government. Brennan's instrumentalist philosophy, with its prongs of a living Constitution, the critical importance of individual rights, and judicial enforcement of such rights, helped to shape the actual malice rule and opened the door to greater protection for criticism of the government. One relatively recent material consequence of such a result is that critics of the Bush Administration's war in Iraq have had the opportunity to voice publicly their concerns about the war.

The actual malice rule did not have to be the doctrinal result in *Times v. Sullivan*. If a justice with a non-instrumentalist philosophy had authored the opinion of the Court, the result could have been notably different. For example, had a justice with a formalist, Holmesian or natural law philosophy penned the opinion, observers reasonably could have expected a fit into the previous 173 years of First Amendment history. Instead, Brennan, with the consent of a majority, re-wrote the traditional rules of defamation in an effort to promote democratic ideals.

Rodney Smolla has noted that "[f]ree speech is an indispensable tool of self-governance in a democratic society."[206] The successful functioning of democracy calls for informed decision-making, and free speech helps to ensure "that everything worth saying shall be said"[207] so that decision-making can be more informed. Public officials may not always like what citizens say about them, since public criticism can be "vehement, caustic, and sometimes unpleasantly

---

[204]*See* Kelso, *supra* note 133, at 1063.
[205]*See* Kelso & Kelso, *supra* note 112, at 984.
[206]RODNEY SMOLLA, FREE SPEECH IN AN OPEN SOCIETY 12 (1992).
[207]ALEXANDER MEIKLEJOHN, FREE SPEECH AND ITS RELATION TO SELF-GOVERNMENT 25 (1948). For the influence of philosopher Alexander Meiklejohn on the Supreme Court, *see* William J. Brennan, *The Supreme Court and the Meiklejohn Interpretation of the First Amendment*, 79 HARV. L. REV. 1 (1965).

sharp,"[208] but public criticism, along with other types of public discussion, can contribute insight to democratic decision-making. This principle, influenced in part by Justice Brennan's instrumentalist judicial philosophy in *New York Times v. Sullivan*, opened the door for greater democratic discourse in 1964, and such a principle keeps that door open for the same type of expansive democratic discourse today.

[208]*Times v. Sullivan*, 376 U.S. 254, 271 (1964).

Printed in the United States
by Baker & Taylor Publisher Services